POST MORTEM

POST MORTEM

SOLVING HISTORY'S GREAT MEDICAL MYSTERIES

Philip A. Mackowiak, MD, MBA, MACP

American College of Physicians
Philadelphia, Pennsylvania

Associate Publisher, Tom Hartman
Production Supervisor, Allan S. Kleinberg
Senior Production Editor, Karen C. Nolan
Publishing Coordinator, Angela Gabella
Interior and Cover Design, Flatiron
Composition, ATLIS Graphics

Printed in the United States of America by R.R. Donnelley

Library of Congress Cataloging-in-Publication Data
Mackowiak, Philip A.
  Post-mortem : Solving History's Great Medical Mysteries / Phil Mackowiak.
    p. cm.
  Includes bibliographical references.
  ISBN 978-1-930513-89-1 (alk. paper)
  1. Medicine—History. 2. Medicine—Anecdotes. 3. Medicine—Miscellanea. I. Title.

R707.M28 2007
10—dc26

To CGM, SLM and RLM

for love tempered by tolerance

ACKNOWLEDGMENTS

I am indebted to scores of gifted clinicians and historians for the inspiration and the ideas that are this book. I knew few of them personally before I enlisted their help in dissecting these medical mysteries. Many are now close friends. All have given freely of their expertise and, in the process, enriched my understanding with both information and perspective.

In my analysis of Akhenaten, I relied heavily on information provided by Donald B. Redford, PhD (Professor of History, Pennsylvania State University), Victor McKusick, MD (Emeritus Professor of Internal Medicine, the Johns Hopkins School of Medicine) and Robert J. Littman, PhD, (Professor of Classics, University of Hawaii). My investigation of Pericles and the Plague of Athens was also facilitated greatly by Dr. Littman, as well as by David T. Durack, MD, DPhil, FRCP, FRACP, FACP (Consulting Professor of Medicine, Duke University School of Medicine). Eugene N. Borza, PhD (Professor Emeritus of Ancient History, Pennsylvania State University), and David Oldach, MD (Associate Professor of Medicine, University of Maryland School of Medicine) contributed greatly to my understanding of Alexander's life and death, as did Peter Richardson, PhD (Professor Emeritus of Religious Studies, University of Toronto), Ross Kraemer, PhD (Professor of Religious Studies, Brown University) and Jan V. Hirschmann, MD (Professor of Medicine, University of Washington School of Medicine) to those of Herod. Judith P. Hallett, PhD (Professor of Classics, University of Maryland), Richard J.A. Talbert, PhD (Professor of History and Adjunct Professor of Classics, University of North Carolina), Anthony A. Barrett, PhD (Professor of Classics, University of British Columbia), Wayne H. Millan, MA (Researcher, Falls Church, Virginia) and William A Valente, MD (Chairman, Department of Medicine, St. Agnes Hospital, Baltimore) each helped me comprehend Claudius and the Julio-Claudian family. Frank C. Arnett, MD (Professor of Medicine, University of Texas Medical School at Houston, Texas), Charles Merrill, PhD (Professor, Language Department, Mt. St. Mary's University, Emmitsburg, Maryland) and Francesc Albardoner (Columbus Study Center of the Omnium Cultural Foundation, Barcelona, Spain) opened my eyes to the mysteries of Columbus' progressive arthritis and origin. The complicated lives and illnesses of Mozart and Beethoven would have been beyond my comprehension had it not been for critical information received from Neal Zaslaw, PhD (Professor of Music, Cornell University), Faith T. Fitzgerald, MD (Professor of Medicine and Assistant Dean for Student Affairs, University of California, Davis), Maynard Solomon (Professor Emeritus of Music, Julliard School of Music) and Michael S. Donnenberg, MD (Professor of Medicine, University of Maryland School of Medicine). Karen Sullivan, PhD (Associate Professor of Literature, Bard College), William T. Carpenter, MD (Professor of Psychiatry and Director of the Maryland Psychiatric Research Center, University of Maryland School of Medicine) and Robert T. M. Phillips, MD (Adjunct Professor of Psychiatry, University of Maryland School of Medicine) educated me in the details of the life of Joan of Arc and in forensic psychiatry. R. Michael Benitez, MD (Associate Professor of Medicine, University of Maryland School of Medicine), David Keltz (Actor and Poe Scholar) and Jeff Jerome (Curator, Edgar Allan Poe House and Museum of Baltimore) gave me knowledge of Poe. Kathleen L. Wisner, MD, MS (Professor of Psychiatry, Obstetrics-Gynecology and Pediatrics and Director of Women's Behavioral HealthCARE, University of Pittsburgh School of Medicine), Mark Bostridge, MA (Biographer and Critic, London), Thomas L. Murtaugh, PhD (Project Officer, National Center for PTSD) and Alex Attewell (Director, Florence Nightingale Museum, London) gave me critical insight into Florence Nightingale's strange maladies. Jackson T. Wright, Jr., MD, PhD (Professor of Medicine, Case Western Reserve University), W. Fitzhugh Brundage, PhD (Professor of History, University of North Carolina, Chapel Hill) and Mrs. Margaret Washington Clifford (granddaughter of BTW) added immeasurably to my comprehension of the life , legacy and terminal illness of Booker T. Washington. Richard J. Behles, MLS (Historical Librarian, University of Maryland Health Services Library) gave generously of his time and expertise to assist in many of the literature searches that made the following chapters possible.

To all, I am immensely grateful, as I am to Larry Pitrof (Executive Director of the University of Maryland Alumni Association) and Dr. Morton D. Kramer for technical, financial and moral support, without which the conferences on which this book is based would not have been possible; to Tom Hartman (Associate Publisher, American College of Physicians) and Dennis DiClaudio for their critical review of each chapter and invaluable editorial advice; and to Celeste Marousek, Harriet Kerr and Karen Cowley for their encouragement during the decade in which this book was written.

PREFACE

Post Mortem is a derivative of a continuing series of Historical Clinicopathological Conferences I began hosting for the VA Maryland Health Care System and the University of Maryland School of Medicine in 1995. The clinicopathological conference, or "CPC," is a standard medical conference designed to teach physicians and physicians-in-training basic medical concepts and clinical problem-solving techniques. It is a case-based exercise, in which the featured speaker and the audience struggle together to diagnose a particularly challenging illness of some recent patient using only the information included in a clinical summary prepared especially for the conference. That clinical summary, distributed well in advance of the conference, typically contains all of the medical information pertaining to the case in question, except for the definitive, diagnostic test result. That result, known only to the conference organizers, is revealed at the very end of the conference as a validation or repudiation of the presenter's conclusions.

The Historical CPC, at least as I have designed it for the Baltimore conferences, is like its standard counterpart in all respects, except that it concerns an historical rather than a contemporary patient in whom the diagnosis is as yet uncertain. In compiling case summaries for Historical CPCs, I have endeavored to produce the most accurate and comprehensive medical histories possible, and in most cases have been ably assisted in these efforts by internationally renowned authorities on the subjects in question. I have chosen as cases historically prominent persons with enigmatic disorders that are described in reasonable detail in the historical record. These case summaries and the deliberations of the skilled clinicians and noted biographers who have participated in the VA Maryland Health Care System/University of Maryland Historical CPCs are the wellspring from which the following chapters flow.

Each chapter begins with a clinical summary organized according to the standard format used by physicians today in their clinical practices. The history of the present illness (i.e., the illness in question) is given first, followed by the subject's past medical history, family history, social history and physical examination. In current clinical practice, this information alone is sufficient more than 80% of the time to permit a correct diagnosis of the present illness when the medical history is accurate and the physical examination is properly performed.

In none of the cases reviewed in *Post Mortem* is there a definitive diagnostic test result — no critical blood test, no key culture, no salient radiologic, histologic or autopsy result to confirm or invalidate proposed diagnoses. Moreover, the historical records from which clinical summaries are derived differ in important respects from contemporary medical records. In most cases, the only available medical histories were written by non-physicians, whose appreciation for and description of important clinical details was limited. This problem is especially evident in Thucydides' description of the rash exhibited by victims of the plague of Athens. Perhaps more than any other feature of that illness, the rash was the key to diagnosis, and Thucydides' description is ambiguous — so much so, that clinicians have argued for more than a millennium over both the nature of the rash and the diagnosis it signifies.

In some cases, medical histories were almost certainly distorted for personal gain or in deference to political agendas. Dr. J. J. Moran, the physician who cared for Poe during his final illness, was almost certainly guilty of the former distortion in a second published account of the poet's illness. Some historians suspect that Josephus was guilty of the latter distortion in his description of Herod's terminal illness, embellishing it with grotesque physical abnormalities, not in the interest of historical accuracy, but as post-mortem punishment for crimes committed during a despotic reign.

Some accounts were written years after the fact, and fading memories may have taken a toll on their accuracy. This is of particular concern with regard to the only detailed description of Mozart's terminal illness, one written by his sister-in-law some twenty-seven years after the fact.

Finally, there is the reluctance of those who look for answers in the medical records of history's illuminati to accept ordinary diseases as causes of the deaths of extraordinary persons, as well as a penchant for diagnosing disorders that are the particular interests of those proffering diagnoses. This is especially true of Beethoven's illness. Although in life the composer exhibited a panoply of relentlessly progressive signs and symptoms that could only be explained by an all too common infection, and on post-mortem examination exhibited additional evidence of the diagnosis, no fewer than eighteen alternative diagnoses have been offered by "medical experts" to explain his illness.

Post Mortem does not close the book on questions surrounding the twelve medical mysteries considered. Rather, it opens the book at a new page — one written by a contemporary academic internist, ably assisted by some of the world's most gifted clinicians and knowledgeable historians, and based on the most comprehensive and objective medical histories compiled to date.

TABLE OF CONTENTS

HUMANOID PRAYING MANTIS

Of all the mysteries lying buried in the dust of ancient Egypt, this patient was among the greatest. Not only was he one of the strangest of all of the pharaohs, he was also one of the most controversial. He was a monotheist, perhaps the very first in history, and although Aten, not Jehovah, was his one-and-only god, some suspect he was a mentor to Moses, possibly even an early avatar of Christ. He was also so physically deformed that some believe his father hid him from the public for much of his reign. And yet, when the patient became Pharaoh, he seemed to revel in his strange appearance, one likened to that of a "humanoid praying mantis."[1] Perhaps he recognized that while individually his features, in the many statues and reliefs he commissioned, were spectacularly ugly, together they possessed a certain foreboding, other-worldly beauty that heightened his mystery and served as a challenge and warning to those who might oppose him.

When the patient ascended the throne of his ancestors circa 1377 B.C.E.,[2] the kingdom of Egypt had already existed for over eighteen centuries. Seventeen dynasties had come and gone (Table 1-1). Another fourteen would follow before Ptolemy I was crowned in 323 B.C.E., inaugurating the era of Greek suzerainty (Table 1-2).

It was the twilight of the 18th Dynasty, the last days of the house of the Thutmosids.[3] Isaiah, Elijah and Moses were not yet born. Athens was then an insignificant outpost on the frontier of the civilized world and would have to wait almost a millennium to enter its golden age; Rome was a marshy wilderness barely fit for human habitation.

1

TABLE 1-1   Manetho's List of Dynasties

Dynasty	Period	Approximate Date (B.C.E.)
I-II	Archaic	3168-2705
III-VII	Old Kingdom	2705-2230
VIII-X	First Intermediate	2230-2035
XI-XIII	Middle Kingdom	2035-1668
XIV-XVII	Second Intermediate	1720-1540
XVIII-XX	New Kingdom	1540-1070
XXI-XXXI	Late	1070-332
Ptolemaic	Greek	332-30
Emperors	Roman	30-AD 395

Adapted from Aldred C. *Akhenaten. King of Egypt.* Thames & Hudson. London: 1988, p. 9-10.

TABLE 1-2   The Eighteenth Dynasty (Ahmosides)

Nomen	Prenomen	Date (B.C.E.)	Chief Queen
Amosis	Nebpehtirē	1540-1515	Ahmose-Nefertari
Amenophis I	Djeserkarē	1515-1494	Meritamum (?)
Tuthmosis I	Aakheperkarē	1494-1482	Ahmose
Tuthmosis II	Aakheperenrē	1482-1479	Hatshepsut
Hatshepsut	Maetkarē	1479-1457	
Tuthmosis III	Menkheperrē	1479-1425	Hatshepsut Meritrē
Amenophis II	Aakheperurē	1427-1393	Tia
Tuthmosis IV	Menkheperurē	1394-1384	Mutemwiya
Amenophis III	Nebmaetrē	1384-1346	Tiye
Amenophis IV	Neferneferuaten-Nefertiti		
Akhenaten	Neferkheperurē	1358-1340	Nefertiti
Neferneferuaten/ Smenkhkarē- Djeserkjeperu	Ankhkheperurē	1342-1340	Meritaten
Tutankhamum	Nebkheperurē	1340-1331	Ankhesenamun
Ay	Kheperkheperurē	1331-1326	Tey
Haremhab	Djeserkheperurē	1326-1299	Mutnodjme

The kingdom the patient inherited from his father over three thousand years ago, however, was remarkably modern.[4] We know this because of intimate details of his reign preserved in an astonishing cache of cuneiform-inscribed clay tablets unearthed at the site of his ancient capital in 1887 C.E. These "Amarna letters," as they have come to be known, represent diplomatic dispatches of Asiatic envoys assigned to the patient's court. They describe a society with labor strikes and fact-finding committees appointed to investigate them; inflation and crime in the streets; taxes and tax evasion. People married and divorced. They were hired and fired. They bought and sold goods and left detailed wills. They went to parties and drank too much. Old folks complained that times just weren't what they used to be and that youngsters no longer respected their elders. People read love poems, short stories, devotional works, "how to" books and horoscopes.[5] In short, people then were remarkably similar to people today.[6] But not the patient. He was different, a "first individual in history."[7]

He was the second son of Amenophis III[8] and ascended the Horus throne of the living only because an older brother died young of unknown cause. Many believe that when he donned the white and red crowns of Upper and Lower Egypt, the patient was ill-prepared to rule the most powerful empire on earth, having until then been excluded from court functions because of his appearance. Some suspect he had a congenital ailment[9] that robbed him of his self-confidence and caused him to reject the ancient families that had administered the empire for generations in favor of parvenus lacking experience. Certainly, he had none of the fear-inspiring qualities of his father and tended to rationalize weakness as fairness, all of which served to embolden his enemies. Although some speculate that excessive inbreeding caused both his physical and mental handicaps, others disagree, pointing out that he was the product of a gene pool that had not been polluted by close intermarriage for at least two generations.[1]

During the seventeen years he ruled, the patient fomented revolution within his own kingdom by legislating the existence of a one-and-only god.[10] Before him, Egypt had worshipped many gods and goddesses: *Amun*, the supreme one; *Osiris*, ruler of the underworld; *Iris*, goddess of fertility; *Re*, the ancient sun god; *Khnum*, the creator; *Thoth*, scribe and patron of the arts; *Min*, god of fertility; *Hathor*, goddess of love, beauty and femininity; *Sekhmet,* lioness-headed goddess of pestilence; and *Shu*, god of the atmosphere and air, and father of earth (*Geb*) and sky (*Nut*).[11] The patient elevated Aten, the Sun-disc, above them all, eclipsing even the all-powerful Amun, who had ruled in Thebes as king of the gods for centuries. All of the other gods, according to his decrees, ceased to be effective. Only the Sun-disc retained its power.

In the course of his revolution, the patient declared himself the image of Aten, his father in heaven, and proclaimed his own *beauty* that of the Sun-disc itself.[12] He also gave Nefertiti (see Figure 1-1), his chief wife (whose exquisite limestone bust unearthed in 1912 brought her fame surpassing that of the patient himself), greater influence in religious matters and in affairs of state than perhaps any queen had ever enjoyed.[13] Together, they presided over a religious upheaval that shattered centuries of tradition. What motivated them is not known. However, by the fifth year of the patient's reign, tension with the powerful Theban clergy devoted to Amun was intolerable. The patient would say only that what he experienced at their hands was worse than anything he or his ancestors had ever had to endure. His response was to anathemize Amun, close his temple in Thebes and move the capital from Thebes to a huge, new city one hundred eighty miles to the north on the eastern bank of the Nile. The patient named it Akhetaten, "the horizon of Aten."[14]

All these efforts to establish Aten as his kingdom's one true god left little time for other matters of state, in particular, time to deal with the defense of Egypt's borders and provinces against hostile incursions.[15] The patient's failure in this regard was grave. Even so, it was his heresy that inspired his successors to systematically obliterate every trace of his existence little more than a decade after his death.[16]

Smenkhare, Tutankhamun (King Tut), Ay and Horemheb, the last of the Tutmosids, followed. Horemheb was the one who finally

4

FIGURE 1-1. Queen Nefertiti of Egypt. Limestone from workshop of Thutsmosis, ca. 1350 BCE. Photo: Margarete Buesing. Aegyptisches Museum, Staatliche Museen zu Berlin, Berlin Germany. Photo Credit: Bildarchiv Preussischer Kulturbesitz/Art Resource, NY.

closed the temples of the Sun-disc, which had been allowed to function side-by-side with the reopened shrines of the other gods after the patient died. During twenty-seven years as Pharaoh, Horemheb was relentless in his efforts to erase all traces of the patient and his reign. Walls of the patient's new capital were torn down to their foundations, mud bricks pillaged, and steles and statuary hopelessly smashed. Shards of the ruined edifices were then quarried for over a century as fill for the foundations of new structures built across the river at Hermopolis.[16]

So complete was the destruction of Akhetaten, we are told, that when Horemheb had finished literally no stone of the city was left upon another.[17] Although the reliefs and steles that were the principal record of the patient's existence were systematically dismantled, fortunately they were not smashed beyond recognition. More than one hundred thousand of the blocks of the masonry (talatat) used to build his temples survived in foundations of structures erected by later pharaohs. Through reliefs preserved on these and a few other artifacts, we have rediscovered the patient and the bold new artistic style that for many is his greatest legacy.

While the survival of these talatat[18] offer some illumination of the patient's mysterious history, much darkness remains.[19] The talatat indicate that near the third anniversary of his accession to the throne, the patient gathered around him his chief sculptors, including one Bek, and decreed that, henceforth, "[His] form was to be portrayed in such a way to emphasize the attributes that differentiated him from a traditional royal subject — his youth, musculature and beauty."[20] The works of art that followed are unflattering, even by ancient standards, depicting a monarch with spindly arms, heavy thighs, and an oddly triangular head with pointed chin who differs radically in appearance from the idealized images of his ancestors.[9]

The distinctive physical features depicted in statues and reliefs are at once odd, strikingly diverse and inconsistent. In existing statuary, the patient appears more natural and life-like than in reliefs.[1] Moreover, likenesses produced at the beginning of his reign, and then again at the end, depict him in traditional pharaonic guise with little to distinguish his image from the perfect physiques of other pharaohs of the 18th Dynasty. Only after he concentrated his worship on Aten was the patient portrayed in his new (realistic?) image. That image, at its most florid, is androgynous, with striking abnormalities of the head, chest, abdomen, hips, extremities and spine.

The patient's skull, in some (but not all) representations, is malformed, with an elongated head, almond-shaped eyes, lantern-like jaw, protruding teeth and large ears.[21] The neck is inordinately long and serpentine. In some representations the chest has a deeply depressed sternum (*pectus excavatum*) and in others, a protruding sternum characteristic of a pigeon breast deformity (*pectus carinatum*). The breasts are sometimes as large and round as a woman's (*gynecomastia*), as are the hips and buttocks. These feminine characteristics are all the more striking because, more often than not, they are accompanied by a belly as prominent as that of a pregnant woman, as if to emphasize the patient's fertility and to validate his claim that he was "the Nile which fills the entire land."[22] Moreover, the only nude statue of the patient known to exist lacks a phallus. In fact, unlike that of at least one other pharaoh, a nude statue of King Hor I, the patient's statue shows no evidence of external genitalia whatsoever. In many representations, the shoulders are gaunt, the arms and legs long and spindly, with flat feet (*pes planus*), spider-like fingers and toes (*arachnodactyly*) and knee joints that flex posteriorly (*genu recurvatum*). In some (but not all) representations, these distortions of the head, body and extremities are also shown in the patient's children, his wife, and some members of his entourage. The striking departure of these images from the idealistic, even heroic, portraits of earlier royalty would not likely have occurred without the patient's insistence. No artist, regardless of how talented or creative, would have dared produce such unflattering likenesses of the god-king and his family without having been instructed to do so. In fact, the patient's chief sculptor, Bek, affirms this in describing himself as "the apprentice whom his majesty taught."[23]

Only a bit more is known of the health of the patient or of his family. He had six children by his principal wife, Nefertiti; all were daughters. They gathered together in the twelfth year of his reign for a magnificent reception for foreign ambassadors who had come to Akhetaten to pay tribute to the patient. It was to be the family's last official function together. Within two years, the patient's second child was dead of unknown cause. She was scarcely more than eleven

7

years old when she died. Other family members died in rapid succession shortly thereafter: first the patient's second wife, Kiya, then Tiy, the queen mother, along with the patient's three youngest daughters. The reason for these sudden deaths is unknown; however, plague was ravaging the Levant at the time and might also have invaded Egypt to decimate the royal family.[24] The patient survived the plague only to die at Akhetaten in the summer of 1359 B.C.E. under obscure circumstances.[25] He was not yet forty and had ruled the land of Egypt for seventeen years as Neferkheprure Amenophis IV, Amenhotep IV, Akhenaten (son of the dazzling sun disk) (Figures 1-2, 1-3).[26]

***

FIGURE 1-2. Colossal head of Akhenaten. From the Aton Temple at Karnak. Egypt, 18th dynasty. Museum, Luxor, Thebes, Egypt. Photo Credit: Wener Forman/Art Resource, NY.

FIGURE 1-3. Akhenaten (right) and family. Aegyptisches Museum, Staatliche Museum zu Berlin, Berlin, Germany. Photo Credit: Bildarchiv Presussischer Kulturbesitz/Art Resource, NY.

In the recovered fragments of his demolished temples, Akhenaten has reemerged as "the most controversial figure in Egyptian history."[27] The many traces of his reign uncovered by archaeologists reveal astonishingly little, however, of who this strange potentate was.

To express his abstract monotheistic concept of godhead, Akhenaten instigated a novel style of art, one that aroused great interest among scholars who first reencountered it during the 19th century in the ruins of Akhenaten's capital city at Tell el-Amarna in Middle Egypt.

Tell el-Amarna, the modern village after which the Akhetaten archeological site is named, is actually a misnomer, since there is no single *tell* or great mound marking the ancient site. Scholars now generally refer to it as "El Amarna" or simply "Amarna."

Aldred maintains that the forces that gave rise to the new, realistic style of art were already gathering strength in the last decade of the reign of Amenophis III, suggesting, at least to some scholars, the existence of a long co-regency between Amenophis III and Akhenaten. In full flower, the new art form celebrated Akhenaten's claim to a considerable share of the Aten's godhead and replaced images of the old gods of the Egyptian pantheon with representations of the new divine ruler and his family (Figure 1-4). According to Aldred, the Amarna art forms illustrate "the significant acts of a Holy Family, the visible intermediaries between man and the godhead supreme, the invisible sun-god whose symbol predominates at the summit of every composition."[28]

Of all the mysteries surrounding Akhenaten, his appearance in the representations produced during the Amarna period is the most arresting. Because the statues and reliefs are so unflatteringly bizarre, they are presumed to be realistic, but are they?[23] The plaster cast of Akhenaten's head excavated in the studio of the master sculptor Djhutmose at Amarna in 1912-13 C.E. only vaguely resembles the pharaoh's appearance in the statues and reliefs that have been most influential in fueling speculation about a deforming congenital disorder. Therefore, one must wonder if the other deformities (of the neck, breast, hips, etc.) in the Amarna images truly represent the subject's appearance. If they do, are the images portraits of a deforming disease or simply those of an extraordinarily odd-looking man? If the statues and reliefs are symbolic rather than realistic, what is it they are meant to symbolize?

In *Aspects of Monotheism: How God is One*, Egyptologist D.B. Redford[21] writes that the art Akhenaten favored was supercharged with

FIGURE 1-4.   Akhenaton (right) and Nerfertiti offering to the sun god Aten. Egyptian Museum, Cairo, Egypt. Photo Credit: Scala/Art Resource, NY.

a symbolism expressive of his divinity. He suspects, as do many Egyptologists, that the key to unlocking Akhenaten's many mysteries lies in understanding the peculiar imagery used to depict him. Some have suggested that Akhenaten's images are actually those of a woman in disguise or a eunuch brought back from the Sudan.[29]

Proponents of a symbolic interpretation of the Amarna images believe that Akhenaten had himself depicted in that form simply to convey the concepts of androgyny and fertility which were the essence of his status as both father and mother of all mankind,[30] and also to reinforce the idea that he was the embodiment of a god "who himself gave birth to himself."[21] It has also been suggested that in the early years of his reign, when Akhenaten fought as a young radical against established religion, exaggeration was one of the devices he used to topple more than a thousand years of orthodoxy in both art and religion.[28] For some scholars, the Amarna images are just such an exaggeration, used principally to portray Akhenaten's power artistically and to differentiate him from his subjects; for others, they are simply the exuberant distortions of artists celebrating a brief respite from the disciplined style they had been forced to endure for generations.[31]

If the Amarna images are faithful representations of Akhenaten, how might one explain the many odd, almost surreal, physical anomalies depicted? One of the earliest proposals is that Akhenaten's strange appearance was the result of an endocrine disorder first described by A. Fröhlich in 1901 C.E.[32] The technical term for the disorder, *adiposogenital dystrophy*, reflects the adipose and genital abnormalities that are its most striking features. Fröhlich syndrome is a disorder of the pituitary gland, the small, oval structure at the base of the brain which regulates the production of most of the hormones produced by the body's endocrine glands. The syndrome primarily affects males and is characterized by obesity, delayed puberty and underdeveloped genitalia. Adult males with the disorder are typically impotent, mildly retarded and have soft skin and effeminate thighs and breasts. Although there are many potential causes of such traits, Fröhlich syndrome is appropriately diagnosed only when the traits are the result of a tumor of the hypothalamus (the area immediately adjacent to the pituitary), which disrupts both the appetite-regulating function of the hypothalamus and the sex hormone–regulating function of the pituitary. Because the body's thermostat is located in the hypothalamus, patients with Fröhlich syndrome occasionally also have difficulty regulating their body temperatures.[33]

Although Fröhlich syndrome might explain the feminine physique, protuberant belly and, perhaps, the absence of genitalia in the Amarna representations, it would not explain Akhenaten's peculiarly shaped head, serpentine neck, sternal abnormality, spindly extremities or hyperflexible joints. Moreover, Akhenaten was a sun-worshipper literally as well as figuratively. All of his official meetings and ceremonies were conducted entirely in the sun, in heat so oppressive that foreign dignitaries actually feared for their lives. If Akhenaten had had difficulty regulating his body temperature because of Fröhlich syndrome, it is unlikely that he could have tolerated the extreme heat during such functions routinely conducted in direct sunlight.[34] Moreover, although many scholars believe that Akhenaten was by no means an intellectual heavyweight,[35] his accomplishments as religious reformer and builder were incompatible with mental retardation. His apparent innate intelligence and fertility (as evidenced by his six daughters) are, perhaps, the strongest evidence that he did not suffer from Fröhlich syndrome.

A disorder known as "Marfan syndrome" also has been proposed as the cause of Akhenaten's strange appearance[1] and, in many respects, is a better fit than Fröhlich syndrome. Marfan syndrome is an inherited disorder of connective tissues, the matrix tissues that provide support for virtually all of the structures of the body. It is a condition typically passed from one generation to the next as an *autosomal dominant* trait, meaning that only one (rather than two) abnormal chromosome is sufficient to produce the disorder. In its most florid state, Marfan syndrome is associated with a diverse array of abnormalities, many of which were exhibited by United States President Abraham Lincoln, who some authorities believe had the disorder. Those involving the heart (valvular abnormalities and aneurysms) are especially dangerous and, prior to the advent of corrective surgery, were largely responsible for a shortened life span in which half of affected males died before the age of forty. Typically, patients with Marfan syndrome are tall and have disproportionately long limbs compared with the trunk. Most also have abnormally long, spider-like fingers and toes (arachnodactyly), anterior chest deformities (both *pectus excavatium* and *pectus carinatum*) and hyperextensible joints. Curvature of the spine, flat feet (*pes planus*) and dislocated lenses are common. The lens abnormality frequently leads to myopia (near-sightedness). Intelligence is normal.[36]

Thus, Marfan syndrome has many features in common with Akhenaten's appearance in the Amarna images, including the serpentine neck, flat feet, spider-like fingers and toes and hyperextensible joints. Moreover, unlike Fröhlich syndrome, Marfan syndrome is not associated with either infertility or mental retardation. As noted above, it is associated with myopia, a condition Burridge[1] believes might explain Akhenaten's love of light, and, perhaps, also the frequency with which he was shown holding the hand of Nefertiti and/or his daughters, whose assistance he might have needed when ambulating because of poor vision. One of the pernicious cardiovascular complications of Marfan syndrome might even explain Akhenaten's death before age forty.

Marfan syndrome, however, does not typically cause deformities of the head or a lantern-like jaw. Nor in men is it associated with gynecomastia, feminine hips and buttocks, absent (or poorly developed) genitalia or a pregnant-appearing abdomen. Therefore, if Akhenaten had Marfan syndrome, it likely would not have been his only medical problem. Some other disorder would have to have caused these additional deformities: one associated with cirrhosis, such as schistosomiasis (Bilharzia), for example.

Schistosomiasis is an infestation by parasitic worms (blood flukes) belonging to the genus *Schistosoma*.[37] Man is the worm's definitive host (i.e., the host within which the worm matures into adulthood and reproduces). A second (intermediate) host is required for the schistosome to complete its life cycle and survive in nature. Fresh water snails fulfill the role of intermediate host by providing a suitable environment for newly hatched offspring to develop into dart-shaped, infective forms (cercaria) capable of penetrating the intact skin of humans unfortunate enough to bathe in infested waters. Once within the human body, cercariae find their way to the veins that drain the bladder and intestine, where they mature, copulate and begin to produce eggs. The life cycle is complete when eggs migrate from abdominal veins into the lumen of the bladder or intestine and are excreted into water inhabited by receptive fresh water snails. Many of the eggs, however, become trapped within abdomi-

14

nal veins and are swept into the sieve-like vascular network of the liver, where they cause chronic inflammation, which over time, especially in heavy infestations, produces cirrhosis with its associated complications of anemia, emaciation, ascites, gynecomastia and testicular atrophy (see Chapter 8).

Schistosomiasis is common in Egypt and probably always has been.[38] A recent autopsy of a sixteen-year-old weaver who lived at the time of Rameses III found evidence of both heavy schistosome infestation and cirrhosis. Simms[39] has theorized that Akhenaten might have been similarly afflicted and that the likely source of his schistosomal infestation and that of the unfortunate sixteen-year-old weaver who lived a little over a century later was a lake excavated by Akhenaten's father (Amenophis III) in front of his palace at Malqata.

Schistosomal cirrhosis thus might explain Akhenaten's gynecomastia, his genital atrophy, and his swollen belly, but none of the other striking deformities of the Amarna images. Moreover, if Akhenaten had had cirrhosis severe enough to produce ascites, it likely also would have caused dependent edema, most pronounced in the ankles and calves, rather than in the hips and thighs. For this reason, cirrhosis, even if superimposed on Marfan syndrome, is an unlikely explanation for the array of physical abnormalities depicted in the Amarna images.

If Akhenaten did not have Fröhlich syndrome, Marfan syndrome or cirrhosis, what medical condition could he have had which might account for his strange appearance in the Amarna statues and reliefs? The answer is a condition called Klinefelter syndrome, a genetic disorder in which the normal XY sex chromosome pattern of males is distorted by the presence of one or more extra X chromosomes.[40] Afflicted males typically possess forty-seven (rather than the usual forty-six) chromosomes owing to the presence of an XXY (rather than XY) sex chromosome pattern. Because of the influence of the extra X chromosome, affected males are typically tall and infertile, and exhibit gynecomastia, a eunuchoid body habitus, sparse facial and body hair and small testes. These features, however, generally do not become evident until after puberty. Although the head circumference of affected adults is normal, the face tends to be long and slender with a prominent jaw. Muscles usually are weak. Sexual development progresses normally throughout childhood. However, by mid-to-late adolescence, most males with the 47, XXY chromosome pattern begin to show evidence of arrested testicular growth and low sperm counts. As a result, they are generally infertile. Rare fertile cases, however, have been identified and are thought to represent incomplete (mosaic) forms of the disorder.[41]

Many Klinefelter patients exhibit mild derangements of intelligence, personality and behavior. Although intellectual development is generally normal, slight delays in the evolution of motor and language skills are common, as are poor muscle tone, incoordination and mild cognitive disability (primarily verbal). Affected boys are characteristically shy, unassertive and immature. Poor verbal skills tend to limit their interactions with peers, adding to their immaturity and isolation. Some experience serious emotional and behavioral difficulties, sometimes manifested as depression and at others as mania. The social isolation many Klinefelter patients feel as a consequence of their genetic disorder is vividly illustrated by the following excerpt from a personal account written by one such patient for the *Lancet* in 2004:

> About 30 years ago I began to search for an explanation for why I was different from other teenagers. I had just finished high school, which had been an academic and social struggle. By 6th grade (12 years of age) my unusual physical appearance — 6 ft. tall (1.80 m) and skinny frame — made me an easy target for the taunts of other children. My slow academic progress and my need for special tuition contributed to my image as a nerdy social outcast. Socially, I never made it as far as my peer group, and my appeal to girls was limited to causing them to point and giggle at my gangly awkwardness. Many psychological tests throughout my adolescence led my teachers to only one conclusion: I was lazy. Life after high school was a sequence of jobs, none of which I held down for long. A lack of upper-body strength for manual work left me short of

stamina. Social interaction with work colleagues was not easy. In many ways, my working life seemed to be an extension of my depressing high-school experience. At the age of 35, I became ill with symptoms that included an irregular heart beat, sleep apnoea, cold sweats, and extreme fatigue. No diagnosis was forthcoming. Too ill to continue working, I moved back home to live with my parents in California.....[42]

Varicose veins, venous stasis ulcers and venous thrombosis affect up to a third of Klinefelter patients. Diabetes and disorders of the heart, lungs and gastrointestinal tract are also common. As a result, such patients are at considerable risk of dying prematurely.[43]

Thus, of all the disorders that might explain Akhenaten's bizarre appearance in the Amarna images, none offers a better fit than Klinefelter syndrome. It could explain his misshapen head and jaw, his gynecomastia, his tall gangly appearance and his feminine physique (see Figure 1-5). It might also explain why, time and again, he is shown in the Amarna images lounging limply in a chair or on a stool, eating and drinking at a table groaning with food; never hunting, doing battle or engaging in any other strenuous activity in the heroic style of his forbearers. If he had Klinefelter syndrome, the image of "refined sloth" which permeate his representations,[44] and the protuberant belly, might have been the result of poor muscle tone resulting from the genetic defect.

Klinefelter syndrome's psychological effects also might have had a role in creating the sense of alienation which caused Akhenaten to reject the Theban clergy[45] while becoming increasingly dependent on his wife, Nefertiti.[46] It would not have impaired his intellect to a degree incompatible with his artistic and religious accomplishments. Moreover, if he had the incomplete (mosaic) form of the disorder, he would not necessarily have been infertile. Klinefelter syndrome would not explain the abnormalities of the anterior chest or the absent genitalia in the painted sandstone colossus excavated from the site of the Gempaaten temple at East Karnak.[47] Nor would it explain the representations of Nefertiti, Akhenaten's daughters

FIGURE 1-5. Statuette of Akhenaten. Ca. 1345 BCE. Egypt, 18th dynasty. From Tell el-Amarna. Alabaster. Photo: Margarete Buesing. Aegyptisches Museum, Staaliche Museen zu Berlin, Berlin, Germany. Photo Credit: Bildarchiv Preussischer Kulturbesitz/Art Resource, NY.

and members of his entourage exhibiting deformities similar to his own.[48] It is highly improbable that they all had the same disorder. Rather, it is more likely that under Akhenaten's influence, the Amarna physiognomy became the artistic ideal and as such fashionable for both the king's relatives and his followers to adopt.

Because Klinefelter syndrome is the result of a genetic accident that is neither inherited from the preceding generation nor passed on to the next, no examination of the mummies of Akhenaten's close relatives[49] can help to confirm or refute the diagnosis. Only his remains might serve this purpose, and they have yet to be recovered. If his mummy were recovered, gross examination and radiologic studies might verify the physical abnormalities depicted in the Amarna images. If they did exist, careful examination of the testes for evidence of arrested growth and fibrosis might produce further support for Klinefelter syndrome. The definitive diagnostic test would be the examination of an intact cell with a well-preserved nucleus for the presence of two X chromosomes and a Y chromosome using appropriate molecular probes. Unfortunately, the likelihood of finding such a cell in a 3,300 year-old mummy is vanishingly small.

Because Akhenaten's instructions to his artists, like those of the other pharaohs, would have been explicit, it is reasonable to assume that his sculptors accurately depicted the Pharaoh's actual appearance (Figure 1-5). If so, and we discount the possibility that Akhenaten was simply born extraordinarily ugly, of the known genetic disorders, only Klinefelter syndrome can explain more than a few of the Amarna abnormalities.

Notes

1. Burridge A. Did Akhenaten suffer from Marfan's syndrome? *Akhenaten Temple Project News Letter.* No. 3, September 1995.
2. The dates of the Egyptian dynastic periods are uncertain. They have been established, for the most part, by working forwards and backwards from one or two key points determined from chance recordings of astrological phenomena. The further one reaches into the past, the less accurate they become (Alfred C. *Akhenaten. King of Egypt.* Thames & Hudson. London: 1988, p.9,10). Redford has proposed both 1377 B.C.E. and 1352 B.C.E. as the year Akhenaten became Pharaoh (see notes below), Aldred 1358 B.C.E.

3. There were over thirty dynasties in all according to Manetho, High Priest of the sun god in Heliopolis, who was commissioned by Ptolemy I in the third century B.C.E. to write a history of Egypt. See Table 1-1 for his dynasty list.
4. Op cit (Alfred) p. 52.
5. Redford D.B. Akhenaten. *The Heretic King.* Princeton U. Press. Princeton; 1984, p. 3-4.
6. Medicine in Akhenaten's Egypt was, likewise, surprisingly modern. Eight medical papyri, which are the source of what we know of the practice of medicine in ancient Egypt (see Table 1-3 for a list of the chief Egyptian medical papyri), describe a medical profession with roots extending back to 3000 B.C.E., a profession which reached its zenith during the 18th Dynasty. The papyri demonstrate clearly that the physicians of ancient Egypt were keen and accurate observers, who possessed a systematic method of examination, an interest in the principles of diagnosis and an appreciation for prognosis and the natural course of untreated disease. They also contain an extensive pharmacopoeia, which was used rationally by physicians of that era in the treatment of disease. Many of the preparations described in

TABLE 1-3 The Chief Egyptian Medical Papyri

Name	Approximate Date (B.C.E.)	Location
Kahun	1900	London
Edwin Smith	1600	New York
Ebers	1550	Leipzig
Hearst	1550	Berkeley
Erman	1550	Berlin
London	1350	London
Berlin	1350	Berlin
Chester Beatty	1200	London

Adapted from Leake CD. *The Old Egyptian Medical Papyri.* Univ. Kansas Press, Lawrence: 1952, p. 7-44.

the papyri can be found in medical formularies and recipe books as recent as those produced during the Middle Ages and Renaissance. Supernaturalism was, by comparison, relatively unimportant in ancient Egyptian medical practice, with incantations recorded in the papyri used primarily as "prayers" for skill and guidance in managing patients.

7. Breasted JH. *A History of Egypt.* Charles Scribner and Sons, New York: 1937.

8. Akhenaten, the second son of Amenophis III, was the tenth pharaoh of the 18th Dynasty. The complete list of the 18th Dynasty potentates is shown in Table 1-2.

9. Op cit (Redford) p. 57-8.

10. Redford offers a negative view of Akhenaten's revolutionary cult, pointing out that Akhenaten excised much more from the traditional religion of his day than he added. He did away with service to the gods and watched their temples decay in desuetude. Moreover, in Aten, his one and only God, he offered no mythology to replace that of the displaced gods. What he offered his people instead "was not a 'god' at all, but a disc in the heavens....[The equivalent of] a fanatical Christian priest denying Christ, the Trinity, and the saints in favor of the Cross." [Op cit (Redford) p. 170, 226]

11. Op cit (Redford) p. 236-241.

12. Op cit (Redford) p. 179.

13. Op cit (Redford) p. 78.

14. Op cit (Redford) p. 140-2.

15. Until the twilight years of Amenophis III, the army had campaigned continuously in the field under the leadership of valiant pharaohs. Under Akhenaten, however, it became an instrument of centralized domestic policy, more concerned with laboring in quarries and construction projects than in waging foreign wars. As a result, Akhenaten's reign was marked by a series of defeats which culminated in the loss of a principality in Lebanon. [Op cit (Aldred) p. 282-3]

16. Op cit (Redford) p. 227.

17. Op cit (Redford) p. 63-71.

18. The masonry blocks with which Akhetaten was built were dubbed "talatat" by the inhabitants of Karnak. The term is Arabic for the plural of the word "three" and presumably alludes to the fact that these building blocks are three handbreadths in length. [Op cit (Redford) p. 68]

19. Carter H. *The Tomb of Tut-ankh-Amen.* Cooper Square Publishers Inc. New York: 1963, vol 2, p. 20

20. Op cit (Redford) p. 63.

21. Redford DB. The monotheism of Akhenaten. In Shanks H, Meinhardt J, eds. *Aspects of Monotheism. How God is One.* Biblical Archaeological Society. Washington, D.C.: 1997, p. 11-26.

22. Redford DB. The Sun-Disk in Akhenaten's program: Its worship and antecedents II. *JARCE.* 1980; 17:21-50.

23. Akhenaten's less bizarre representations in the latter years of his reign raise the possibility that the grotesque aspects of his appearance in earlier monuments owe more to artistic expression than actual pathology. Late models and sketches found in sculptors' studios at Amarna lack the exaggerated physical features of the earlier style. Moreover, model reliefs used to guide workmen constructing buildings during the last year of his reign present more orthodox portraits of the royal family than earlier reliefs. Op cit (Aldred) p. 234-5.

24. Op cit (Redford) p. 186-7.

25. Op cit (Redford) p. 193.

26. "Amenophis" ("Amun is satisfied"), the Greek version of "Amenhotep" was discarded for "Akhenaten" (Son of the dazzling sun disk") as part of the religious revolution.

27. Op cit (Redford) p. 215.

28. Aldred C. *Egyptian Art in the Days of the Pharaohs. 3100-320 BC.* Thames and Hudson, London: 1985. p. 168-75; Gore R. Pharaoh's of the sun. *National Geographic.* 2001; April: 34-60.

29. Op cit (Redford) p. 4.

30. Redford DB. Preliminary report of the first season of excavation in East Karnak, 1975-76. JARCE. 1977;14:9-32.

31. Hawkes, J. The First Great Civilizations: Life in Mesopotamia, the Indus Valley, and Egypt. New York, Alfred A. Knopf, Inc., 1973, p. 438

32. Op cit (Aldred) p. 231-6.

33. Wilkins L. *The Diagnosis and Treatment of Endocrine Disorders in Childhood and Adolescence.* 3rd ed. Charles C. Thomas, Publisher. Springfield:1966, p. 262-3.

34. Op cit (Redford) p. 235.

35. Op cit (Redford) p. 233.

36. Pyeritz RE. Marfan syndrome and other disorders of fibrillin. In Rimoin DL, Connor JM, Pyeritz RE, Korf BR, eds. *Emery and Rimoin's Principles and Practice of Medical Genetics.* 4th ed. Churchill-Livingstone, London: 2002, p. 3977-4010.

37. Mahmond AA. Trematodes (schistosomiasis) and other flukes. In Mandell GL, Bennett JE, Dolin R, eds. *Principles and Practice of Infectious Diseases.* 5th ed.) Churchill-Livingstone. Philadelphia: 2000, p. 2950-3.

38. The Egyptian medical papyri (see Note 6) catalogue a long list of disorders that were apparently common in ancient Egypt. In addition to schistosomiasis, which was almost certainly responsible for frequent references to hematuria (bloody urine), the papyri mention exanthematic fevers (fevers with rashes), dysentery, worms (most likely both tapeworms and round worms), heart disease (including angina pectoris and aneurysms), edema, rheumatism, excessive urination (diabetes?), intestinal obstruction, lung abscess, burns, blisters, "eating" ulcers, infected nails, wounds, impotence, hernias, scurvy, dental disorders, cancers, buboes and abscesses. [Ghalioungui P. *Magic and Medical Science in Ancient Egypt.* Hodder and Stoughton, London: 1963, p. 51-7]

39. Simms TM. The Amarna kings, anaemias and parasitic liver disease. *Proc Amarna Centennial Symposium.* 1988

40. Allanson JE, Graham GE. Klinefelter syndrome. In Rimoin DL, Connor JM, Pyeritz RE, Korf BR. *Emery and Rimoin's Principle and Practice of Medical Genetics.* 4th ed. Churchill-Livingstone. London:2002, p. 1189-91.

41. Laron Z, Dickerman Z, Zamir R, Galatzer A. Paternity in Klinefelter's syndrome: a case report. *Arch Androl.* 1982;8:149-151; Terzoli G, Lattala F, Lobbiani A. Fertility in a 47, xxy patient: assessment of biological paternity by deoxyribonucleic acid fingerprinting. *Fertil Steril.* 1992;58:821-22.

42. Grace RJ: Klinefelter's syndrome: a late diagnosis. *Lancet.* 2004;364:284.

43. Lanfranco F, Kamischke A, Zitzmann M, Nieschlag E: Klinefelter's syndrome. *Lancet.* 2004;364:273-83.

44. Op cit (Redford) p. 234.

45. Op cit (Redford) p. 175-6.

46. Op cit (Redford) p. 165-7.

47. Akhenaten scholars are divided as to the significance of the absent genitalia in the colossus. Redford has commented: "For my own part, I can imagine that this image might have been clothed with some sort of applied garment. In any case, it need not be pointed out how ill-advised it is to read profound meaning into such a flimsy piece of evidence." [Op cit (Redford) p. 104]

Aldred, on the other hand, has written:

A theory to account for this epicene form [the nude king without genitals] has suggested that this colossus, and other more fragmentary examples in the series, are manifestations of the bisexual aspect of the sun-god, the demiurge, 'the father and mother of mankind', who impregnated himself in Chaos in order to create the diversity of the universe from the oneness of his self. The most plausible explanation, however, has been offered by J.R. Harris, who takes the view that some at least of the colossi represent not Akhenaten but Nefertiti wearing a close-clinging garment. The holding of kingly scepters, and the wearing of a heavy beard in each case does not vitiate this argument, since there are other instances where such masculine adjuncts are occasionally arrogated by heiress-queens, particularly by Hatshepsut. Unfortunately, no complete range of stylistic details has survived on these statues which would clinch his argument. There are no feet to show evidence of a lower hem of the garment: and the upper part of the crown is also missing, thus thwarting any attempt to decide whether the queen's double uraeus was worn, and what the exact design of the headgear should be. [Op cit (Aldred) p. 235]

48. Op cit (Aldred) p. 232.

49. The remains of several of Akhenaten's close relatives have been recovered including those of his father and (possibly) his mother, his paternal grandfather and both maternal grandparents. Most scholars believe that Akhenaten's own remains were destroyed in antiquity. [Op cit (Aldred) p. 96-109]

HELLENIC HOLOCAUST

2

*S*uch was the misery to which the Athenians being fallen, were oppressed; having not only their men killed by the Disease within, but the Enemy also laying waste to their Fields and Villages without. In this sickness also, (as it was not unlikely they would) they called to mind this Verse, said also of the elder fort to have been uttered of old: A Doric War shall fall/And a great Plague withall.[1]

The 5th century B.C.E. was the golden Age of Athens, perhaps of all western history. It was then that Aeschylus, Sophocles, Aristophanes and Euripides wrote their immortal works; Pheidias created some of mankind's most sublime examples of sculpture and architecture; Herodotus and Thucydides wrote treatises that are the basis of the science of history; modern medical concepts first began to flower under the influence of Hippocrates; and democracy, as we know it, was born. It was also the period over which this patient reigned as political and military leader and as cultural leader as well (see Figure 2-1).

This patient's name is indissolubly linked to Athens' Golden Age because he more than any other was the man responsible for gathering and nurturing the illuminati who were the Golden Age. He was also personally responsible for inaugurating construction of the Parthenon and other public buildings that comprise the principal architectural legacy of Classical Greece. Moreover, his funeral oration for Athenians who perished during the first year of the Peloponnesian War, one of the greatest speeches ever delivered, became not just the credo of his city, but also of the 18th century's Age of Enlightenment and of the democracy of Thomas Jefferson and Benjamin Franklin.

FIGURE 2-1. View of the Parthenon, construction of which was supervised by Pheidias from 447 to 431 BCE. Photo Credit: Scala/Art Resource, NY.

Sadly, he and his Golden Age lasted but a short time. Both were swept away by war and pestilence. The former was, in large part, a product of the patient's hubris and of the financing of his Golden Age with monies purloined from a league of Greek city states united in defense against renewed aggression by the Persians after their defeat at the battle of Marathon in 490 B.C.E. The patient transformed the league into an instrument of his own imperial ambitions, imposing his will and that of his people on it and openly appropriating its funds for Athenian purposes. When Sparta could tolerate the role of Athenian subordinate no longer, war erupted and was followed almost immediately by a plague, the nature of which persists to this day as one of the great mysteries of antiquity.

The plague arrived the summer the Spartans and their allies invaded Attica (the region surrounding Athens).[2] It first appeared among the Athenians only days after the Spartan coalition commanded by Archidamus began ravaging the countryside beyond the city walls. Although there had been other epidemics, none was

nearly as extensive or destructive of human lives; for this one resisted all known treatments. In fact, physicians who dared to minister to the stricken themselves quickly fell victim to the disease and
perished. At first, the Athenians resorted to supplications to the
gods and inquiries of the oracles, but when these proved to no avail,
they were overwhelmed by the magnitude of the calamity and lost
hope.

No one knows for certain where the disease originated. Some say
it began in Ethiopia and then descended into Egypt and Libya before spreading throughout the eastern Mediterranean. It entered
Athens suddenly, through its port at Peiraeus, so suddenly, in fact,
that residents of Peiraeus thought the Peloponnesians (Sparta and
its allies) had poisoned their cisterns. It later spread to the city
proper, however, and gained in murderous strength.

The plague descended on Athens in a year that otherwise had
been unusually healthy. In fact, it seemed as if all other diseases
temporarily had relaxed their grip on the city in anticipation of the
plague's arrival, so that when the patient came down with the illness, he and his sister, like so many others, began their sudden and
rapid decline from a state of apparent excellent health.

If, in a democracy, one man can be described as indispensable,
this patient was such a man. An aristocrat, born five years before the
battle of Marathon, he emerged as political leader of the Athenians
in 463 B.C.E. Around 454 B.C.E., he became *strategos,* or general,
and dominated Athenian political, military and cultural life thereafter, until his death in 430 or 429 B.C.E. His was a reign marked
by intellectual ferment, in which Sophists, historians, ethnogra-
phers and physicians engaged in an intense period of enlightened
inquiry into the human condition. It witnessed the birth of rational-
ism, humanism and science,[3] during which man first began to comprehend his place in the universe, to appreciate the power of
invention that would enable him to advance from a state of nature
to one of culture, and to recognize that he was himself an object
worthy of scientific investigation.[4] When the patient died during
the first year of the plague's three-year rampage, Athenian élan

ebbed, and the city's strategy for the war against the Spartan coalition failed. More than their political and military leader, he was their inspiration — the wellspring from which the ideals that defined their age seemed to flow.

The illness struck the patient when he was 65 years of age. Until then, he had remained hale and sturdy and vigorous of purpose and retained a well-preserved physique, even for his age, and an extraordinary brain housed in an elongated skull shaped like a hatchet.[5] He was married, with two fine sons, both of whom also perished in the carnage wrought by the plague. A third son by his mistress, his namesake, survived the epidemic, only to be executed by his own people in the final days of the war as one of many scapegoats blamed for the series of defeats that doomed the Athenian empire.

The patient's illness, if it was typical of the one that ended the lives of so many of his fellow Athenians, began with intense heat of the head and redness and inflammation of the eyes. His throat and tongue would have been blood red as well, his breath fetid. Sneezing and hoarseness typically followed and then violent coughing, marking the descent of the disease into the chest. The stomach was next. When the disorder settled there, vomiting and intractable retching resulted. Although victims were not particularly warm to the touch, their skin was red, livid and covered with small blisters and ulcers. Moreover, they complained of such intense internal heat they could not tolerate even the lightest covering. Rather, they preferred to remain uncovered or, better yet, submerged in cold water. Indeed, many who were left unattended threw themselves into cisterns to relieve both their internal heat and an unquenchable thirst. Whether the patient did so is not known.[1]

The disorder brought restlessness and sleepless nights. And yet, those afflicted did not become wasted or lose their strength until the very end. If they died, they generally did so on the seventh or the ninth day. Some survived this phase of the illness only to have the disorder descend into their bowels where it caused profuse diarrhea. In some cases, the disease attacked and destroyed the fingers, toes and genitalia. In others it took the eyes. Some patients recovered from this phase too, but only at the cost of memory so impaired that they could not recognize themselves, their friends or even common, everyday objects. The patient's disease was like no other previously encountered. For one thing, the birds and other scavengers that normally feed on carcasses would not come near the bodies of victims, even though scores of dead men, women and children littered the streets of the besieged city. And if scavengers did feed on the diseased carrion, they also died.[6,7]

Physicians prescribed baths and purgatives and bled some victims. The patient likely received such treatments, but to no avail. Nothing seemed to slow the disorder as it advanced relentlessly, killing the illustrious and the insignificant, the just and the wicked with equal implacability. Sometimes death was the result of neglect; at others, it came despite the best care possible. Those who ministered to the afflicted themselves became ill and died, leaving many of the sick to perish uncared for, alone in their houses. Even so, there were those who made it a point of honor to visit sick friends and relatives without regard for their own safety. More often, those who had recovered from the illness were the ones who did so. The disease never attacked the same person a second time, at least not with fatal results.

With refugees pouring into Athens, crowding became intolerable. Housing was quickly exhausted, forcing new arrivals to live in huts that provided little protection. Refugees perished in such wild disorder that bodies of the dead and dying littered the streets, one on top of another. The greatest numbers accumulated around fountains, where victims had been driven by their thirst, and in temples, where, in vain, they had sought divine intervention. Even the streets of the city's affluent districts became corridors of horror. Abandoned dogs ranged the city in packs, amplifying the hellish atmosphere with their howling and snarling. The dead and dying choked the once grand boulevards, metamorphosing them into gauntlets of despair.

The magnitude of the calamity eventually killed even social order. So overwhelmed were the Athenians by the plague that as soon as they developed the first signs of the illness, they immediately lost hope and gave up all attempts to resist the disorder. When it became apparent that neither their gods nor the state could turn the tide of death, they became careless of all laws, sacred as well as profane.

Funeral services were among the first casualties of the social disintegration wrought by the epidemic. With no spaces to plant the dead, burial parties stacked unclaimed corpses in public places throughout the city. Families lacking proper funeral materials threw bodies of lost loved ones onto the pyres of others and lit them; some threw the bodies of family members onto the already burning pyres of strangers and then disappeared. Common decency too seemed to disappear in those funeral pyres. As English poet Thomas Sprat would later put it:

> Hell forth its magazines of Lust did call,
> Nor would it be content
> With the thick troops of souls were thither sent.
> Into the upper world it went,
> Such guilt, such wickedness,
> Such irreligion did increase
> That the few good who did survive
> Were angry with the Plague for suffering them to live,
> More for the living than the dead did grieve[8]

Lawlessness and brazen indiscretion became the norm. People saw how quickly fortune could turn on both the prosperous, who died suddenly, and the destitute, who in a moment might go from nothing to possession of another's great wealth. And so the citizens of Athens became obsessed with immediate pleasures, especially those that would satisfy their lusts. Self-denial was no longer practiced in the interest of honor. What good was honor or public esteem if one were doomed? Pleasures of the moment became paramount, and anything conducive to such pleasures came to be regarded as both honorable and expedient. Neither fear of the gods nor respect for the law of men restrained the beleaguered Athenians. Why should one fear the gods or respect the law if the pious and the just perished as quickly as the profane? In any case, no one expected to live long enough to be called to account, much less to pay the penalty for misdeeds. On the contrary, most believed that the penalty already decreed against them and hanging over their heads was far heavier than any the gods or the courts might impose.

The patient would have wept had he witnessed the civil destitution brought about by the plague that accompanied his war with Sparta. It destroyed not just the lives of a quarter of the citizens of Athens, but also their moral compass and with it the utopian society they had come closer to achieving than any people before or since. When the plague of Athens claimed Pericles, it signaled not only his end, but also the end of the golden age that was his personal legacy to mankind[9] (see Figure 2-2).

***

The story of the plague that claimed the life of Pericles is actually many stories intertwined. It is the tale of one of the most mysterious and significant epidemics in occidental history, one which has much to tell about epidemics in general and about their effects on civilizations. It is a tale of Pericles and his golden age, of Thucydides and a new method of recording history, and of Hippocrates and the birth of modern medicine.

The cause of the epidemic has defied identification for almost two and a half millennia, with no diagnosis offered explaining all of the features of the illness described by Thucydides. There are several reasons why this might be so. The most logical explanation is that for all his talent as an historian, Thucydides was unequal to the task of producing a sufficiently comprehensive or accurate clinical description of the plague to allow even the most astute modern medical expert to discern its cause. Although he had the personal insight of one who had contracted and recovered from the plague, his own experience might have distorted rather than clarified his view of the disorder by instilling in him a belief that his symptoms were necessarily typical of all those who suffered from the illness. His personal

33

FIGURE 2-2. Bust of Pericles. Museo Pio Clementino, Vatican Musseums, Vatican State. Photo Credit: Scala/Art Resource, NY.

bias in this regard might have been compounded by the nearly two decades which elapsed between the time of the plague and the writing of his account. And then there is the problem of translation. Modern-day clinicians who struggle to diagnose Pericles' illness are at the mercy not only of Thucydides and his case history, but also of subsequent translations of his work.[10] No where are the limitations of such translations more evident than in the question of the meaning of "phlyktainai," the term used by Thucydides to describe the rash which appeared during the course of the illness. Because the rash, perhaps more than any other feature of the illness, is the key to its diagnosis, confusion over the precise meaning of phlyktainai (variously translated as: blain, bleb, blister, bulla, eruption, pustule, vesicle, pimple and welk) has been, in many respects, the most significant obstacle to identifying the etiology of Thucydides' illness.

There are other reasons why the etiology of the plague of Athens might continue to defy diagnosis. The disease might have been unique, arising de novo in a world long gone, never to be seen again. If so, it would not be the first epidemic disease to appear just once in the historical record. In the early years of the 20th century, for example, a massive outbreak of a previously unknown form of encephalitis suddenly appeared. Before the epidemic was over, more than a million people worldwide developed the disorder, which came to be known as von Economo's encephalitis.[11] Shortly thereafter, it vanished, just as mysteriously as it had appeared, never to be seen again.

Alternatively, Thucydides' plague might have been a disorder that transmogrified during the course of the epidemic to such an extent that subsequent visitations have born little resemblance to the original syndrome. Epidemic diseases are especially virulent when first introduced into "virgin soil" populations (that is, populations having no prior experience with and, hence, no immunity against, the infectious agent). It has been suggested that the illness described by Thucydides might have been the first epidemic of a particular infectious agent among the residents of Athens which never again returned with the ferocity of its original visitation because the Athenians were never again a "virgin soil" population with respect to the infectious agent responsible for the epidemic.[12] During one such virulent outbreak of measles in the "virgin soil" population of Fiji in 1875, there were reports of patients seeking relief from their discomfort by jumping into water. Although this interesting parallel with the plague of Athens has been offered by some as support for a diagnosis of measles, for reasons enumerated below measles is an unlikely etiology of the disorder described by Thucydides.[13] It is also possible that the plague of Athens was not a single epidemic, but rather two or more epidemics which raged simultaneously within the walls of the beleaguered city. If so, then Pericles' illness might have remained undiagnosed after all these years because Thucydides' description is of a conflation of more than one disorder, impossible to tease apart from a distance in time of over two millennia.

The correct diagnosis, if it can be determined, must explain the clinical features of the illness described by Thucydides: those present as well as those notable for their absence, the peculiar epidemiologic characteristic of the outbreak, and its sudden appearance in and equally sudden departure from the historical record. Of the diagnoses advanced to date, typhus and smallpox are the most likely. Bubonic plague, anthrax and measles are distant possibilities. None is a perfect fit. All are infections, apropos of Thucydides' report that second attacks of the illness were rare, suggesting induction of immunity of the kind seen in response to an infectious disease.

What were the characteristics of the epidemic that claimed Pericles? According to Thucydides, the illness began with "intense heat of the head" (more than likely headache) and inflammation of the eyes and throat. These were followed by sneezing and hoarseness and then violent coughing. Vomiting and retching were next and finally a generalized rash, the precise nature of which, as noted above, is uncertain. There was low-grade fever, restlessness, sleeplessness and extreme thirst. There was also an aversion to covers and clothing, and a desire to submerge oneself in water. High fever was not described, nor was physical wasting or altered mentation, at least not until the final stage of the disorder. Those who died generally did so on the seventh or ninth day. The average duration of illness in non-fatal cases is not known. In fatal cases, diarrhea was a prominent, terminal complaint. In at least some cases, there was loss of vision, in others, necrosis of digits and/or genitalia. In some of those who recovered, there was profound amnesia.

The epidemiologic features of Pericles' illness are equally striking.[7,14] The epidemic was explosive; it was thought to have originated in Africa, somewhere south of Egypt. It first appeared in
summer; arrived in Athens only after sweeping through the eastern
Mediterranean; affected the Athenians to a substantially greater extent than the besieging Peloponnesians; raged for two to five years
(although the first year was by far the deadliest) and then disappeared. All segments of Athenian society were affected; close contact with ill victims and overcrowding magnified the risk of
acquiring the disease. The disorder was deadly, with an estimated
case/fatality ratio of twenty-five percent.

Finally, there is the epidemic's historical context. It was not history's first great plague, nor its worst, and certainly not its last. It
arrived in 430 B.C.E. from the south (from Africa, according to
Thucydides), unlike one that came from the north some ten years
later in 419-416 B.C.E. The later one invaded Greece from barbar-
ian territories beyond Illyria and Paeonia and was the one against
which Hippocrates is purported to have intervened. Since word of
this later epidemic exists only in the Hippocratic tradition, its au-
thenticity is uncertain. It is of interest because, with the passage of
time, it came to be confused with Thucydides' great plague, engendering the myth that Hippocrates ended the epidemic by lighting
great fires to purify the air when no evidence exists of his involvement in the plague described by Thucydides.[15] There was also an
earlier outbreak of pestilence among Greek confederates besieging
Crisa during the First Sacred War at the beginning of the 6th century B.C.E.[16] History, in fact, is rife with accounts of great plagues,
which challenge the ability of even the most learned scholars to distinguish apocrypha from fact. As a result, many have remained undiagnosed to this day, as much because of limitations of the
historical record as the absence of sophisticated clinical test results.

In the ancient world, there were the ten plagues of Egypt mentioned in the Bible[17] and a series of Roman epidemics,[18] the most
important of which was the Antonine plague of 165 C.E. to 180
C.E.[19] The medieval period had its black death, the Renaissance its

great pox (syphilis). In the New World, an epidemic named huey cocoliztli, probably a viral hemorrhagic fever, created a Mesoamerican holocaust which left a shattered native population of colonial Mexico in its wake and dashed the hopeful beginnings of an intercultural society.[20] Cholera spilled onto the world stage in 1817 with successive epidemic waves. Influenza, in the form of the "Spanish flu" of 1918-1919, gave mankind one of its most awesome epidemics. In the short span of just eighteen months, it claimed the lives of an estimated twenty million people.[21] And, of course, our own generation has seen the advent of the AIDS epidemic caused by the human immunodeficiency virus.[22]

If one looks for a recurring theme among these epidemics, one finds several features in common. All have been infections. War, famine and social disruption have been frequent causes and consequences of these pestilential visitations. In some cases, epidemics developed because old diseases (infections) had metamorphosed into new and deadly variants through unknown mechanisms. The Spanish flu of 1918-1919 is an example. In others, such as the current AIDS epidemic, disorders not previously encountered have exhibited a deadly force that is as much a product of the immunological naiveté of the populations they attack as of the microbe's innate virulence.

Additional insight into why it has been so difficult to translate Thucydides' clinical description into a modern diagnosis can be obtained by considering the historian himself, the nature of the medical theory to which he was exposed and the subsequent evolution of epidemic disease concepts. Thucydides (ca 460 to ca 400 B.C.E.) was an eyewitness to and a participant in Athens' war with Sparta and the Peloponnesian alliance. He was an historian, as well as a victim, of the plague he recorded for posterity. He was also a military commander, exiled from Athens during the course of the war for failing to save the city of Amphipolis from the Spartans. While in exile, he wrote his account of the plague of Athens, returning to Athens in 404 B.C.E., some twenty years after the war, and dying shortly thereafter.[12]

Thucydides was not a physician. Nonetheless, his description of the great plague is replete with medical terms common to that era, at least some of which were confined largely to medical treatises.[23] His terminology and the perspective from which he wrote his account are rooted in concepts just then being promulgated by the Hippocratic school. Like students of that school, he shunned supernatural references in his description of events and his interpretation of their causes.[24] He devoted his efforts instead to accurately and objectively recording and interpreting his observations. In his account of the Athenian plague, he closely adhered to the Hippocratic format for clinical documentation with a general introduction, a description of symptoms, and the illness' crisis.[25]

Although Hippocratic writers were concerned most with prognosis (those features of an illness which predict its course), that is not to say that they had no interest in diagnosis or treatment.[26] They introduced concepts of inspection, palpation and auscultation, which are fundamental parts of the physical examination even today. Many of their treatments also continue to be used, such as salicylates (the forerunner of aspirin), incisions, cauterizations, evacuations, dietary interventions and exercise.

When confronted with epidemics, Hippocratic physicians recommended the following, which might well have been their approach to Pericles at the time of his fatal illness:

[Patients] should not change their regimen, as it is not the cause of their disease, but rather take care that their body be as thin and as weak as possible, by diminishing their usual food and drink gradually. For if the change of regimen be sudden, there is a risk that from the change too some disturbance will take place in the body, but regimen should be used in this way when it manifestly does no harm to a patient. Then care should be taken that inspiration be of the lightest, and also from a source as far removed as possible; the place should be moved as far as possible from that in which the disease is epidemic, and the body should be reduced, for such reduction will minimize the need of deep and frequent breathing.[27]

The principles and practices of the Hippocratic school are pre-served in a collection of texts attributed to Hippocrates and are therefore referred to as the Hippocratic Corpus.[25] Hippocrates, long regarded as both the founder of the school and the father of modern medicine, was born on the island of Cos in 460 B.C.E. He belonged to the Coan branch of the Asclepiad school of medicine. According to legend, Asclepius, the founder of that school, first communicated the art of medicine to his two sons, Podalirius and Machaon, who, in turn, initiated a process whereby medical knowledge was then passed down from one generation of disciples (Asclepiads) to the next. Although Hippocrates was, thus, neither the father of medi-cine, as regarded by many today, nor the founder of the Coan school, his teachings conferred a lasting and exceptionally lustrous reputa-tion upon the school which came to bear his name. Over time, his image has passed into legend, one no less compelling today than in the time of Pericles. "The Oath" taken by most American physicians upon graduation from medical school today is in fact derived from one attributed to him by the ancients.[28]

The Hippocratic Corpus is a curious and often fragmented col-lection of more than sixty treatises of varying style and content, of which the most widely cited, *Aphorisms,* deals with prognosis, diag-nosis, and treatment. The Corpus was the clinician's bible until the 18th century C.E. and, although named for Hippocrates, the large number of its treatises and their varying styles and content make it unlikely that the great physician himself, or even his disciples of the school of Cos, produced it in its entirety. Clearly some of its text comes from other sources and later periods.[29]

The essence of Hippocratic concepts of health and disease is em-bodied in the "humoral theory," according to which:

> The body of man has in itself blood, phlegm, yellow bile and black bile; these make up the nature of his body, and through these he feels pain or enjoys health. Now he enjoys the most perfect health when these elements are duly proportioned [métriôs] to one an-other in respect of compounding, power and bulk, and when they

40

are perfectly mingled. Pain is felt when one of these elements is in defect or excess, or is isolated in the body without being compounded with all the others. For when an element is isolated and stands by itself, not only must the place which it left become diseased, but the place where it stands in a flood must, because of the excess, cause pain and distress."[30]

It would be overstating the case to suggest that the humoral theory was the alpha and the omega of Hippocratic doctrine. Unlike Thucydides, who rejected completely the notion of divine intervention in determining the course of events, Hippocratic physicians believed that at least some phenomena had (divine) causes independent of nature which might possibly be influenced by the intervention of a particular deity.[31] There was also a general belief that certain days in the course of illness are fortunate or fatal, while others are indifferent. The first, the fourth and the seventh days of illness were thought to be critical, which might explain why Thucydides reported that during the plague of Athens, victims generally died "on the seventh *or* ninth" day of illness, rather than "*between* the seventh and ninth" day of illness. Nevertheless, the humoral theory was the heart of Hippocratic concepts responsible for health and disease. According to it, health and the absence thereof are dictated by a delicate balance between the four vital humors: blood, phlegm, yellow bile and black bile. Health was thought to exist when the four humors are in equilibrium, illness when domination of one over the others results in disequilibrium.[32]

In concert with precepts of the humoral theory, when there were imbalances between the four humors, treatment was designed to return the humors to proper balance, much as modern clinicians do today when, for example, confronted with an abnormally high blood glucose, they initiate treatments designed to lower the glucose to the normal range. Treatment was, in many respects, an exercise in opposites, as are today's treatments. Today, if a patient is cold, he is warmed; if anemic, he is transfused with blood; if his pressure is high, he is given antihypertensive medications; and so on. Hippocratic physicians' philosophy in this regard is reflected in the following passage from the *Nature of Man* (one of the Hippocratic texts):

> Furthermore, one must know that diseases due to repletion are cured by evacuation, and those due to evacuation are cured by repletion; those due to exercise are cured by rest, and those due to idleness are cured by exercise. To know the whole matter, the physician must set himself against (*enantion histasthai*) the established character of diseases, of constitutions, of seasons and of ages; he must relax what is tense and make tense what is relaxed. For in this way the diseased part would rest most, and this, in my opinion, constitutes treatment.[32]

The term "epidemic" likewise has its roots in the Hippocratic doctrine.[33] It is derived from "demo," meaning people, and "epi," meaning upon. The prefixes "en" (with) and "pan" (throughout) are added to "demo" to distinguish disorders that smolder within populations (endemic) from those that sweep through the global community (pandemics). "Epidemics" are outbreaks of disease which lie somewhere between endemic disorders and pandemic eruptions. Thucydides' plague, which at the very least spread throughout a significant portion of the known world (from Africa throughout the eastern Mediterranean), would more appropriately be viewed as a "pandemic" than an "epidemic."

According to Hippocratic doctrine: "When a large number of people all develop the same disease at the same time, the cause must be ascribed to something common to all."[33] However, at no place in the Hippocratic Corpus is epidemic disease connected with the idea of contagion, nor any suggestion that epidemic disease might be transmitted from one affected person to another. Rather it was believed that epidemics were due to the influence of the same general factors in each one of the persons affected by the disease, such as miasmas present in the air they breathed, the seasons, exposure to the elements, and so on.[34] Before the advent of the Hippocratic doctrine, epidemics were ascribed to the wrath of the gods, or in the case of proponents of the ancient pseudoscience of astrology, to the "influence" of heavenly bodies (giving rise to the name of one of our most important epidemic diseases, "influenza").[33] At other times in history, human scapegoats have been invoked to explain the mysterious appearance of epidemics: the Jews, for example, during the black plagues of the Medieval period, the Irish during the 1832 outbreak of cholera in the United States, and the Italians during an epidemic of poliomyelitis in 1916.[33] However, the miasma theory, to which Hippocratic physicians of Pericles' day subscribed, attributed contagion to bad air. It was the dominant theory of epidemics until the age of microbiology, when the microbial etiology of epidemic disease finally came to be recognized.

Given Thucydides' background and how it might have influenced the nature of his account, what can be said of the likely etiology of the epidemic he described? Hans Zinsser, one of the foremost microbiologists of the 20th century, on contemplating this question, wrote: "It is important to remember that in any great outbreak, while the large majority of cases may represent a single type of infection, there is usually a coincident increase in other forms of contagious diseases; for the circumstances which favor the spread of one infectious agent often create opportunities for the transmission of others. Very rarely is there a pure epidemic of a single malady."[35] If Zinsser was correct, then at least some of the victims of Thucydides' plague might have succumbed to disorders other than the principal one responsible for the epidemic.

Conditions in Athens in 430 B.C.E. were ripe for just such a great outbreak. Large armies were camped in Attica, causing the population within Athens itself to swell to a level approaching that of the concentration camps of more recent times. Communicable diseases are close companions of such conditions, as is starvation. However, the disorders related to the latter condition, such as scurvy and ergotism, do not induce immunity to second attacks of the kind described by Thucydides.

No one has yet succeeded in relating the plague that claimed Pericles to a single known epidemic disease. To some scholars, epidemic typhus (a rickettsial infection) offers one of the best fits. It is a disease long associated with war and famine. During the two great wars of our own era, for example, over fifty-five million people are believed to have contracted typhus. The infection is transmitted from one person to another by the body louse, and its spread is potentiated by crowding and privation, both of which favor proliferation of the arthropod vector.[36] The tiny intracellular bacterium responsible for the infection, *Rickettsia prowazekii*, infects body lice causing an illness no less dire for them than for the human host. The lice pass their rickettsial burden on to humans while feeding. If the disorder responsible for ending the life of Pericles and most of his family was typhus, the Peloponnesians might have been less affected than the Athenians because they were not subjected to the same level of crowding or to conditions nearly as unhygienic.

Clinically, there is much to support typhus as the cause of Pericles' disorder. It is a devastating infection, even today, in which pathogenic bacteria (rickettsia), highly adapted to the intracellular environment, damage a wide variety of cells throughout the body, especially those lining the inner surfaces of blood vessels. The action of rickettsia on these endothelial cells causes diffuse vascular damage, characterized first by dilatation of capillaries, then thrombosis of progressively larger blood vessels. Rupture of affected vessels results in localized hemorrhages. In the skin, this process first manifests as a flat (macular) or slightly raised (papular) rash, later as a hemorrhagic rash. Infection of the blood vessels of the brain produces one of the disorder's earliest and most prominent symptoms, excruciating headache. In severe cases, inflammation of cerebral vessels can cause stroke, as well as altered consciousness and amnesia. If vessels supplying the optic nerve are affected, blindness can ensue, and if the vasculitis is severe and involves the larger vessels of the extremities or the genitalia there can be necrosis of fingers, toes and genitalia.

In spite of the many features typhus shares with the illness described by Thucydides, Zinsser, who made typhus his life's work and became its foremost authority, did not believe it was the infection that killed Pericles.[35] For one thing, Thucydides' description of the rash is inconsistent with the disorder. According to him, it was a generalized eruption composed of small blisters ("phlyktainai," a term ancient Greek writers also used for blisters found on a loaf of bread and for those on the hands of rowers[7]). The rash of typhus never blisters and does not typically ulcerate. Moreover, upper respiratory tract symptoms and coughing are atypical. Although necrosis of the extremities occurs in severe cases of typhus (see above), this complication is seen primarily during winter epidemics,[35] and the Athenian outbreak struck during the torpid days of summer. Finally, the epidemic began almost immediately after the Peloponnesians began their siege, too soon for the residents of Athens, who were by nature hygienic, to have become lousy.

If the rash of the plague of Athens was generalized and composed of small blisters and ulcers as Thucydides claimed, smallpox is a more likely diagnosis. Smallpox is a systemic infection caused by the variola virus, a member of the Poxviridae family. It no longer plagues mankind because of the persistent and ultimately successful efforts of an intensive global eradication program implemented by the World Health Organization, thanks to whose efforts, no naturally acquired case of the infection has been seen since 1977. The virus lives on, however, in stocks maintained in microbiology laboratories at the Centers for Disease Control and Prevention (CDC) in Atlanta, and the State Research Center of Virology and Biotechnology (the Vektor Institute) in Novosibirsk, Russia, raising concerns that one day it might fall into the hands of terrorists and re-emerge in epidemic form.[37]

Smallpox has an incubation period (the interval between infection and onset of symptoms) of a week to seventeen days.[37] The illness begins abruptly with an initial phase of two to three days (the prodrome) of severe headache, backache and fever. At first the fever is high but then subsides over two to three days. Next, there is inflammation of the tongue, mouth and throat and shortly thereafter the appearance of the characteristic rash. The rash begins as small, reddish spots (macules) which, over the course of one to two days, become raised (papular) with diameters of two to three millimeters. It appears first on the face and extremities and gradually spreads to cover the entire body. As it matures, the rash transforms into pustules (pus-filled blisters) with diameters of four to six millimeters. These first appear four to seven days after the rash's onset and remain for five to eight days before crusting and then healing. A second, lower-grade fever sometimes develops five to eight days after the appearance of the rash, especially in cases with secondary bacterial infections. Of the patients with severe infections who survive, sixty-five to eighty percent are permanently scarred with pockmarks. These pitted residua of the pustular eruption are particularly prominent on the face. In one percent of cases, inflammation of the eyes, either as a result of the viral infection itself or as a secondary bacterial infection, leads to blindness. Arthritis develops in two percent of infected children, encephalitis (infection of the brain) in another one percent of cases. Although cough is not usually prominent, in severe cases respiratory symptoms and pneumonia may develop. Gastrointestinal complaints such as vomiting and diarrhea may be a feature of terminal toxemia in fatal cases, but otherwise are not prominent.

Smallpox typically has a case fatality rate (percent of infected patients dying) of thirty percent. In atypical cases, in which the rash is flat and evolves slowly or becomes hemorrhagic, the case fatality rate can approach one hundred percent. In such cases, death generally occurs within the first seven days of the illness.

Smallpox spreads primarily via respiratory aerosol, although infected clothing or bedding can also serve as vehicles for transmission. It is less contagious than measles, chickenpox or influenza, and its spread is often limited to close contacts such as family members and health care workers. Patients who have severe infections, especially those with involvement of the respiratory system, are highly contagious.

Although the historical record indicates that smallpox was common throughout North Africa by the 6th century C.E., earlier reports of the disorder in the Mediterranean basin are more difficult to substantiate.[35] Nevertheless, the similarities of the illness described by Thucydides with smallpox are inescapable. Moreover, Diodorus Siculus described an almost identical epidemic among the Carthagenian army besieging Syracuse in 396 B.C.E. (less than forty years after the plague of Athens), suggesting that if the epidemic in which Pericles died was a Mediterranean outbreak of smallpox, it was by no means an isolated event. According to Diodorus: "First, before sunrise, because of cold breeze from the water, they had chills; in the middle of the day, burning heat. During the first stage of the disease there was a catarrh; followed by a swelling in the throat; shortly after this, fever set in; pains in the back and a heavy feeling in the limbs; next, a dysentery and blisters upon the whole surface of the body." After this, some victims became delirious and died on the fifth or sixth day. The death rate was enormous and caused the siege to be raised and the army dispersed.[18]

One can find evidence in Thucydides' account of the Plague of Athens to support typhus, bubonic plague, anthrax, measles, scurvy and ergotism. However, no diagnosis explains as many of the clinical, epidemiological and historical features of Pericles' illness as smallpox. Typhus is unlikely for the reasons mentioned above and because it is an endemic, occasionally epidemic, disorder. Because of the critical role of the body louse in transmitting typhus from one close contact to another, pandemic spread of the infection in the absence of a world war is not likely to occur. Bubonic plague is also unlikely because Thucydides made no mention of buboes (enlarged, painful lymph nodes in the armpits, groin and neck), which are the hallmark of "bubonic" plague.[25] Anthrax does not produce a generalized rash of the character reported by Thucydides, nor do measles, scurvy or ergotism.

In modern times, severe backache has been a frequent complaint of patients with smallpox (see above). Therefore, if Thucydides' description is both comprehensive and accurate, and the clinical manifestations of the infection have not changed over more than two millennia, the absence of backache argues against smallpox. The apparent absence of pockmarks among those who recovered from the disorder is even more troublesome.[25] If smallpox was the cause of

Thucydides' plague, pockmarks should have been so common and so prominent among survivors that Thucydides could not possibly have missed them. If they were present but not described, the only reasonable explanation is that as a product of the Hippocratic school, Thucydides was more interested in prognosis (features of a disorder that predict its course) than diagnosis. Pockmarks are the residua of past infection and as such, have no value in predicting the course of an active infection.

The apparent absence of widespread illness among the besieging Peloponnesians is equally difficult to explain, whatever the cause of the plague, particularly so because it devastated not only the Athenians but also other peoples of vast areas of the eastern Mediterranean. Moreover, during the Peloponnesian War, sieges tended to be porous affairs, with regular intercourse between line troops of opposing sides, during which food, valuables, women and sometimes even armor were exchanged.

Thucydides might have minimized the effect of the plague on the Peloponnesians in his account to rationalize the Athenian defeat. If so, his primary purpose in describing the epidemic might not have been to provide an accurate description but rather to dramatize the tragic plight of the Athenians.[38] It is also possible that the agent responsible for the epidemic was only moderately contagious, in which case measles, influenza[39] and pneumonic plague, all highly contagious agents in susceptible populations, can be excluded. Smallpox and typhus, on the other hand, are not nearly as contagious, unless there is crowding to the degree to which the citizens of Athens were subjected during the siege.

The Peloponnesian War proved to be the longest, most vicious and destructive war ever fought among Greeks. When the conflict began, few believed it would last long. Sparta previously had sallied north and engaged in a few months of desultory pillaging before leaving with a negotiated settlement. The Peloponnesian War, however, was different. In prior conflicts, the Spartans incinerated vines and groves, toppled walls and destroyed crops: this time they sheared plants to the nub and sowed fields with lime. They burnt houses, cottages and barns and slaughtered stock indiscriminately. Such was the nature of this new war, which brought to an end all that was fair and gentle between the Greek states.

When war broke out, Athens was at the height of her glory. Her navy had turned the Aegean into an Athenian millpond. Tribute flowed to her from hundreds of states as conqueror, empire and cultural capital of the world. Pericles, appreciating the ephemerality of such power, envisioned war with Sparta long before it developed, prepared for it and, ultimately, instigated it, even as he helped to create his city's golden age. He was the architect of the Athenian strategy for conducting the war, some might say also of the war itself. He fortified Athens' harbors and extended its battlements (its "Long Walls") four and a half miles on one side, nearly the same on the other, linking the upper city to the harbor at Piraeus and creating a nearly impregnable municipal fortress. His strategy for conducting the war was to withdraw the citizenry behind these Long Walls, while permitting the enemy to ravage farms without until their lust for warfare had been sated. Meanwhile, the city, which controlled the sea, could procure its needs by ship from its empire, secure behind its walls. The other key element of his strategy was to halt expansion of the empire until the war's conclusion.

Pericles' loss during the plague was a critical setback for the Athenian cause because he was replaced by men of lesser military and political ability.[12] His death amplified his glory, even though his role in precipitating the war made him no less an assassin of the Golden Age than leaders of the other side.

The war raged on for over twenty years after Pericles' death and the end of Thucydides' plague. In view of the epidemic's devastating effect on the Athenian military, it is unlikely that Athens could have denied the Spartans victory for so long after the epidemic had done its worst, had the plague not also decimated the Spartan war machine. Similarly, because the Athenian defenders continued their struggle for over two decades after the end of the epidemic and the death of Pericles, neither Thucydides' plague nor the death of Pericles can fully explain Athens' surrender in 404 B.C.E.

After more than two thousand years we continue to ponder the cause of the plague that took Pericles and so many others during the first years of the Peloponnesian War. If smallpox was the cause, skeletons dating to 430 B.C.E., which recently have been uncovered in Athens, might provide proof of the diagnosis when subjected to molecular analysis.[6] If not, we will continue to be haunted, and taunted, by Thucydides' challenge:

> Now let every man, Physician or other, concerning the ground of this sickness, where it sprung, and what causes he thinks able to produce so great an alteration, speak according to his own knowledge, for my own part, I will deliver but the manner of it and lay open only such things as one may take his mark by, to discover the same if it come again.[9]

Notes

1. Major RM. *Classic Descriptions of Disease* (Translation of Thomas Hobbes: 1588-1679). Springfield, Ill: Charles C. Thomas, 1945, p. 73-6.
2. The Peloponnesian War, which began in the summer of 431 B.C.E. and continued until 404 B.C.E., pitted Athens and her allies against a coalition of forces derived primarily from Sparta, Thebes and Corinth. The war had several causes, perhaps the most important of which concerned Pericles' (who was then the Athenian leader) diversion of funds intended for the general defense of Greece against the Persians to construction of the Parthenon and other public buildings in Athens. The Spartan coalition was also enraged by Athens' intervention on behalf of Kerkyra (Corfu) in a dispute with Corinth in 433 B.C.E. and its attack on the Corinthian colony of Potidaea in 432 B.C.E. After unsuccessful attempts at a negotiated settlement, Sparta and her allies invaded Athenian territory in 431 B.C.E. According to Thucydides, the truest cause of the war was Sparta's anxiety

over the growing power of Athens. (Rose M. Fallen heroes. Bones of Pericles' soldiers come to New York for Analysis. *Archaeology.* 2000; March/April: 42-5).

3. Jouanna J. Hippocrates. Trans. By DeBevoise MB. Baltimore. Johns Hopkins Univ. Press, 1999, p. 179-80.

4. Ibid p. 210.

5. Godolphin FRB. The nemesis of Cratinus (Notes and Discussions). *Classical Philology.* 1931;26:423-6.

6. According to Morens and Littman, Thucydides was ambiguous in implying that the plague affected animals as well as humans. They maintain that although Thucydides never claimed to have seen ill dogs or birds, some authorities have cited this passage as proof that the outbreak involved animals. For their part, Morens and Littman believe the structure of the passage implies a literary attempt to explain the unexpected absence of birds and dogs which is not necessarily based in fact. (Morens DM, Littman RJ: Epidemiology of the plague of Athens. *Trans Am Philol Assoc.* 1992;122:271-304).

7. The notion of epidemics simultaneously attacking several life forms (human, animal, vegetable) was not new in Greek literature. In Thucydides' time, it was already a legacy of archaic, epic literature. In the *Iliad*, for example, Homer describes a pestilence which befalls the Achaeans camped outside the gates of Troy; it first strikes the animals (mules and dogs) and then the men. [Op cit (Jouanna J) p. 204-5].

8. Sprat T. *The Plague of Athens.* London: Henry Brome, 1665, p. 3-4.

9. There have been many translations of Thucydides' account of the plague of Athens. The version presented in this chapter is derived largely from Thomas Hobbes' 17th century translation (see Note 1), with modifications suggested by Dr. Robert Littman of the Classics Department, University of Hawaii, Honolulu, Hawaii.

10. Even names of diseases used in Thucydides' time which are still in use today are potentially problematic because modern

applications of ancient medical terms do not always correspond to the same entities. Thus, even for astute clinicians, retrospective diagnosis of ancient diseases is all the more difficult because of problems involved in translating early clinical descriptions. (Op cit. footnote 5, p 143-4).

11. von Economo's encephalitis (encelphalitis lethargica) caused a global pandemic estimated to have involved more than a million cases of severe neurologic disease during the decade 1919-1928. It was responsible for more than a half million deaths and thousands of cases of postencephalitic parkinsonism in the decades following the original outbreak. No similar outbreak is known ever to have occurred. Although the etiology of the disorder is still debated, this unique form of epidemic encephalitis was most likely a late sequella of infection with the highly virulent 1918 strain of influenza (see below) (Ravenholt RT, Foege WH: 1918 influenza, encephalitis lethargica, parkinsonism. *Lancet.* 1982; 2:860-4).

12. Durack DT, Littman RJ, Benitez RM, Mackowiak PA. Hellenic holocaust: a historical clinicopathological conference. *Am J Med.* 200; 109:391-7.

13. Shrewsbury JDF. The plague of Athens. *Bull Hist Med.* 1950;24:1-24.

14. Morens DM, Littman RJ: "Thucydides syndrome" reconsidered: new thoughts on the "plague of Athens." *Am J Epidemiol.* 1994;140:621-7.

15. Op cit (Jouanna J) p. 32-3, 208.

16. Op cit (Jouanna J) p. 13.

17. In the book of Exodus, ten plagues of Egypt are described. They would have occurred circa 1250 B.C.E. In the first, the Nile river turned to blood (possibly as a result of microbes or red earth); then in succession: frogs covered the land and then died off; dust became "lice" in man and in beasts; swarms of flies invaded the houses of Egypt; the cattle of Egypt died in great number; boils broke forth with blains upon man, and upon beast; hail smote throughout the land of Egypt destroying

crops, animals and human lives; locusts came up upon the land of Egypt and ate every herb of the land, even all that the hail had left; darkness descended over the land of Egypt for three days; and the first born in the land of Egypt died in great number.

18. The Latin words *pestis* and *pestilentia* have the same meaning and were often used to indicate misfortune of any sort. This is one of several reasons why many of the plagues of antiquity have been so difficult to diagnose. In Roman history, there were five great periods of pestilence. One, which followed the eruption of Vesuvius in 79 C.E., caused widespread disease in Campagna. A plague of Orosius in 125 C.E. killed an estimated thirty thousand Roman soldiers sent to defend the colony. The plague of Antonius struck in 164 C.E. (see Note 16). The plague of Cyprian, which lasted from 251 to 266 C.E. is thought to have been an epidemic of smallpox because of the frequency with which the disorder attacked the eyes. And in 312 C.E., there was another massive outbreak of a disorder thought to have been smallpox. (Patrick A. Diseases in antiquity: ancient Greece and Rome. In Brothwell D, Sandison AT, eds. *Diseases in Antiquity.* Springfield, Ill: Charles C. Thomas, Publisher. 1967: 238-46.

19. The Antonine plague was a prolonged and destructive epidemic which struck the Roman empire during the reign of Marcus Aurelius. It began in Mesopotamia in 165-6 C.E. during Verus' Parthian campaign. Within a year it had spread to Rome, where it continued at least until the death of Marcus Aurelius in 180 C.E., more likely until 189 C.E. (during the reign of Commodus). Although the plague's significance as a factor in Rome's decline is questionable, it holds an important place in history because of its association with Galen. Galen, who more than any other physician immortalized the teachings of Hippocrates, described the epidemic with sufficient attention to the physical affects of the disease to convince R.J. Littman and M.L. Littman that the cause of the disorder was smallpox.

(Littman RJ, Littman ML: Galen and the Antonine plague. *Am J Philol.* 173;94:243-55.

20. An epidemic illness known as "huey cocoliztli" decimated the native people of Mexico between 1545 and 1548 C.E. The epidemic killed an estimated five million to fifteen million people, or close to 80% of the indigenous population of Mexico. It was a swift and highly lethal disease characterized by high fever, severe headache, dizziness, black tongue, dark urine, dysentery, chest and abdominal pain, nodules in the neck and behind the ears, neurologic complaints, and profuse bleeding from the nose, eyes and mouth. Death frequently occurred in three to four days. A growing body of epidemiologic evidence indicates that indigenous, viral hemorrhagic fevers transmitted by rodent hosts and aggravated by extreme drought conditions were responsible for the epidemic. (Acuna-Soto R, Stahle DW, Cleaveland MK, Therrell MD: Megadrought and megadeath in 16th century Mexico. *Emerg Infect Dis.* 2002; 8:360-2).

21. During the 20th century C.E., there were three major influenza pandemics. The most recent, in 1968, was caused by the Hong Kong strain of influenza A. It killed an estimated 98,100 people over a four-year period. In 1957, an epidemic caused by the Asian strain of influenza A caused an estimated 115,700 deaths. The overall impact of these two pandemics paled by comparison with that of the 1918 pandemic caused by the so called "Spanish" strain of influenza A. During this outbreak, perhaps the most virulent plague of all time, an estimated 20 million people worldwide succumbed to the infection between the fall of 1918 and the spring of 1920. The infection was especially lethal for healthy, young adults, aged twenty to forty years. The specific features of the virus responsible for its extraordinary virulence have yet to be identified. (Luk J, Gross P, Thompson WW: Observations on mortality during the 1918 influenza pandemic. *Clin Infect Dis.* 2001;33:1375-8).

22. As of 2002 C.E., forty million people throughout the world have been infected with the human immunodeficiency virus

(HIV); twenty million have died from the adult immunodeficiency syndrome (AIDS) caused by the virus; and 750,000 babies are currently born each year infected by HIV. Predictions are that during the coming two decades, seventy million people will perish in the epidemic (Clark S: Experts predict global devastation due to HIV/AIDS. *Lancet.* 2002;360:145). Like the agent responsible for Thucydides' epidemic, the one responsible for the current AIDS pandemic (the human immunodeficiency virus) appears to have originated in sub-Saharan Africa. Africa is also currently suffering the greatest impact of the AIDS epidemic, with an estimated 25.3 million sub-Saharan Africans infected as of the end of 2000 C.E.. In Botswana, the country with the highest prevalence of AIDS in the world, over 35% of the adult population is infected with the human immunodeficiency virus. Virtually all are expected to die of their infection. (Gow J: The HIV/AIDS epidemic in Africa: complications for U.S. policy. *Health Affairs.* 2002;21:57-69).

23. Page DL. Thucydides' description of the great plague of Athens. In Galbraith VH, Mynors RAB, eds. *Nelson's Medieval Texts.* Edinburgh, Nelsons Publishers, 195, p. 97-119.

24. Op cit (Jouanna J) p. 181.

25. Littman RJ, Littman ML. The Athenian plague: smallpox. Trans Proc *Am Philol Assoc.* 1969; 100: 261-73.

26. Op cit (Jouanna J) p. 155-75.

27. Op cit (Jouanna J) p. 207.

28. In its original form, the Hippocratic oath was as follows:

> I swear by Apollo Physician, by Asclepius, by Health, by Panacea and by all the gods and goddesses, making them my witnesses, that I will carry out, according to my ability and judgment, this oath and this indenture. To hold my teacher in this art equal to my own parents; to make him partner in my livelihood; when he is in need of money to share mine with him; to consider his family as my own brothers, and to teach them this art, if they want to learn it, without fee or indenture; to impart precept, oral instruction, and all other instruction to my own sons, the sons of my

teacher, and to indentured pupils who have taken the physician's oath, but to nobody else. I will use treatment to help the sick according to my ability and judgment, but never with a view to injury and wrong-doing. Neither will I administer a poison to anybody when asked to do so, nor will I suggest such a course. Similarly I will not give to a woman a pessary to cause abortion. But I will keep pure and holy both my life and my art. I will not use the knife, not even, verily, on sufferers from stone, but I will give place to such as are craftsmen therein. Into whatsoever houses I enter, I will enter to help the sick, and I will abstain from all intentional wrong-doing and harm, especially from abusing the bodies of man or woman, bond or free. And whatsoever I shall see or hear in the course of my profession, as well as outside my profession in the intercourse with men, if it be what should not be published abroad, I will never divulge, holding such things to be holy secrets. Now if I carry out this oath, and break it not, may I gain for ever reputation among all men for my life and for my art; but if I transgress it and forswear myself, may the opposite befall me. [Op cit (Jouanna J) p. 10,17,39,42, 369, 401]

29. Galen, a Greek native of Pergamum (a city now in Turkey), did more than any other physician to perpetuate the influence of the Hippocratic school. After completing his medical education in Alexandria, he lived and practiced medicine in Rome for two extended periods (first from 162 C.E. to 166 C.E. and then for an additional thirty years beginning in 168 C.E.). [Op cit (Jouanna J) p. 353-7].

30. Op cit (Jouanna J) p. 326.

31. Op cit (Jouanna J) p. 190-1.

32. Op cit (Jouanna J) p. 342.

33. Yankauer A. Reacting to epidemics: past and present. *Pharos.* 1998; Summer: 17-22.

34. Op cit (Jouanna J) p. 152.

35. Zinsser H. *Rats, Lice and History.* Boston: Little, Brown and Co, 1963.

36. Kelly DJ, Richards AL, Temenak J, et al. The past and present threat of rickettsial diseases to military medicine and international public health. *Clin Infect Dis*. 2002; 34(Suppl 4):S145-69.

37. Breman JG, Henderson DA. Diagnosis and management of smallpox. *N Eng J Med*. 2002; 346:1300-8.

38. Parry A: The language of Thucydides' description of the plague. *BICS*. 1969;16:106-18.

39. In 1985, Dr. Alexander Langmuir, one of the founding fathers of the U. S. Centers for Disease Control in Atlanta, Georgia, revived an earlier theory that Thucydides' plague was influenza. He and his co-authors maintained that features of the outbreak which were atypical of influenza itself could yet be explained by a complication of the influenza infection: toxic shock syndrome resulting from a secondary staphylococcal infection. (Langmuir AD, Worthen TO, Solomon J, et al. The Thucydides' syndrome. A new hypothesis for the cause of the plague of Athens. *N Engl J Med*. 1985;313:1027-30). In 1992, Morens and Littman reported the results of an epidemiologic evaluation of the Athenian outbreak in which they concluded that the protracted course of the epidemic was incompatible with a highly contagious respiratory infection such as influenza (see Note 5).

3 DEATH OF A DEITY

In 334 B.C.E., this patient crossed the Hellespont with a little over thirty thousand men to conquer the known world. In ten years' time, he subjugated Egypt and the eastern Mediterranean and then routed Persia's King Darius III to become "Lord of Asia." He was invincible, and at the height of his power, claimed to be the son of the king of the gods. However, four months shy of his thirty-third birthday he was dead. Some say he was poisoned, a victim of the many powerful enemies he had created during his twelve years and eight months in power. Others say he drank himself to death. He was drunk when he torched the palace of the Persian monarchs in 330[1] and when in 328 he murdered Clitus, who years before had saved his life.[2] Still others say that he simply gave up. After the death of his lifelong friend and lover, Hephaestion, the patient seemed to care little for the fragile thread Atropos would sever less than a year later.

Throughout his life the patient had been in all ways extraordinary. He had great personal beauty,[3] incomparable power of endurance and a singular intellect. However, he used his body savagely in his relentless pursuit of fame and was wounded at least ten times during his conquests. At Issus, his shank was shattered by an arrow and splinters of bone had to be removed from the wound.[4] On another occasion, he received a blow to the nape of the neck of such force that he had difficulty seeing for some time thereafter.[4] At Granicus, the Persian warrior, Spithridates, hit him hard enough with a battle axe to shear the plumes from his helmet and in the process, graze the very hair on his head. Had his loyal subject,

Clitus, not run Spithridates through with his spear just as he was about to strike again, the patient surely would have been dispatched with a second stroke of Spithridates' axe.[5]

At Multan in what is now Pakistan the patient received perhaps his most serious wound.[6,7] During the siege of that Mallian town in 326 B.C.E., an arrow found its way through the patient's cuirass, between his ribs and into the vicinity of his heart. It was so deeply embedded in the bone that it was extracted with great difficulty; and when it was at last removed, blood mixed with air bubbled from the wound, suggesting that the lung had been punctured. Months passed before the patient was well enough to continue his journey back to his new capital, Babylon.

Like battle wounds, disease was the patient's constant companion. For nearly a decade, he drove himself and his men through some of the most disease-infested regions of the globe. There is little doubt that he contracted malaria during his eastern campaign or that his army suffered constantly from the infection. A febrile illness incapacitated him for two months in Cilicia in 333 B.C.E. Darius, whom he was then pursuing, attributed his inactivity to cowardice.[8] In all likelihood, it was malaria that detained him, causing symptoms so severe none of the patient's physicians dared treat him for fear they might be blamed if he should die. Unfortunately for Darius, he recovered.

On the march, the patient and his men regularly drank from streams so foul dysentery was not only inevitable but probably an all but constant affliction. And yet, to accomplish what he did, the patient could not permit his army to be delayed by disease. In fact, he once pursued a Scythian force beyond the river Orexartes for over a hundred furlongs, suffering the whole time from diarrhea.[4]

The patient was fortunate to have been derived from hearty stock. Although he later claimed to be the son of Zeus Ammon, Philip was his actual father. Philip too was gifted physically and mentally but, like his son, a mortal. Assassination at the hand of Pausanias proved that in 336 B.C.E.[9]

The patient's mother, Olympias, was alive and well when he developed his fatal illness, as was Cleopatra, his younger sister.[10] He had an older half brother, Arrhidaeus, who was Philip's son by an obscure woman named Philinna. Although Arrhidaeus showed a happy and promising enough character as a child, his intellect weakened as he grew, some say because Olympias gave him drugs that ruined both his health and his understanding.[11]

The patient was bisexual, with three wives,[12] the newest of whom was pregnant with his only child, and at least two male partners. Hephaestion was his oldest friend, lover, and most trusted commander.[13] Some argue that the patient also had a sexual relationship with Bagoas, a Persian eunuch who had formerly served Darius.[14] Nevertheless, prior to his return from India, he had always indulged in the pleasures of the body with moderation. He had also been temperate as to his diet. It seems that only in his pursuit of knowledge and glory did he indulge himself to excess.

Regarding the patient's mental state, we know that he was brave and adventurous, but he was also strict in his observance of religious duties. Toward the end of his life, however, he was gripped by paranoia and increasingly turned to diviners and priests to sacrifice and purify and to guarantee his future.

The patient's final illness began in the summer of 323 B.C.E. He had been agitated since his return from India, and drinking heavily since Hephaestion's death. By some accounts, he had caroused almost continuously for nearly seven months. Some say he was egged on by sycophants, including Medius, who came to enjoy a special relationship with the patient. How this came to be is not known, for Medius was only a trireme commander. Even so, it was at a drinking marathon at Medius's house that the patient developed the first signs of his fatal illness. Details are sketchy, but most likely the illness began with high fever and abdominal pain.

The first day, the patient bathed and then slept in the bath house because of his fever. The next, he felt well enough to play dice with Medius and again bathed, sacrificed and ate a hearty dinner. During the night, the fever returned and increased in intensity over the next several days. Initially, the patient was vigorous enough to engage his admiral, Nearchus, in a discussion of naval strategy for a planned

Arabian campaign, however, by the fourth day of illness, his strength began to ebb. On the seventh day, his condition was so desperate he had to be carried from his bed and assisted with his daily sacrifices. Guards were posted. Then he was taken back to the palace, where he slept little because of his fever. Before long, his speech began to fail. His troops, fearing the worst, demanded an audience. As they filed by in silent review on the tenth day of the illness, the patient struggled to raise his head, but could do little more than follow with his eyes as each man passed. Shortly, thereafter, Alexander III of Macedon, Alexander the Great (see Figures 3-1 and 3-2), perhaps the greatest military commander of all time, was dead. It was the evening of the eleventh day of the illness. In the confusion that followed, six more days elapsed before the embalmers reached him. It has been said that when they did, they found the body uncorrupted in spite of the summer heat and prepared it with such skill that on viewing it three centuries later, Caesar Augustus remarked on its beauty.[15]

***

The cause of Alexander's death remains a mystery even today, after over two millennia of scrutiny and speculation. Inconsistencies in the historical record have been, in no small part, responsible for the difficulty in diagnosing his illness. Contemporary accounts of the disorder are long lost, and those secondary accounts that remain were written centuries after the fact. The two most important, by Plutarch and Arrian (1st-2nd century C.E.), are based on the *Royal Ephemerides,* the so-called "Royal Journals" (journals allegedly written by Macedonian historians during Alexander's lifetime and covering the last ten years of his reign), and on the long lost texts of contemporary historians, Ptolemy and Aristobolus. These accounts describe a fatal illness lasting eleven days and characterized by fever, progressive weakness, loss of the power of speech (aphonia) and death. According to Plutarch and Arrian, the illness began suddenly with high fever shortly after heavy drinking at a feast given by Medius, and following another held earlier that same evening in honor of Nearchus, Alexander's naval commander. Plutarch maintained that Alexander did not have pain, as others had written, positing instead that this

62

FIGURE 3-1.   Portrait bust of Alexander the Great from the Acropolis circa 340-335 BCE. Acropolis Museum, Athens, Greece. Photo Credit: Nimatallah/Art Resource, NY.

symptom had been added to the clinical record to render Alexander's death as tragic and as moving as possible.[16]

Diodorus Siculus (1st century B.C.E.) and Justin (3rd century C.E.), the two other principal sources of Alexander's clinical history, maintain that pain was a prominent initial symptom, although they do not mention its location. According to their accounts, it was severe and penetrating in character and began immediately after Alexander had consumed a massive draft of wine, suggesting, at least to Justin, that the wine had been poisoned.

FIGURE 3-2. Detail of Alexander from the Battle of Ussus mosaic, from House of the Faun, Pompei, c.80 BCE.

Based on these accounts, it can be concluded with reasonable certainty that Alexander died of an acute illness marked by high fever and progressive weakness with terminal immobility and loss of speech. He might also have had abdominal pain. He had been drinking heavily at the time and most likely for a considerable period before. Although of remarkably strong constitution, he had sustained numerous, severe battle injuries in his lifetime, not the least of which was a hemopneumothorax (blood and air in the chest cavity resulting from a punctured lung) three years prior to his terminal illness. During the same campaign in which he received these wounds, he was exposed to, and more than likely contracted, an argosy of communicable diseases including both malaria and dysentery. A little less than a year before his own death, Alexander's friend and lover, Hephaestion (see Figure 3-3), died of an acute febrile illness, having at least some of the features of typhoid fever. If Curtius (1st century C.E.) is to be believed, when Egyptian and Chaldean embalmers were summoned several days after Alexander died, they were afraid to approach, so life-like was the body, even though it had languished in the sultry Mesopotamian air for nearly a week.[17]

What could have caused such an illness? In the centuries since Alexander's death, many theories have surfaced. None has been universally accepted, because no diagnosis offered to date has explained all the disparate features of Alexander's illness.

FIGURE 3-3. Head of Hephastion. Courtesy of The J. Paul Getty Museum, Villa Collection, Malibu, California. Used with permission.

An early theory proposed that Alexander was poisoned, perhaps by Antipater, one of Philip's ablest and most trusted lieutenants, who Alexander appointed regent of Macedonia while campaigning in Asia from 334 to 323 B.C.E. Antipater was powerful, talented and ambitious, all of which rendered him especially vulnerable to the fate which befell a score of other officials, satraps and military commanders who lost their posts and their heads on Alexander's return from India. Therefore, it is not surprising that Antipater was suspected almost immediately of complicity in the king's death.

Aristotle, who had tutored young Alexander,[18] was also an early suspect. According to the poison theory, Aristotle joined the assassins, because he feared for his own life after Callisthenes, the son of his niece, died in prison after having been implicated in an assassination plot.[19] The poison, although never specified, was reputed to have been so toxic no vessel could hold it, and it had to be transported to Babylon in the hoof of an ass. Antipater's son, Cassander, was believed to have carried it to Alexander's court, where it was administered to the king by his taster, Iolaus, at the banquet of Medius.

Although both Arrian and Plutarch were skeptical of the poison theory, it deserves consideration, if for no other reason than many, including Antipater, would have welcomed Alexander's death in 323 B.C.E. Alexander had offended many of his fellow Macedonians, Clitus for example, by adopting the dress and customs of the vanquished Persians. His plans for yet another campaign, this one around the horn of Arabia and along the coast of North Africa, must have been greeted with alarm by his exhausted army.[20] The king was neurotically suspicious of independent achievement. Moreover, his claim to be the son of Zeus-Amon was abhorrent to the Macedonians, not just because of the absurdity of his claim to divine status, but also because it was an insult to the memory of Philip, their former king. And perhaps most important, Alexander was surrounded by an extremely able and ambitious staff which included the likes of Ptolemy, Craterus, Perdiccas and Antipater. History would prove them all prepared to kill former brothers-at-arms for their own

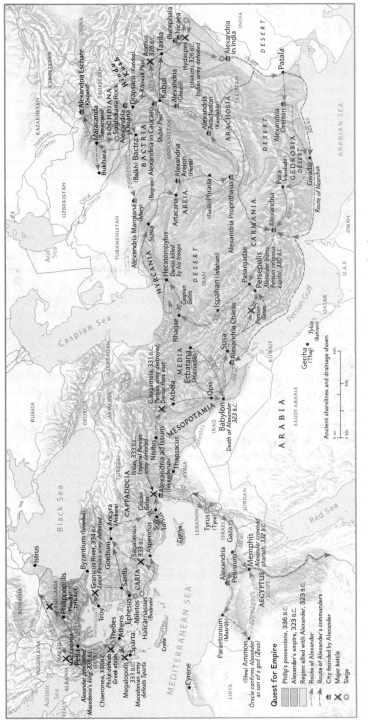

FIGURE 3-4. Alexander's conquests. Photo Credit: Copyright © National Geographic Society. Used with permission.

share of the empire.[21] For when Alexander died, internecine warfare erupted. In the battles that ensued, Ptolemy consolidated his hold on Egypt, creating a dynasty the would last almost three hundred years (see Chapter 1). Antipater succeeded in holding together the remainder of the kingdom until his death in 319 B.C.E., when renewed warfare led to its dismemberment. Thus, for many of Alexander's closest and most powerful associates, his death would seem to have been both timely and highly desirable.

Of the poisons which might have been used by Macedonian conspirators, arsenic is worth considering, only because it causes at least some of the symptoms evinced by Alexander during his terminal illness (i.e., his abdominal pain and progressive weakness). It is also water-soluble (as a salt), and thus readily dissolved in beverages such as wine. Moreover, arsenic oxide, which has the appearance of sugar, is practically tasteless.

In acute poisonings, gastrointestinal symptoms predominate early and generally begin within an hour of ingestion. However, symptoms may be delayed by as much as twelve hours if arsenic is ingested with food, which retards its absorption. Burning lips, constriction of the throat and difficulty swallowing develop first. Excruciating abdominal pain, vomiting and profuse diarrhea follow. In some cases, blood and protein appear in the urine and then the kidneys fail entirely. Victims often complain of severe muscle cramps and intense thirst. They become dehydrated. Their end is marked by convulsions, coma and death. Death can occur within an hour of ingesting the poison, but more often is delayed by at least a day. Fever is not a feature of acute arsenic intoxication.

Thus, Alexander's eleven-day illness would have been unusual for acute arsenic intoxication. It did not have the appropriate clinical characteristics nor did it follow the typical time course of acute arsenic intoxication. What of chronic poisoning, repeated doses of arsenic administered over several days?

The most common early signs of chronic arsenic poisoning are weakness and muscle aches, pigmentation and thickening of the skin (especially of the neck, eyelids, nipples and axillae), and swelling of the extremities. Gastrointestinal complaints are less prominent than in acute poisoning. The breath and perspiration smell of garlic. With repeated doses of arsenic, salivation and sweating increase and the mouth and throat become inflamed. These are followed by generalized itching, tearing, numbness, burning or tingling of the arms and legs and patchy loss of hair and skin pigmentation. These symptoms may begin insidiously with weakness, languor and loss of appetite, less often with nausea, vomiting and diarrhea or constipation. Occasionally, the skin begins to peel. Sometimes the liver enlarges and jaundice develops. As the intoxication advances, the nerves become inflamed, causing progressive numbness and weakness. The latter process might explain Alexander's increasing weakness, but not his unremitting fever. Neither arsenic nor, for that matter, any poison causes fever as a prominent toxic effect. Moreover, because arsenic was not isolated until 1250 C.E., most authorities doubt that it was used as a poison prior to the 13th century C.E.[22]

Alexander drank heavily the night he became ill[23] and, in all probability, had been doing so for at least seven months.[24] For this reason, the possibility that alcohol was either the proximate cause of his terminal illness or, at least, a contributing factor must be considered.

Three acute disorders are commonly associated with heavy alcohol consumption: peptic ulcer disease, alcoholic hepatitis and acute pancreatitis. With regard to the first disorder, alcohol damages the inner lining of the stomach and the upper small intestine (or duodenum) by impairing its capacity to resist the destructive effects of gastric acid and digestive enzymes. When the damage is severe, ulcers develop, causing abdominal pain and dyspepsia (nausea, loss of appetite and vomiting). Such ulcers can bleed, and when they do, they produce bloody vomitus and bowel movements composed of partially digested, black blood. They can also burrow through the entire wall of the stomach or small intestine, releasing digestive juices and bacteria into the abdominal cavity. If this happens, sepsis, shock and death ensue unless the defect is repaired surgically and the infected abdominal cavity cleansed.

Alcohol is directly toxic to the liver as well, causing both acute (hepatitis) and chronic (cirrhosis) damage. Alcohol-induced hepatitis is indistinguishable from other types of hepatitis, such as those caused by the hepatitis viruses. Jaundice (a condition well known to clinicians of Alexander's day but not mentioned in his case history), loss of appetite and brown discoloration of the urine are some of its most prominent features. Nausea and vomiting occur, although less frequently than with alcohol-induced inflammation of the pancreas (pancreatitis). Fever accompanied by a tender liver is more common than in viral hepatitis and may be intense. However, although debilitating, alcohol-induced hepatitis is not usually fatal, at least acutely, especially if alcohol is avoided while the liver is inflamed.

The pancreas is the other digestive organ damaged by alcohol. It lies against the spine in the upper abdomen and is a principal source of digestive enzymes. When the pancreas is inflamed by alcohol, such enzymes ooze from its surface into surrounding tissues, causing intense pain in the upper abdomen, which often seems to penetrate into the back. Typically, the pain is accompanied by nausea and vomiting. Fever is not usually prominent unless there has been hemorrhaging into the pancreas or the pancreas has become secondarily infected. In severe cases, the release of pancreatic enzymes into the blood stream may activate a systemic inflammatory process that can fatally damage the heart, lungs and other vital organs.

Thus, Alexander's acute abdominal pain (if, indeed, he had such pain), mounting fever and death might have been the result of complications of an alcohol-induced peptic ulcer or pancreatitis. Alcohol-induced hepatitis is less likely. None of these diagnoses could account for the progressive weakness, culminating in loss of the power of speech, or the reputed incorruptibility of Alexander's corpse.

Alexander's physicians would have diagnosed his condition as *pyretos* (πυρετος), the ancient Greek word for fever, which by the 5th century B.C.E., was used chiefly as a term for malaria.[25] The ancients associated *pyretos* with marshy areas and a propensity for seasonal attacks, both features now recognized as typical of malaria.

Moreover, they recognized that such fevers were frequently periodic and often accompanied by enlargement of the spleen (splenomegaly). Based on documentation of these observations in Hippocratic works and in the medical writings of the succeeding four centuries, it is clear that clinicians of Alexander's day were well enough acquainted with malaria to describe its symptoms in terms readily recognized by modern day physicians. Was their description of Alexander's illness compatible with malaria?

Malaria is an illness caused by parasitic microorganisms belonging to the genus, *Plasmodium*, which are transmitted to humans by the bite of infected anopheline mosquitoes. The critical role played by mosquitoes in transmitting the disorder is responsible for malaria's association with both marshy areas and warm months of the year. The parasite principally attacks red blood cells and liver cells during different stages of its life cycle to produce a highly distinctive illness.[26]

Initially, the patient complains of chills, violent shivering (rigor) and headache. The skin grows pale and cold. Goose bumps appear and the lips and fingernails turn blue. Within minutes to a few hours, this "cold phase" of the illness is followed by a "hot phase" in which the temperature soars to levels as high as 105°-106°F. Then the skin becomes warm and dry to the touch; the heart races; respirations increase; and the patient exhibits signs of systemic toxicity, such as cough, nausea, vomiting, headache, backache, abdominal pain and delirium. Some time thereafter, surface vessels dilate, releasing internal heat through the skin surface. In three to six hours the attack ends, almost as abruptly as it began, with profuse sweating and a precipitous drop in body temperature, and sometimes the blood pressure as well. Such exhausting paroxysms are characteristically followed by sleep. Upon awakening, the patient feels well until a next attack repeats the whole process in another forty-eight or seventy-two hours. The intermittent nature of the attacks is dictated by the parasite's life cycle, which takes either forty-eight hours or seventy-two hours to complete (depending on the species of plasmodium parasite causing the infection). Although malaria is easily recognized in its classic form, the infection sometimes mimics other diseases (as, for example, bacterial sepsis), making it difficult to diagnose.[27] A malignant form of malaria caused by *Plasmodium falciparum* is notorious in this regard and is also frequently fatal.

If Alexander's terminal illness was malaria, it would almost certainly have been the falciparum variety. Falciparum malaria causes fever with a hectic, unpredictable pattern, lacking the periodicity of the fevers of other forms of malaria. Alexander likely was exposed continuously to malaria, both during his conquests (see Figure 3-4) and his final days in Persia. Moreover, many of his symptoms, his hectic fever, weakness, abdominal pain and his death are typical of falciparum malaria. However, falciparum malaria, again, would not explain Alexander's loss of speech or the incorruptibility of his corpse.

One of the more innovative explanations for Alexander's terminal illness was recently posited by Marr and Calisher in the journal, *Emerging Infectious Diseases.*[28] They believe Alexander might have died of West Nile virus encephalitis, a viral infection of the brain, which sometimes induces a flaccid paralysis. They base their theory on both Alexander's progressive weakness and a previously overlooked incident described by Plutarch, in which a flock of ravens exhibiting bizarre behavior died at Alexander's feet as he entered Babylon on his return from India. Birds are the principal reservoir for West Nile virus, and like humans, develop a sometimes fatal encephalitis. Corvine species, such as ravens and crows, are especially susceptible to the infection. Thus, the West Nile virus might explain both Alexander's illness (his fever and his progressive weakness) and the apparent corvine epidemic that greeted him at the gates of Babylon. However, in humans, West Nile encephalitis is rarely fatal unless the victim is old or otherwise debilitated. Moreover, Plutarch had a penchant for avian augeries, which he frequently used to heighten the drama of critical events.[29] He reported, for example, that wild birds perched in the forum in anticipation of Caesar's assassination; that a flight of crows croaked and pecked at the ropes of Cicero's vessel shortly before he was murdered; that a flight of birds directed Romulus and Remus to the site at which they founded Rome; that the lost grave of Theseus was revealed to Cimon by an eagle tearing up the earth with its talons; and that an owl foretold the defeat of the Persian armada at Salamis by flying to the right of Thermistocles' fleet before landing on the top mast of his flag ship.

A final possibility, one which might explain all of Alexander's abnormalities (his fever, his progressive weakness, his abdominal pain, his loss of the power of speech, and his post mortem incorruptibility) is typhoid fever complicated by ascending paralysis.[15] Typhoid is an acute, systemic infection caused by the bacterium, *Salmonella typhi*. The bacterium infects only humans, traveling from person to person, most often as a food-borne contaminant. It is a scourge of third world countries, as well as a shadowy companion of warfare and social disintegration. Prior to modern concepts of public health, which recognize the importance of clean drinking water and proper sewage disposal, typhoid was an urban blight. More than likely it killed Hephaestion, and, no doubt, scores of Alexander's subjects as well. All of them, including Alexander himself, were likely victims of poor sanitation of that era, which allowed their food and/or water to become contaminated with human feces, in some instances derived from patients with typhoid fever and other gastrointestinal infections.

The infection causes general debilitation, headache, fever, weakness and abdominal pain. Initially the fever increases in intensity day by day in a stair-step fashion. After a week, it plateaus and becomes a continuous or mildly remittent fever of 103° to 104°F. A rash is present in many cases, but tends to be subtle and evanescent and is easily missed.

Prior to the discovery of antibiotics in the mid-20th century, typhoid was a diseased marked by prolonged fever and progressive debilitation. In rare instances, the infection was accompanied by an ascending paralysis involving first the legs, then the arms, and finally, the area of the brain that controls breathing. This form of paralysis, the so-called Landry-Guillain-Barré syndrome,[30] is virtually universally fatal when due to typhoid fever. Intestinal perforation (specifically, rupture of the terminal segment of the small intestine, a preferred site of attack by the typhoid bacillus) is another potentially fatal complication of typhoid fever, one some authorities believe took the life of Alexander's oldest and closest friend, Hephaestion.[31]

Alexander exhibited many of the classic signs and symptoms of typhoid fever during the course of his terminal illness: fever which seemed to rise from one day to the next in stair-step fashion, abdominal pain, malaise and generalized weakness, weakness which progressed in a pattern suggesting ascending paralysis. First, he had difficulty walking, then could not perform daily sacrifices without assistance. Ultimately, he lost even the power of speech as progressively higher nerve centers fell prey to the ascending paralysis.

If Alexander's corpse was surprisingly fresh when approached by embalmers almost a week after his death, only two explanations seem plausible. Either the story is apocryphal, or Alexander actually died later than his attendants appreciated. In the later case, typhoid-induced, Landry-Guillain-Barré syndrome might have created the appearance of death prior to the actual event, in a patient whose extraordinary pre-morbid constitution enabled him to teeter at the very precipice of death without food or water for a considerable time before finally succumbing to the inevitable consequence of the illness.

Highly effective drugs are available today to treat both typhoid fever and malaria. However, in 323 B.C.E. little could be done for either infection.[32] Traditional interventions consisted of prayers and sacrificial offerings, both of which were employed by Alexander to no avail. Such interventions were based on concepts ascribing disease to divine retribution. At the time Alexander died, these concepts were being supplanted by more objective constructs promulgated by the Hippocratic school (see Chapter 2) which were to become the seeds from which the scientific spirit and ethical ideals of today's medical practice would germinate.

Alexander more than likely survived his many battle wounds, at least in part, because of therapeutics developed under the influence of Hippocrates and his followers. Regarding the treatment of wounds, Hippocratic doctrine maintained that "they should never be irrigated except with clean water or wine, the dry state being nearest to healthy, the wet to the diseased." The aseptic advantages of extreme dryness were promoted by avoiding greasy dressings and by efforts to reunite the edges of fresh wounds, sometimes with the help of astringents. Rest and immobilization were believed to be of capital importance in the recovery process. Water used for irrigation had to be either very pure or else boiled. Surgeons were admonished to cleanse hands and nails and to conduct their work in operating rooms which were well illuminated and staffed by capable assistants.

Although Hippocratic physicians had access to many drugs, they firmly believed that the primary focus of therapeutics was to assist nature in the healing process. Therefore, the mainstays of therapy were generally expedients such as fresh air, nourishing diet, purgation, tisanes of barley water (a concentrate of water and other ingredients still popular in Britain today), wine, massage and hydrotherapy. Black hellebore (*Helleborus niger*) was the universal purgative; white hellebore (*Veratrum album*), the universal emetic.

Because Alexander would have been deemed incurable in the latter phase of his illness, Hippocratic doctrine would have proscribed against further treatment at that point. Medicine, according to the doctrine, was an art, by means of which sufferers might be freed of their ailments and severe attacks of disease might be mitigated. Since the art could be of no help in terminal cases, physicians were obliged to discontinue treatments once patients were overwhelmed by their illnesses. To do otherwise, they might violate ethical standards by receiving fees or raising hopes based on false inducements.

When Alexander returned from India, he was not the same man who had crossed the Hellespont to become Lord of Asia.[33] A decade of the carnage of uninterrupted conquest had reduced him to a state of paranoia in which "he gave way to fears of the supernatural....[and became] so disturbed and easily alarmed that if the least unusual or extraordinary thing happened, he thought it a prodigy or a presage,[16] "symptoms which today would lead to a diagnosis of *post-traumatic stress disorder* (see Chapter 11). Although he dreamed of renewed conquest around the Arabian peninsula and across North Africa, more than likely, his psychological collapse had ended his days as military commander well before his fever (one most consistent with typhoid fever complicated by ascending paralysis) took his life. In many respects, it is remarkable not that he died so young, but that he survived so long in the face of extended periods of extreme privation, rampant communicable diseases, heavy alcohol consumption and intense court intrigue.

Notes

1. According to Plutarch, "From hence designing to march against Darius, before he set out he diverted himself with his officers at an entertainment of drinking and other pastimes, and indulged so far as to let every one's mistress sit by and drink with them. The most celebrated of them was Thais, an Athenian mistress of Ptolemy, who was afterwards King of Egypt.....[she asked] if, while the king looked on, she might in sport, with her own hands, set fire to the court of that Xerxes who reduced the city of Athens to ashes, that it might be recorded to posterity that the women who followed Alexander had taken a severer revenge on the Persians for the sufferings and affronts of Greece, than all the famed commanders had been able to do by sea or land. What she said was received with such universal liking and murmurs of applause, and so seconded by the encouragement and eagerness of the company, that the king himself, persuaded to be of the party, started from his seat, and with a chaplet of flowers on his head and a lighted torch in his hand, led them the way, while they went after him in a riotous manner, dancing and making loud cries about the place....all agree that he soon repented of it, and gave order to put out the fire. (Plutarch. *The Lives of the Noble Grecians and Ro-*

mans. Translated by J. Dryden and revised by A. H. Clough. The Modern Library. New York:1979, p. 828-9.)

2. During the course of an acrimonious exchange and after much drinking, the king ran a spear through Clitus, killing him instantly. They had been arguing over a number of issues. Clitus, like many of his countrymen, bridled at the king's claim to be the son of Zeus, and the king's insistence that he be "adored" as such. Moreover, Clitus felt that the king had become so enamored of his Persian subjects, that Macedonians were being forced to petition their former foes for access to him. (Plutarch. *Lives*, p. 837-8.)

3. "....he was fair and of a light colour, passing into ruddiness in his face and upon his breast.... Aristoxenus in his Memoirs tells us that a most agreeable odour exhaled from his skin, and his breath and body all over was so fragrant as to perfume the clothes which he wore next him; the cause of which might probably be the hot and adust [sic.] temperament of his body." (Plutarch. *Lives,* p. 803.)

4. Plutarch. *Lives*, p. 834.

5. Plutarch. *Lives*, p. 811-12.

6. According to Arrian, the king's chest was penetrated by a great arrow, and the wound, which nearly killed him, issued forth both "blood and breath." (Arrian. *The Life of Alexander the Great.* Translated by Aubrey de Sélicourt. Penquin Books. Baltimore: 1958 p. 202-3.)

7. Plutarch, *Lives*, p. 846.

8. Plutarch, *Lives*, p. 813-4.

9. ".... Pausanias, having had an outrage done to him [by Cleopatra, Philip's daughter]...., when he found he could get no reparation for his disgrace at Philip's hands, watched his opportunity and murdered him..... Alexander was twenty years old." (Plutarch, *Lives*, p. 807-8.)

10. Not to be confused with Egypt's last queen of the same name, who lived some three hundred years later.

11. Plutarch. *Lives*, p. 854.

12. In the spring of 324 B.C.E., Alexander married two women simultaneously in a move to consolidate his position within the empire. One was Darius' daughter, Statira, whom he had captured along with her mother and grandmother at Issus. The other, Parysatis, was the daughter of Artaxerxes III, who had occupied the Persian throne before it was usurped by Darius III. His first wife, to whom he was still married, was Roxana.

13. "....for Hephaestion, [he had] a love which persisted even beyond the grave." (Arrian. *Alexander*, p. 250.)

14. Bagoas first appears in Curtius, who states: "Nabarzanes, having received a safe conduct, met him [Alexander] bringing gifts. Among these was Bagoas, a eunuch of remarkable beauty and in the very flower of boyhood, who had been loved by Darius, and was afterwards to be loved by Alexander..." (Renault M. *The Persian Boy.* Vintage Books. New York:1988, p. 413-14.) Plutarch too mentions Bagoas in his description of a celebrated incident some six years later: "and one day after he [Alexander] had drunk pretty hard, it is said, he went to see a prize of dancing contended for, in which his favourite Bagoas, having gained the victory, crossed the theatre in his dancing habit, and sat down close by him, which so pleased the Macedonians that they made loud acclamations for him to kiss Bagoas, and never stopped clapping their hands and shouting till Alexander put his arms round him and kissed him." (Plutarch. *Lives*, p. 849.)

15. Alexander's corpse was prepared for interment in Babylon. While en route to Macedonia, it was hijacked and taken to Alexandria where it was placed in a glass sarcophagus and remained on view for the next five and a half centuries. The ultimate fate of Alexander's corpse is unknown. In modern Alexandria, in the Mosque of the Nebi Daniel, there is a cruciform-shaped subterranean crypt which formed part of the foundation of an early Christian church. Legend has it that the church was built over Alexander's mausoleum, and according to

newspaper accounts in the late 19th century, a workman repairing the foundation gazed on the remains of Alexander's crypt. The possibility of gaining permission to excavate this site in search of the remains of an ancient Macedonian king is remote, and thus, Alexander's ultimate resting place remains a mystery. (Oldach DW, Richard RE, Borza EN, Benitez RM. A mysterious death. *N Engl J Med.* 1998;338:1764-9.)

16. Plutarch. *Lives*, p. 853.

17. According to Curtius: "[Alexander's] corpse during those seven days [after he died] was as still alive even as if still breathing, without any signs of decomposition or discoloration, so that the Egyptians and Chaldeans who had been ordered to embalm the corpse did not dare to approach it and, after praying to get strength from the gods, they removed the entrails and filled the coffin with perfume." (Quintus Curtius. *History of Alexander.* Vol 2. Harvard University Press, Cambridge: 1977, p. 12-13.)

18. Philip entrusted the education of his son to Aristotle, "the most learned and most celebrated philosopher of his time, and rewarded him with a munificence proportional to and becoming the care he took to instruct his son." (Plutarch. *Lives*, p. 805.)

19. Callisthenes accompanied Alexander as historian during the Persian campaign. He died in prison after having been implicated in a conspiracy organized by Hermolaus to assassinate Alexander. Some claimed that he was hanged by Alexander's orders; others that he died of sickness in prison. Like Alexander, Callisthenes, the son of Aristotle's niece, had been educated by the great phiosopher. (Plutarch. *Lives*, p. 841.)

20. At the time of his death, Alexander was developing a grandiose plan for conquest in the west. It would have taken his armies around the Arabian peninsula and across the southern Mediterranean all the way to the Atlantic. (Bosworth A.B. The death of Alexander the Great: rumor and propaganda. *Classical Quarterly.* 1971; 21:112-36.)

21. Egypt was to become Ptolemy's share of the empire, Cilicia, Craterus', regent of the kingdom, Perdiccas' and Macedonia, Antipater's. (Bosworth, p. 130.)

22. According to Nelson, arsenic was first isolated by Albertus Magnus in the year 1250. [Nelson K. Session I: Industrial Sources. Introduction in Lederer WH, Fensterheim RJ, Eds. *Arsenic. Industrial, Biomedical, Environmental Perspectives.* Van Nostrand Reinhold Co. New York:1983, p. 1.]

23. According to one report, Alexander drained a bowl of Hercules full of wine (12 pints) at Medius' banquet (Plutarch. *Lives*, p. 853.)

24. Ancient historians differ as to the extent of Alexander's drinking. According to Bosworth, "The most substantial extract, from Aelian, gives a day-to-day account of the king's drinking during the month of Dios, some seven months before his death. What results is a continuous record of carousing with the frequent story that the king slept solidly for one or even two days after his excesses. This last detail is taken up by Athenaeus and Plutarch (in the *Quaestiones Conviviales*).... So either the testimonia are to be rejected out of hand or we must face the conclusion that the Ephemerides recorded a drinking marathon unique in history, in which the king spent his life alternately drinking himself to insensibility and sleeping off the results. Clearly this is the story of Ephippus and Nicobule, who attributed Alexander's death to his excesses at Medius' banquet. In the Ephemerides the final illness seems anticipated by a string of comparable debauches, and the impression to be fostered is no doubt that Alexander ruined his constitution by his drinking and so succumbed easily to the illness thereby induced. (Bosworth, p. 121-2.)

25. Borza EN. Some observations on malaria and the ecology of central Macedonia in antiquity. *Am J Ancient Hist.* 1979; 4:102-24.

26. Anopheline mosquitoes transmit malaria by injecting forms of the parasite called sporozoites into the human host. These

sporozoites then invade liver cells (hepatocytes), in which they develop into the next stage of the parasite, the schizont. Each infected hepatocyte ruptures to liberate 10,000 to 30,000 representatives of yet another stage of the parasite, the merozoite, which invade circulating red blood cells (erythrocytes). Growth and development of the parasites in red blood cells result in subsequent waves of merozoite invasion. This blood cycle repeats every 48 to 72 hours (depending on the species of the malaria responsible for the infection), leading to amplification of parasite numbers in the blood, paroxysms of chills, fever and sweats, as well as other manifestations of the disease. (Adapted from Fairhurst RM, Wellems TE. Plasmodium species [malaria]. In Mandell GL, Bennett JE, Dolin R, Eds. *Principles and of Practice of Infectious Diseases.* 6th ed. Elsevier, Inc. Philadelphia:2005. p. 3122.)

27. Kean BH, Reilly PC Jr. Malaria, the mime: recent lessons from a group of civilian travelers. *Am J Med.* 1976;61:159-64.

28. Marr JS, Calisher CH. Alexander the Great and West Nile virus encephalitis. *Emerg Infect Dis.* 2003;9:online.

29. Oldach D, Benitez RM, Mackowiak PA. Alexander and West Nile virus encephalitis (letter). *Emerg Infect Dis.* 2004;10: 1330-1.

30. Osler W. *The Principles and Practice of Medicine.* 12th ed. D. Appleton-Century Co. Inc. New York: 1935, p. 21; Rich JD, Dickinson BP, Flaxman AB, Mylonakis E: Guillain-Barre Syndrome as a first manifestation of typhoid fever. *Clin Infect Dis.* 1999;28:1171.

31. Plutarch tells us that Hephaestion fell "sick of a fever, in which, being a young man and soldier, too, he could not confine himself to so exact a diet as was necessary; for whilst his physician, Glaucus, was gone to the theatre, he ate a fowl for his dinner, and drank a large draught of wine, upon which he became very ill, and shortly after died. (Plutarch. *Lives*, p. 851.) Hephaestion's febrile illness, like Alexander's, could have been typhoid fever, in this case complicated by

post-prandial perforation of the terminal ileum (lower small intestine).

32. See Garrison FH. *An Introduction to the History of Medicine.* W.B. Saunders Co. Philadelphia: 1924, p. 86-109; and Selwyn-Brown A. *The Physician Throughout the Ages.* Capehart-Brown Co., Inc. New York: 1938.

33. Mackowiak PA. Bagoas. The Pharos Summer/2006: 26-28.

4

WORM'S MEAT

In life, this patient's power grew like a cedar in Lebanon. But while his achievements as warrior/king were considerable, many would argue that his victimization by an unnamed disease in which his flesh literally was consumed by worms was fitting retribution for his many acts of cruelty, not the least of which were the Massacre of the Innocents[1] and the murder of his own sons.

Until his final decade, the patient enjoyed exceptional physical health. As a youth he was a hunter and a horseman of uncommon ability and an all but invincible warrior. He could bend a bow and throw a javelin with great precision. He fought bravely and skillfully in many wars without serious injury. He also survived numerous assassination attempts and natural disasters, all of which seemed to ensure his survival to an old age full of riches and honor.[2]

The patient's youth, however, was not entirely free from physical or mental affliction. When he was thirty he developed his first known illness while traveling in Damascus. Neither the name nor the symptoms of the illness were recorded, but we know that it prevented him from returning to Jerusalem, his capital, to help quell a disturbance. A few years later, during a war against Antigonus, a javelin pierced his side. The wound must not have been severe, however, because he continued fighting.[2]

The patient's most serious illness, prior to his last, followed the execution of Mariamme, his second wife, when he was forty-four and she was not yet twenty-five. Mariamme was beautiful and dignified, though quarrelsome and quick to speak her mind. The patient was driven to murder her by unfounded suspicions of adultery, but quickly came to regret the results of his misplaced passion. He grew delusional with despair over Mariamme's death, and many suspect he never fully recovered, although eventually he was able to resume the work of ruling his kingdom.[2]

During this same time, an epidemic in Jerusalem caused him to flee to Samaria. He still became ill, although it is not certain that his illness was the same one that attacked Jerusalem. The patient's symptoms included an inflammation and a numbness of his neck, apparently combined with a temporary loss of reason. For a time, his condition was so critical his physicians feared for his life.[2]

Only two other illnesses are mentioned in the patient's clinical record. One was a hunting accident in which he fell from his horse and impaled himself on one of his own spears. Neither the location of the wound nor its extent is known. The other was a serious, but otherwise uncharacterized, disorder that befell him when he was sixty-five, shortly before the death of his brother, Pheroras. His family's medical history sheds little light on the source of the patient's own medical problems. His father, also a fierce warrior, was fatally poisoned when in his late fifties; the patient was then thirty years of age. Nothing is known of his mother's health. He had three brothers and a sister. An older brother committed suicide when in his thirties while imprisoned by the Parthians; a younger brother also died in his thirties of war-related injuries; and his youngest brother died in his sixties after contracting an illness of unknown cause. His sister, who lived into her seventies, was alive and in good health at the time of the patient's death. Nothing more is known of her medical history.[3]

The patient was a Jew by birth, with parental roots in Idumaea (father) and Nabatea (mother). The Idumaeans, among whom he was reared, were a semi-nomadic people scattered throughout a relatively small area south of Judea (roughly, present-day Masada) that was bordered on the east by the Dead Sea (see Figure 4-1, a map of Judea, and Note 21). They were a desert people, derived from Esau's tribe of Edom, and traditional enemies of Jacob's tribe of Israel.[3,4] The patient united and ruled them for over three decades as king of

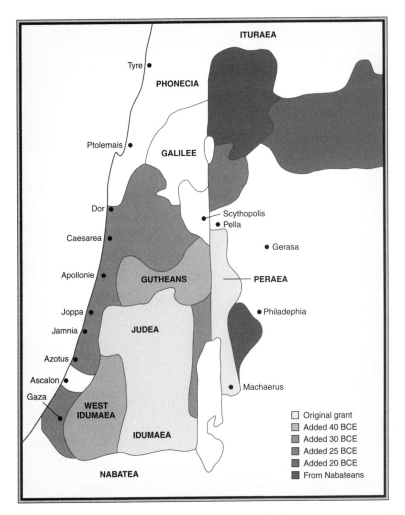

FIGURE 4-1. The patient's kingdom. Adapted from Richardson, P. Herod, King of the Jews and Friend of the Romans. University of South Carolina Press. South Carolina: 1996; p. 149; Map 4. Used with permission.

the Jews and a third-generation descendent of a full and willing proselyte to Judaism.[5] Nevertheless, because during his reign he suppressed the Sanhedrin,[6] appointed and deposed high priests according to his whim, introduced Greek culture into Judea,[7] evicted Jews from positions of authority and replaced them with non-Jews[8], had a Nabatean mother who was not considered a true convert[9] and, most of all, because he bowed to Rome, his Jewishness is questioned even to this day.

The patient's approach to religion was that of a political realist, who ruled a diverse people, some of whom sacrificed to gods other than Yahweh. He allowed them to worship gods of their own choosing in return for loyalty, according to a policy of "religious syncretism" in which his own cult of Yahweh coexisted with those of other semitic deities.[8]

He was a warrior and a monarch who took up the mantle of David and Solomon with a fortitude that allowed him to successfully rule the stubborn and rebellious people who occupied Judea, one of the richest, most populous, vibrant and extensive regions of the Roman empire.[10] For thirty-seven years he maintained peace to a degree not since enjoyed in that region and created an effective buffer for Rome against Parthian aggression.[11]

The patient had ten wives[12] and with them produced fifteen children, only one of whom died of natural (but otherwise unspecified) cause during his lifetime.[13] Good health brought the family little comfort, however, as the patient himself proved to be the biggest threat to his family's well-being. His sons, Alexander II and Aristobulus I, were the first victims of the paranoia that consumed the patient during his final decade. Their supposed crime, planning to assassinate their father in a hunting "accident" so that they might petition Caesar Augustus for his kingdom, was supported only by testimony obtained under torture. Nevertheless, the patient had them both strangled just three years before his own death. Finally, while in the throes of his terminal illness, the patient ordered the execution of his first-born son, Antipater III, giving rise to the celebrated phrase attributed to Augustus: "Better to be [the patient's] pig than his son,"[2] alluding to both the patient's penchant for killing his own children and his conversion to Judaism, which prevented him from eating pork.

There were many other acts of cruelty for which the patient is now widely despised and rejected. In his effort to maintain power, he exterminated legions of opponents and presumed opponents, notably the Hasmonean descendents of Simon Maccabaeus and their supporters, who had ruled Judea from 140 B.C.E. until 37 B.C.E.; the rebel leader, Hezekiah, and his followers; his second wife's brother, Aristobulus III (whom he had drowned); his brothers-in-law, Joseph and Costobar; and the high priest, Hyrcanus II.

This is not to say the patient was without virtue. He had a personal charm and an aptitude for realpolitic that enabled him to become one of the dominant figures of his age, a friend and an ally of the likes of Julius Caesar, Mark Anthony, Caesar Augustus and Marcus Agrippa. Moreover, he became both the lynchpin of Rome's eastern policy and Judea's shield against Roman oppression. As a result of his political prowess, his subjects were exempt from military service and paid no tribute to Rome. Moreover, during his reign, Judea saw little of Roman administrative officials or tax collectors, and the region enjoyed a period of almost uninterrupted prosperity. Trade flourished, cities were transformed, and the prestige and influence of Jews and Judea rose throughout the Roman world.[14] During the famine of 28/27 B.C.E., the patient used his personal wealth to subsidize a massive relief effort, which not only saved large numbers of his subjects from starvation, but also won for him an international reputation for generosity and innovation.[15] Also at his own expense he built the first Judean navy; he secured for Jews in the Diaspora the freedom to worship the god of Israel; he rebuilt the Temple walls and defensive towers of Jerusalem, and constructed numerous palaces, public buildings, shops, a theatre, ampitheatre, aquaducts and cisterns. At Caesarea Maritima, he created the largest harbor of his day on the Mediterranean Sea and at the same time saw to the construction of new cities at Phasaelis, Antipatris, Aggripias, Pente Komai, Gaba Bathyra and Heshbon.[16] Although a Jew of dubious orthodoxy, the patient honored the God of Abraham, Isaac and Jacob with edifices more magnificent and more numerous than those of any Judean monarch before or since (Figure 4-2). When considering his building projects, his principal biographer, Josephus, wrote: "Thenceforth he advanced to the utmost prosperity; his noble spirit rose to greater heights, and his lofty ambition was mainly directed to works of piety."

FIGURE 4-2. Scale model of Jerusalem and the second temple following its expansion by the patient, circa 20 BCE. The picture shows the temple compound. Holy Land Hotel, Jerusalem, Israel. Photo Credit: Erich Lessing/Art Resource, NY.

All this, however, was of little comfort at the end of his life. Precisely when the disease that would dissolve his flesh and undermine his reason began is uncertain.[17] In his sixties he hunted and was able to lead his army in the field. In fact, when he was sixty-three, he was vigorous enough to cover in three days a journey that usually took seven, as the head of a successful expedition against brigands[18] barricaded within the great castle at Raepta.[19]

When his final illness struck, however, it performed its work swiftly. According to Josephus,[20] the onset of the patient's final illness began when he was already seventy years of age and had grown melancholy over the "calamities" brought about by his children. The calamities to which Josephus referred and which caused the patient to murder his own sons seem to have been, at least in part, imagined; the extent to which his illness contributed to the patient's paranoia is uncertain. As it progressed, the illness affected the patient with a wide range of symptoms, including a gentle fever; intolerable itching over the entire surface of his body; continual pains in his colon; a dropsical collection of aqueous and transparent liquor in his feet and lower abdomen; an inflammation of the colon; a putrefaction of his genitals that produced worms; fetid breath; convulsions; and difficulty breathing unless he sat upright.

The diviners claimed that all of these ills were a punishment for the patient's great impiety. Yet, despite his intense suffering, he longed to live and desperately sought methods that might cure him. Accordingly, he went over Jordan to the hot baths at Callirrhoe, which run into Lake Asphaltitis. There, physicians immersed his whole body into a large vessel full of warm oil, whereupon he went blind and might well have died had his servants failed in their strenuous efforts to revive him.

Following the trip to Callirrhoe, the patient's despair of recovery apparently intensified. He was in such a weakened state during a subsequent trip to Jericho that his death seemed imminent. A short time later he was overcome by a convulsive cough and renewed pains so severe he could not eat even though his appetite was intense. Josephus tells us that, in the grip of renewed despair, the patient took an apple, asked for a paring knife, and, looking around to see if anyone was near, prepared to stab himself. Achiabus, his first cousin, rushed to him at the last moment, however, and prevented him from doing so. When word spread throughout the palace that he had killed himself, the patient blamed the rumor on his son, Antipater III, and promptly had him slain.[20] Five days later, physically wasted and no longer in control of his senses, the patient died. It was the month of Nisan, at the end of March or the beginning of April, in the 750th year of Rome (4 B.C.E.). Herod, Herod the Great,[21] King of Judea, Idumaea, Samraritis, Peraea, Heshbon, Gaulantis, Batanea, Trachonitis, Auranitis, Gaza, Hippos and Gadara,[22] the "Idumaean Usurper," had reigned for 34 years since defeating and then executing Antigonus, the last Judean king of pure Jewish blood, to obtain his kingdom, and thirty-seven years since he had been made king by the Romans (Figure 4-3).

***

Herod's story, including the account of his final illness summarized in this chapter, was recorded for posterity by Flavius Josephus, a Jew of Jerusalem and scion of a priestly family and Hasmonean royals.[23] After participating in events that led to the destruction of Jerusalem by the Romans in 70 C.E., Josephus returned to Rome, where as a pensioner of the Caesars, he spent thirty years writing a history of the war (*War*) and another of his people (*Archeology*).[24] In both works, he devoted considerable attention to Herod while writing for Titus, a future Emperor of Rome who took a personal inter-

FIGURE 4-3. Herod the Great. Engraving, 19th century. Courtesy of Hulton Archive/Getty Images. Used with permission.

est in his work and was, to all intents and purposes, its censor. Because of Titus' interest, Josephus was obliged to write a history acceptable not just to him, but also to his Hasmonean mistress, Berenice, the granddaughter of Aristobulus 1 (one of the three sons Herod had executed), and a woman some suspect longed for posthumous revenge on the man who had killed her grandfather, great-great uncle and great-great-grandfather.[25] Her potential influence and that of Titus on Josephus' works have raised concern that the more gruesome details of his account of Herod's final illness might be metaphorical rather than factual.

Herod's demise was indeed gruesome. The last years of his life were marked by paranoia: the depression and paranoia that drove him to murder his own children may well have been the first signs of the disease that was to become for him both a curse and an astonishment. Later, when it emerged in full-flower, it produced a light fever [*pyretos*] which "did not so much indicate symptoms of inflammation [*phlogosis*] to the touch as it produced internal damage." To this it added intolerable itching [*knesmos*] over Herod's entire body and continuous and intense pains in his "intestines," probably "due to ulceration of the bowels [*helkosis to te enteron*]." It produced "tumors in the feet as in dropsy" which had the appearance of "a moist, transparent suppuration of the feet," and "gangrene of the privy parts [*aidoiou sepsis*]" which "produced worms [*skolekas*]," and, as his end drew near, difficulty breathing [*dyspnoia*], especially in the supine position [*orthopnoia*], and foul breath. "Convulsions [*spasmos*] in every limb that took an unendurable severity" developed during the terminal phase of the illness. Whether the "convulsions" were twitching, spasms or full-blown seizures is uncertain. As the severity of the abdominal pain increased, Herod refused all food. Although his symptoms seem to have waxed and waned, none of the modest treatments administered by his physicians provided any obvious relief.[26] Just prior to his death, spasmodic coughing compounded his suffering, and he died in agony as severe as any he had inflicted on his beloved Mariamme, his sons, the Hasmoneans and so many others during his long reign.

Herod's terminal illness has been attributed to a host of disorders,[27] most of which deserve only passing consideration. His promiscuity and the protean manifestation of his terminal illness have led to speculation that syphilis might have been responsible for the torment of his final days.[28] Syphilis, the great imitator, certainly has the capacity to "seize the whole body and greatly disorder all of its parts with various symptoms" of the sort described by Josephus, but it did not exist in the Old World until the end of the 15th century C.E., when Columbus' crew brought it back with them from the Americas on returning from their first voyage of discovery (see Chapter 7).

Because of Herod's intense intestinal complaints and Josephus' reference to "an inflammation of the colon," it has also been suggested that he might have died of either a gastrointestinal cancer or amebiasis, an invasive parasitic infection of the colon associated with poor sanitation that produces painful, bloody diarrhea.[29] Although gastrointestinal cancer might explain the "internal damage" to which Josephus alluded, and might even account for Herod's fever (if the cancer was necrotic) and the intense pains of the intestine (if the cancer was obstructing the bowel), it would not easily explain Herod's "dropsy," gangrene of his penis, foul breath, difficulty breathing or his seizures, unless the cancer had metastasized to virtually every vital organ. Amebiasis would explain Herod's fever, "internal damage," abdominal pain and "ulceration of the bowels" but none of his other complaints.

W.R. Litchfield, writing in the *Journal of the Royal Society of Medicine*,[27] has raised the possibility that long-standing diabetes mellitus complicated by kidney failure, neuropathy (nerve damage), diffuse atherosclerosis and infection might have been responsible for Herod's terminal illness. In fact, diabetes mellitus, if long-standing and inadequately treated, regularly induces all of these complications, which together might produce the entire spectrum of signs and symptoms described by Josephus. However, the hallmarks of the disorder (a voracious appetite and unquenchable thirst, excessive urination [due to a diuretic effect of high blood sugar] and progressive weight loss) are noticeably absent from Josephus' description of Herod's illness. Moreover, before the advent of insulin therapy, patients did not survive diabetes long enough to develop the renal, neurological or advanced vascular complications of the disorder.

One of the more innovative proposals concerning Herod's fatal illness is that he suffered from *dracunculiasis*, an infestation of the subcutaneous tissues (usually of the legs) by twenty-inch-long worms called "guinea worms."[30] The disorder, now largely confined to tropical Africa, is acquired by drinking water contaminated with crustaceans infected with the parasitic worm, *Dracunculus medinensis*. Dracunculiasis, which might explain only one feature of Herod's multifaceted disorder (his "gangrene of the privy parts....[which] produced worms"), like several of the other diagnoses proposed over the years, has more to tell about the special interest and personal expertise of the proposer than about the nature of Herod's illness. Josephus tells us that Herod's agonies were God's work, divine retribution for a lifetime of sowing wickedness and reaping iniquity. Although each of these diagnoses might explain some of Herod's complaints, none offers a better explanation for all of the features of his terminal illness than hypertension and arteriosclerosis complicated by progressive dementia, congestive heart failure and kidney failure.[31]

Arteriosclerosis, also known as *atherosclerosis*, is the most common cause of death today in industrialized societies; however, it is by no means a new disorder. Evidence of it can be found in Egyptian mummies and in case histories recorded in medical texts of ancient Greece.[32] *Atheroma* (derived from the Greek *athere*, gruel), the principal defects of the disorder, are fatty streaks and raised oleaginous plaques that develop in the inner lining of arteries and obstruct blood flow. Any artery can be affected. In the brain, atheroma are responsible for strokes and progressive dementia. In the heart, they produce myocardial infarctions (heart attacks) and heart failure, and in the kidney they cause chronic renal failure.

The most important risk factors for atherosclerosis are a genetic predisposition (as evidenced by a family history of premature atherosclerosis), advanced age, obesity, physical inactivity, diabetes, emotional stress and cigarette smoking. Hypertension is both a cause and an effect of atherosclerosis, just as it can be either the cause or a consequence of progressive kidney failure (see Chapter 12).[32]

Herod was demented during the later stage of his illness and exhibited signs of a gradually progressive dementia for at least a decade before his death. In fact, Perowne[33] maintains that for the last ten years of his life, and at times before that, he was *non-compos mentis.* Dementia is a generic term used to describe chronic or progressive mental dysfunction.[34] Sometimes, as in Herod's case, it is accompanied by depression. It has many causes, the two most common of which are Alzheimer's disease (a form of *presenile* dementia characterized by progressive memory loss, confusion and disorientation beginning in late middle life) and vascular insufficiency (dementia resulting from insufficient blood flow to the brain). The principal risk factors for the latter form of dementia are old age, male sex, hypertension, heart disease, diabetes, generalized atherosclerosis, smoking and high concentrations of lipids in the blood. Herod most likely had at least five of these (advanced age, male sex, hypertension, heart disease and generalized atherosclerosis), and as such would have been highly predisposed to this form of dementia because the presence of multiple risk factors increases the probability of vascular dementia to a greater extent than that of the sum of the individual risk factors.

Herod's "mild fever," his difficulty breathing (especially in the supine position), his swollen feet and scrotum, and his spasmodic cough all suggest that he suffered from congestive heart failure, a condition most often the consequence of atherosclerosis and/or chronic hypertension. Sometimes atherosclerosis of coronary arteries takes the form of focal atheromatous plaques, which cause angina and coronary thrombosis. At others, it involves the coronary arteries diffusely. In the former instance, congestive heart failure typically develops in the aftermath of a myocardial infarction, frequently heralded by years of intermittent, exertional chest pain (angina). In the latter instance, heart failure more often begins insidiously, in the absence of antecedent angina or myocardial infarction. Chronic hypertension promotes atherosclerosis. It also causes heart muscles to hypertrophy and in the process to function less efficiently.

The human heart, like that of other mammals, is composed of four chambers, two small ones called *atria* and two larger and more muscular ones called *ventricles* (see Figure 4-4).[35] One atrium receives

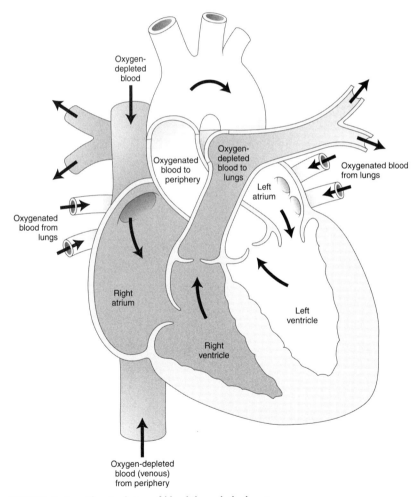

Oxygen-depleted blood

Oxygenated blood to periphery

Oxygen-depleted blood to lungs

Left atrium

Oxygenated blood from lungs

Oxygenated blood from lungs

Right atrium

Left ventricle

Right ventricle

Oxygen-depleted blood (venous) from periphery

FIGURE 4-4. The circulation of blood through the heart.

oxygen-depleted venous blood from the periphery, which it delivers to the smaller, less muscular of the two ventricles, whose responsibility it is to pump the blood into the lungs for re-oxygenation. These two chambers have arbitrarily been designated the *right* side of the heart or, simply, the *right heart*. The *left heart* is composed of the other (left) atrium, which receives re-oxygenated blood from the lungs and the larger, more muscular (left) ventricle, which pumps that blood through the arterial system to tissues throughout the body.

When atherosclerosis damages the left side of the heart, the side responsible for siphoning newly oxygenated blood from the lungs, fluid accumulates in the pulmonary vessels, impairing the process by which blood is oxygenated and causing shortness of breath (dyspnea). In the upright position, the problem is alleviated somewhat because gravity slows the return of blood from the veins of the legs and abdomen to the already congested lungs. This is why, as in Herod's case, patients with left heart failure generally have greater difficulty breathing when lying supine (orthopnea) than when upright.

When the process impairs the right side of the heart, the side into which veins empty their blood so that it can be delivered to the lungs for reoxygenation, venous congestion (and edema) ensue. Such congestion is aggravated by gravity and is most pronounced in dependent areas such as the legs and scrotum. It can become so severe that edema fluid seeping out of congested veins actually begins to bubble through the skin in translucent blisters called "bullae," creating a form of "moist, transparent suppuration" of the kind Josephus described in Herod. In some cases, the congestion may also become so taut and blood flow so compromised by high tissue pressure that necrosis of flesh (or "gangrene") ensues. This, in turn, can cause a "light fever." Patients with congestive heart failure may also have modestly elevated temperatures because of chronic constriction of surface vessels, which prevents the release of internal heat through the skin surface. Based on the signs and symptoms reported by Josephus, Herod most likely had failure of both the left and the right sides of his heart during the terminal phase of his illness.

Chronic renal failure is a consequence, and a cause, of both ather-osclerosis and hypertension; even today it is sometimes difficult to determine which developed first in patients with end-stage kidney disease. Herod's intolerable itching and his foul breath are best ex-plained by chronic renal failure. By themselves, they are not terribly helpful diagnostically, for each has myriad causes. However, in the context of Herod's other signs and symptoms of generalized athero-sclerosis, they emerge as telltale signs of chronic renal failure. Gen-eralized itching (pruritis) is common in chronic renal failure[31] and is occasionally so intractable and intense that it makes life all but un-bearable. Its exact cause has yet to be determined. However, some evidence suggests that it is due to hyperactivity of the parathyroid glands, one of the many metabolic derangments of chronic renal failure.[35]

In the terminal stages of renal failure, waste products normally eliminated in the urine accumulate in the blood and then the saliva and sweat in amounts sufficient to cause them to reek of urine, cre-ating a stench modern clinicians call "uremic fetor." At extremely high levels, the waste products become toxic to nerves, causing them to discharge involuntarily throughout the body creating cas-cades of uncontrollable jerks and twitches identical to Herod's convulsions in his limbs. Generalized brain dysfunction (en-cephalopathy) is the most severe neural abnormality caused by accu-mulation of these waste products and, as in Herod, can manifest as emotional lability, hallucinations, paranoia and, in its most ad-vanced stage, coma.[31]

Herod's intense abdominal pain and inability to eat despite a fe-rocious appetite are, likewise, best explained by atherosclerosis, in this case atherosclerosis of the intestinal arteries. These complaints, although not terribly specific, in conjunction with Herod's other symtpoms, are highly suggestive of a condition called "intestinal angina." Briefly, this is a disorder in which abdominal pain develops because of inadequate blood flow (ischemia) to the intestine. The pain is aggravated by food because digestion is not a passive process but physiologic work that must be supported by oxygen and other blood nutrients. If vessels supplying the intestine are blocked by atheromatous plaques, they may be unable to increase blood flow sufficiently during digestion to meet increased intestinal demands for oxygen and nutrients. This tends to magnify the ischemic state, thereby intensifying the pain of intestinal angina (or intestinal ischemia) in the immediate aftermath of meals. This is why patients with intestinal angina are unable to eat, no matter how fierce their appetite.

Herod's gangrenous penis and its infestation by worms has generated some of the most vigorous speculation about the nature of his illness. It has also raised some of the most serious questions about the credibility of Josephus as an historian (see below). The most likely explanation for the genital gangrene described by Josephus, if it did exist, is that it developed in response to Herod's massive dependent edema and failing heart, both of which critically compromised blood flow to the genital region. The necrosis of genital tissues that ensued then provided an appropriate substrate (rotting flesh) for eggs deposited by flies to develop into *worm-like* maggots.[36]

Infestation of wounds by maggots is one of the more repulsive conditions encountered in clinical practice even today, yet maggots are rarely harmful and may actually perform a useful function in some wounds by debriding devitalized tissue. In fact, military surgeons have long recognized that injured soldiers whose wounds become infested with maggots are less likely to develop infections and die from septicemia and gangrene than those whose wounds do not. Maggots were first used therapeutically during the American Civil War, apparently by J.F. Zacharias, a Confederate medical officer, who claimed that "in a single day [maggots] would clean a wound much better than any agents we had at our command." The value of maggots in this regard continued to be exploited during World War I. The use of such therapy declined in the 1940s when antibiotics became available. However, there has been renewed interest in it in recent years because of the emergence of highly resistant bacteria in wound infections.

Although infestation by maggots (myiasis) is a plausible explanation for the "worms" that appeared in Herod's penis, some authorities have argued that this detail of his illness was fabricated by

Josephus as post-mortem retribution for crimes not punishable during Herod's lifetime because of his position. In fact, several detested rulers of antiquity may well have been subjected to such post-mortem punishment. Antiochus IV Epiphanes (d. 163 B.C.E.), Sulla (d. 78 B.C.E.), Agrippa I (d. 44 C.E.) and Galerius (d. 311 C.E.) each died "worm-eaten" in hostile biographies.[2] Whether Herod truly developed "gangrene of the privy parts which produced worms" in the terminal phase of his final illness can never be known for certain. If he did, the cause was almost certainly myiasis superimposed on genitalia rendered necrotic by the ravages of atherosclerosis and massive dependent edema.

Currently, we use a host of medications to treat the various disabilities with which Herod suffered. However, even today, prevention of hypertension, atherosclerosis and heart failure is much more effective than their treatment. Preventive measures seek to reduce the influence of those risk factors noted above in predisposing to hypertension, atherosclerosis and their complications. Such measures include weight-reduction programs, diets low in saturated fats and sodium, regular exercise and smoking cessation. When these interventions fail to produce the desired effects, anti-hypertensive medications and lipid-lowing agents are employed. In patients whose kidneys fail, chronic dialysis and kidney transplantation are today's ultimate treatment options.

Although Josephus reported that in Herod's efforts to cling to life he "devised one remedy after another".... the only specific treatment he is known to have received was a "thermal cure,"[26] for which he was carried to the warm springs of Callirrhoe, presumably first for hydrotherapy. When the waters provided no salutary effect, his physicians decided to raise the temperature of his whole body with hot oil, and so, "lowered [him] into a bath full of that liquid, whereupon he fainted and turned up his eyes as though he were dead." There are several reasons why Herod might have fainted when lowered into the hot oil. The most likely is that the extreme heat caused a sudden acceleration of his heart rate (tachycardia) either because of the pain it caused or because it produced a generalized dilatation of

FIGURE 4-5. Tomb believed to be the burial place of Mariamne (King Herod the Great's wife) and possibly also of Herod. Entry is blocked by a Rolling Stone. Jerusalem, Israel. Photo Credit: Erich Lessing/Art Resource, NY.

cutaneous vessels, either of which would have caused a pronounced drop in blood pressure.

Jewish physicians of Herod's era were greatly influenced by the Hippocratic school of medicine (see Chapter 2). Hydrotherapy and thermal treatments were important components of their therapeutic armamentarium. However, they also employed preparations of a number of plants and roots with medicinal properties. *Balsam* was one such product. Throughout antiquity, and also during the Middle Ages, the "balm of Gilead," later known as "balm of Jerusalem" was one of the most renowned products of Palestine. Honey, "priestly ointments," rue, mandrake, bitumen and oil were also part of the Judean Materia Medica. Music therapy was employed as a form of psychotherapy, as alluded to in the Bible when it was used to treat King Saul's raving fits.[26]

Herod's mortal afflictions ended long ago, but his name endures, more because of his depiction in the Gospel of Mark than his accomplishments as ruler of Judea.[37] He was a man of strife and contention, and to what extent these contributed to the evolution of his hypertension, atherosclerosis and kidney failure is debatable. Even today, blood pressure experts are not sure if psychological stress has a role in causing hypertension or increasing the likelihood or severity of its complications (see Chapter 12).

Because of the many acts of cruelty Herod committed during his lifetime, his reputation will not likely ever "see when the good cometh; but shall [forever] inhabit the parched places in the wilderness."[38] Josephus, who was an insightful historian, must have foreseen this and, therefore, appreciated that he could not possibly inflict additional punishment by perverting his description of Herod's horrific final illness, one that is wholly consistent with a diagnosis of hypertension complicated by generalized atherosclerosis and kidney failure (Figure 4-5).

Notes

1. At least some historians doubt the veracity of the biblical account of Herod's slaughter of the innocents, suggesting that it represents a standard Christian canard against Herod rather than actual history. For one thing, Matthew and Luke differ with respect to this incident in their accounts of the birth of Jesus. More importantly, it is not mentioned by Josephus in either of his monumental works. For these reasons, it has been

suggested that in contriving his description of Herod's ordering the murder of boys under the age of two in the vicinity of Bethlehem at the time of Jesus' birth, Mathew distorted the facts surrounding Herod's actual succession problems and execution of his own three children to develop a plausible explanation for the holy family's flight to Egypt. [Richardson P. *Herod, King of the Jews and Friend of the Romans*. Fortress Press. Minneapolis:1999; p. 297-8.]

2. Kokkinos N. Herod's horrid death. *Biblical Archaeol Rev.* 2002 (Mar/Apr) 28-35.

3. Op cit (Richardson) p. 6, 7, 54-57, 116.

4. Ibid p. 1.

5. Ibid p. 56.

6. Highest judicial and ecclesiastical council of the ancient Jewish nation, composed of seventy to seventy-two members.

7. Herod's Hellenization of Judea is reflected in his own education in Greek philosophy, his support of gymnasia, his patronage of Olympic Games and religious architecture and in his tolerance of cults dedicated to Apollo, Hermes, the Dioscuri and Kore. Even the names he chose for some of his children (Philip, Olympias, Alexander and Roxana) recall Hellenic lore. His own name is derived from "*heroides,*" Greek for "hero." [Op cit (Kikkinos)]

8. Lazore D: False testament. Archeology refutes the Bible's claim to history. *Harper's Magazine.* 2002 (Mar) p. 39-45.

9. Op cit (Richardson) p. 52.

10. Perowne S. *The Life and Times of Herod the Great*. Arrow Books. London:1960, p. 108.

11. The Parthians, who dwelled in an area just beyond the Euphrates, were a constant menace to Rome's interests in the Levant. They were fierce warriors who relied on two types of cavalry in overwhelming their enemies: one composed of heavily armored horsemen and another of light, rapid squadrons capable of swooping down on a foe and firing a volley of arrows as they advanced and then another as they rode off, the famous

"Parthian shot." Ten years before Herod's reign, the Parthians invaded Judea and succeeded in occupying its capital. More distressing to Rome, many Judeans became their willing collaborators. Herod held the Parthians in check throughout his reign. This is one of several reasons why he received Rome's gratitude and unwavering support for over three decades. [Ibid p. 112]

12. The Jewish family of Herod's day was an endogenous unit characterized by equality of brothers, cohabitation of married sons with parents, frequent marriage between cousins, and polygamy (with kings having as many as eighteen wives). [Op cit (Richardson) p. 40-1]

13. Op cit (Perowne) p. 184.

14. Ibid p. 191-213.

15. Op cit (Richardson, p. 222-3).

16. Op cit (Richardson, p. 315-8).

17. Op cit (Perowne) p. 175.

18. For over two thousand years, those who governed in the Levant have had to deal with rebels posing as martyrs. Herod was no exception. During his reign, he clashed repeatedly with zealot-brigands in Galilee who bridled against his rule in the name of religion. His actions were directed against the brigands' politics and not their religion. [Ibid p. 125-6]

19. Ibid p. 179.

20. Wheston W. (Trans.) Josephus. *Complete Works.* Kregel Publications. Grand Rapids: 19xx. p. 364-9. Josephus gives a slightly different account in his *Archeology* from this one which appeared in *War.* In it he says:

> Herod's distemper greatly increased upon him after a severe manner: a fire glowed in him slowly, which did not so much appear to touch outwardly, as it augmented his pains inwardly; for it brought upon him a vehement appetite for eating which he could not afford to supply with one sort of food or another. His entrails were also exulcerated, and the chief violence of his pain lay in his colon; an aqueous and transparent liquor also had settled about

his feet, and a like matter afflicted him at the bottom of his belly. Nay, farther, his privy member was putrefied and produced worms; and except when he sat upright he had a difficulty of breathing, which was very loathsome, on account of the stench of his breath, and the quickness of its returns; he had also convulsions in all parts of his body, which increased his strength to an insufferable degree. [Op cit (Perowne) p. 222]

21. Herod never referred to himself as "The Great" and Josephus uses the title only once to distinguish Herod from his sons and descendants. [Op cit (Perowne) p. 209]

22. Map of Herod's kingdom is from Richardson Op cit. Map 4.

23. Josephus is believed to have based his account of Herod's life on the works of Nicolas of Damascus, a close relative of Herod and friend of the emperor, Augustus. Unlike Nicolas, Josephus severely censured Herod for his crimes (Sandison AT: The last illness of Herod the Great, king of Judea. *Medical Hist.* 1967;11:381-8). Josephus, who was not a physician, relied on Jewish written and oral tradition in writing his histories. He was most likely influenced by Thucydides (Chapter 2), who was in turn a student of the Hippocratic school. (Kottek SS. *Medicine and Hygiene in the Works of Flavius Josephus.* E.J. Brill. Leiden: 1994. p. 160.)

24. Op cit (Perowne) p. 16.

25. Ibid p. 176.

26. Op cit (Kottek) p. 125-39, 187-8.

27. Litchfield WR: The bittersweet demise of Herod the Great. *J Roy Soc Med.* 1998;91:283-4.

28. Holzapfel RN. King Herod. *Brigham Young University Studies.* 1996-1997;36:35-73.

29. Sandison AT. The last illness of Herod the Great, King of Judea. *Med Hist.* 1967;11:381-8.

30. McSherry JA: Worms, diabetes and King Herod the Great. *J Med Biogr.* 1997;5L167-9.

31. Hirschmann JV, Richardson P, Kraemer RS, Mackowiak PA: Death of an Arabian Jew. *Arch Intern Med.* 2004; 164:833-9.

32. Libby P. The pathogenesis of atherosclerosis. In Braunwald E, Fauci AS, Kasper DL, et al. *Harrison's Principles of Internal Medicine*. 15th ed. McGraw-Hill: 2001, p. 1377-82.

33. Op cit (Perowne) p. 213.

34. Ritchie K, Lovestone S. The dementias. *Lancet*. 2002;360: 1759-66.

35. Hampers CL, Katz AI, Wilson RE, Merrill JP. Disappearance of "uremic" itching after subtotal parathyroidectomy. *N Engl J Med*. 1968;279:695-7.

36. Boon H, Freeman L, Unsworth J. Healthy eating. Wound healing with maggots. *Nursing Times*. 1996; 92:63-80.

37. The precise date of Jesus' birth is uncertain. Nor is it clear that Herod knew of the birth. Richardson has concluded that Jesus was most likely born in 7 B.C.E., based on the probable date of the celestial event referred to in the tradition of the Magi. Although the precise date of Herod's death is also uncertain, Richardson believes it occurred just before Passover in 4 B.C.E., which would mean that Herod's connection with Jesus was limited to a brief period of no more than three years. [Op cit (Richardson)

38. (Isaiah 17:6).

CAVEAT CENANS![1]

Of all the Julio-Claudians, this patient was the most enigmatic. As emperor, he gave Rome enlightenment, justice and hope, and also trammeled her with barbarism, corruption and despair. He gave her two new aqueducts and a safe winter harbor at Ostia, which ensured her bread year-round. He crossed the English Channel to complete the conquest of Britain left unfinished by his uncle, Julius Caesar, and consummated the island's full-scale annexation as a Roman province.[2] He added Morocco to the empire as well. He wrote several erudite treatises, including ones on Etruscan and Carthaginian history. He repaired much of the damage done to the empire by the excesses committed during the reign of his nephew, Caligula. He revised and enlightened Rome's legal system and extended Roman citizenship to loyal provincials. He built hundreds of miles of new roads and, according to one biographer, might even have avenged one of imperial Rome's most crushing defeats at the hands of the German, Arminius, during the reign of Augustus.[2-5]

With the best of intentions, however, he became a tyrant no less oppressive than the worst of his imperial family.[4] Whether he excogitated the dark side of his legacy alone or did so as a passive accomplice of succubae and corrupt freedmen on whom he relied in dealing with a hostile Senate[6] is less important than the fact that after becoming emperor, he "killed as easily as you get a low roll of the dice."[7] The killing began immediately upon his coronation with the execution of Caligula's assassins, and when it was over, the patient's victims included thirty senators, two hundred twenty-one knights, a wife, father-in-law, mother-in-law, nieces, sons-in-law, a secretary, a dancer and others "to the number of the grains of sand and specks of dust."[7] Many of those executed by the patient were convicted *in camera* in closed-door trials. Thus, when his life was ended, if the patient was "hauled to heaven on a hook," as reported by Dio,[8] like some common criminal dragged by his executioner from the forum to the river for disposal, his fate would not have been unjustified.[7]

The patient was born in Lugdunum (Lyons) in transAlpine Gaul (France) on the Kalands of August in the 744th year after the founding of Rome (August 1, 10 B.C.E.), the 767th year after the First Olympiad and the 20th year of the reign of his grandfather (by marriage), Caesar Augustus. Although born prematurely, he seemed normal enough as an infant. However, throughout his childhood and youth, he suffered severely from various obstinate disorders, which seemed to sap the vigor of both his mind and his body to such an extent that by the time he reached manhood, he was deemed incapable of conducting either public or private business of any consequence. So pronounced were his disabilities, for a considerable portion of his early years, he was hidden from the public for fear that his ridicule would become the imperial family's as well.[9]

As a child he was a veritable battleground of diseases, "who seemed to survive only because the competing disorders could not agree as to which should have the honor of carrying him off."[3] To begin with, his foster mother's milk disagreed with him, causing his skin to break out in an ugly rash. He contracted malaria and then measles, which left him slightly deaf in one ear. Erysipelas and colitis were next, and finally, infantile paralysis, which shortened one leg and condemned him to a permanent limp.[3]

His physical disabilities were real enough, although precisely when they first manifested or in what manner or rate they progressed is uncertain. He possessed majesty and dignity of appearance, but only when he was standing still or sitting, and especially when he was lying down. He had an attractive face, becoming white hair and a full neck, and was tall, though corpulent. When he made the least exertion, however, his head shook; he dragged his foot, and his knees gave way under him with such regularity, he was the first Roman noble to be transported in a covered chair. He had other disagreeable traits as well: he was hard of hearing; his laughter was unseemly and "his anger even more disgusting": when he was excited, he would foam at the mouth, trickle at the nose and stammer uncontrollably.[7]

Because of his many physical infirmities, the patient's mental abilities were also generally assumed to be defective,[9] however, he studied constantly, wrote well and, on rare occasion, even exhibited excellent oratorical skill. Even so, because of constant reminders of the embarrassment his appearance brought upon his family, he pursued life in the background of imperial affairs until elevated to emperor, feigning a stupidity greater than was really the case as a defense against the treachery of the imperial court that cost not a few of his relatives their lives. In contrast to the likes of Julius Caesar, Caligula and his brother, Germanicus, who fell victim to assassins during the bloody years of the Julio-Claudian dynasty, the patient managed to survive the political intrigues of the reigns of Augustus, Tiberius and Caligula by being ignored as a dim wit and an embarrassment.[9]

The patient's family, one of imperial Rome's most ancient and prominent, arrived in the city from the Sabine country in the 250th year after Rome's founding. His father, Drusus the Elder, was the younger brother of the emperor, Tiberius; his mother, Antonia Minor, a niece of Caesar Augustus. On his father's side, he claimed as grandparents both a sister of Augustus, Octavia the Elder, and Julius Caesar's close friend, Mark Antony. On his mother's side, he had as grandmother, Livia Drusilla, who divorced his maternal grandfather (while carrying the patient's father) to become both the second wife and the most trusted confidant of Caesar Augustus.[2-4]

The family was generally healthy, with no prior history of physical disabilities similar to the patient's. His father died at age twenty-eight of injuries resulting from a fall from his horse while on campaign. His mother, apparently filled with shame over the excesses of her grandson, Caligula, whom she had helped to raise, committed suicide when she was seventy-three. The patient's brother, Germanicus, died at age thirty-four after a brief but highly successful career as a military commander. He died amid mysterious circumstances of a bizarre illness marked by progressive wasting and a rash, the exact nature of which was not recorded. He is suspected of having been poisoned, possibly by the ambitious senator, Gnaeus Calpurnius, who was then governor of Syria. The patient's only sister, Claudia Lulia Livilla, was executed for adultery when she was thirty-four. She was starved to death, possibly by her own mother, after being discovered having an affair with Sejanus, commander of the Praetorian Guard under Tiberius, who was himself executed for plotting to seize the throne.[2-4]

The patient was married four times and had three children, all of whom were well at the time of his final illness. He was promiscuous, with numerous extramarital, heterosexual relationships, at least some of which were with prostitutes. His third wife, Messalina, was promiscuous too, causing some historians to suspect the patient had doubts that Britannicus, a son by her, was really his own.[4] This might at least explain why he adopted Nero and fatally compromised Britannicus' claim to the throne. It might also have been that he saw qualities in Nero that made him regard the boy as better suited to rule than his own son.

When the patient was fifty, his young nephew, the emperor Caligula, was assassinated. In the chaos that followed, the patient, who, all sources seem to agree, was by nature a coward, was found hiding behind a curtain in the palace, taken by soldiers to the Praetorian barracks and crowned emperor before the Senate could enact plans to restore the republic. Although his accession to power in January of 41 C.E. in the aftermath of his cousin's assassination is often characterized in this manner as a fluke of circumstances, it is also possible that it represented a concerted *sub rosa* effort on the part of his family and their allies to bring stability back to Roman affairs-of-state. For although at times cruel and even manic, his reign of fourteen years also proved in many ways to be a throwback to the enlightened governing style of his great-uncle, Augustus. As emperor, the patient was willing to share power with members of the Senate and to defer to more experienced men in military matters. Moreover, during the first half of his reign, he added Britain to Rome's provinces, the most substantial addition to the Imperial territory since Julius Caesar's conquest of Gaul a century earlier.

The patient's coronation had a decidedly salutary effect on his health. While emperor, he suffered only from attacks of heartburn.[9] This is not to say that these attacks were trivial, however. Many times his indigestion was severe enough to all but drive him to suicide. The heartburn was especially cruel because the patient was eager for food and drink at all times and in all places. He gave frequent and grand dinner parties, where as many as six hundred guests were entertained at one time.[9] During these affairs, he would break wind frequently, convinced that a man "ran some risk [of internal injury] by restraining himself through modesty."[7] He hardly ever left the dining room until both stuffed and soaked, at which point he would fall asleep immediately, while lying on his back with his mouth open.[9] According to most accounts, this was his condition when the Parcae cut the thread from their "ugly spool" to end his "doddering life."[7]

Reports differ as to the precise sequence of events surrounding the patient's death. According to Suetonius, one of his principal biographers, most of the patient's contemporaries believed he was poisoned. When it was done and by whom, however, was never certain. His taster, the eunuch Halotus, might have given him the deadly draught as he was banqueting on the Capital with priests the day before he was carried off. A more widely held theory is that his fourth wife, Agrippina, served him the poison with her own hand in mushrooms, a dish of which he was extravagantly fond (see Figure 5-1). Neither the precise nature of the poison nor the manner in which it killed him is known for certain. One account maintains that as soon as he swallowed the poison, the patient became speechless, and after suffering excruciating pain all night, died just before dawn. In another, he first fell into a stupor, then vomited up the whole contents of his overloaded stomach and was given a second

FIGURE 5-1. Portrait head of Agrippina the Younger. Courtesy of The J. Paul Getty Museum, Villa Collection, Malibu, California. Used with Permission.

dose of poison, perhaps in gruel, under the pretence that he should be refreshed with food to allay his exhaustion; or it was administered in an enema, supposedly to evacuate his intestines.[9]

Dio claimed that Agrippina killed the patient to secure the throne for her son, Nero. His account differs from that of Suetonius, but only slightly. In his account, Suetonius reports that owing to the great quantity of wine the patient drank and the stringent measures he, like all the emperors, adopted for his own protection, he could not easily be harmed. Agrippina, therefore, sent for Lucusta, a famous dealer in poisons. Agrippina instructed her to prepare a poison of subtle and slow enough action to avoid discovery and yet, not so slow that as the patient's end approached, he might discover the treachery and take steps to thwart her ultimate purpose by naming Britannicus, rather than Nero, his heir. Taking the poison prepared for her by Lucusta, Agrippina put it in a dish of mushrooms. After first partaking of the dish, she offered her husband the one containing the poison, which was the largest and finest of all. Sometime thereafter, the patient was carried from the banquet apparently quite overcome by strong drink, looking very much like he had after dining many times before. However, during the night the poison took effect and, according to Dio, the patient passed away without having been able to say or hear a word.[8,9]

Tacitus must have studied the same sources, for he incriminated not only Agrippina, Lucusta and the patient's taster, Halotus, but also the physician, Xenophon, claiming that Lucusta prepared the poison, which Halotus sprinkled on a particularly succulent mushroom. However, because the patient was drunk, the poison's effect was delayed, and before it could act, evacuation of his bowels seemed to have saved him. Agrippina was horrified but also prepared for such an exigency, having already enlisted Xenophon as an accomplice. According to Tacitus, while pretending to help the patient vomit, Xenophon put a feather dipped in a quick poison down his throat, finally ending the life of the penultimate Julio-Claudian emperor of Rome,[10] Tiberius Claudius Drusus Nero Germanicus (Claudius), who died on the thirteenth of October, 54 C.E., aged 63 years, two months and 13 days (see Figure 5-2).

***

The circumstances surrounding Claudius' death were recorded for posterity by three ancient historians, Tacitus, Suetonius and Cassius Dio, all three of whom were born after the events in question. Although Suetonius directed Rome's imperial libraries and correspondences and is thought to have had access to imperial records in

FIGURE 5-2. Bust of Claudius, 1st century CE. Museo Arquelogico, Tarragona, Spain. Photo Credit: Vanni/Art Resource, NY.

writing his biography, none of the actual sources used by the three historians is known for certain. Lucius Annaeus Seneca also provided an account of the death of Claudius. A contemporary of Claudius and tutor to his successor, Nero, Seneca was an intimate of the imperial circle with an insider's knowledge of what actually happened on the 12th and 13th of October, 54 C.E. Unfortunately, he left only an account veiled in satire, as a prudent evasion of one who knew more than he might safely reveal. Each of these historians offers a slightly different view of Claudius' medical history (summarized above) and yet a consistent and detailed enough description to permit diagnosis of his disorders with reasonable confidence.[11] What might these diagnoses have been?

Given his age, unhealthy life-style and underlying disabilities, Claudius might well have died of some natural cause, such as a myocardial or intestinal infarction. However, there are many reasons to believe his biographers were correct in claiming that he died of poisoning instead. To begin with, there is the timing of his death.[12] Claudius was in the twilight of his reign and about to name his successor. Was he to be Britannicus, his natural son by his third wife, Messalina, or Nero, the recently adopted son of his then current wife, Agrippina? Claudius never revealed his choice, because his sudden demise, *ipso facto*, left the decision to his alleged assassin, Agrippina.

The absence of Narcissus at the time of the emperor's death is also significant.[13] Narcissus was the most trusted of many freedmen Claudius relied on in dealing with a hostile Senate as emperor. He was also a shrewd strategist, who would have been aware of the struggle over succession which was about to reach its stormy climax and guarded his master with the care of one whose life depended on it, all of which suggests that had he been present in Rome in October 54 C.E., Claudius' assassins would not likely have succeeded. But Narcissus was away the day Claudius died, having been persuaded by Agrippina to travel to the baths at Sinuessa to treat his gout.

Finally, there is the epigram attributed to Nero, Claudius' successor and the last of the Julio-Claudian emperors.[8,9] At a certain banquet during Nero's reign, in which mushrooms were served, one of the guests is reputed to have alluded to the saying, common at the time, that mushrooms were "the food of the gods." To this (according to both Suetonius and Dio) Nero replied: "True enough; my father was made a god by eating a mushroom." Thus, there is considerable circumstantial evidence that Claudius died of poisoning and that mushrooms were the vehicle used to administer the poison, if not the lethal agent itself.

The use of poisons for hunting, warfare and assassination more than likely predates recorded history. The Ebers papyrus (circa 1500 B.C.E.) refers to several known poisons, including hemlock (the state poison of the Greeks), opium (used as both a poison and an antidote) and metals such as lead, copper, and antimony. There is also evidence that the toxic effects of plants containing substances similar to belladonna alkaloids and digitalis were known. Hippocrates (circa 400 B.C.E.) identified a number of poisons and also first introduced concepts of clinical toxicology pertaining to bioavailability and overdosage.[14]

The first work devoted specifically to poisons is generally credited to Nicander of Colophon, who lived from 204 to 135 B.C.E.[15] Although largely fanciful, the work describes the toxic effects of snake venom, hen bane, colchicum, aconite and conium and recommends antidotes for each. Dioscordes, a Greek surgeon who served under Nero, produced the definitive ancient text on poisons,[16] one, in fact, which was the standard reference on the subject for sixteen centuries. In it, Dioscordes catalogued a long list of poisonous animal, vegetable and mineral products. These included certain crustaceans, toads, salamanders and serpents; mandragora, aconite, colchicum (meadow saffron), opium and hemlock; and arsenic, cinnabar, litharge and white lead.

Thus, if Lucusta, Agrippina and Xenophon did conspire to assassinate Claudius as reported in the historical record, they had access to a host of poisons. The actual list from which they chose their agent is a secret Lucusta carried with her to the grave.[17] "Aconite," a term used by Tacitus and other ancient historians to refer to any poisonous plant, was almost certainly on it. The specific agent chosen might have been opium, cantharides, vitriol or mushrooms, each of which were mentioned in the literature of the time as instruments of both murder and suicide.[15]

If the poison given to Claudius induced a state of terminal intoxication in which Claudius "passed away, without having been able to say or hear a word," as reported by Tacitus, opium could have been the culprit. If he suffered "excruciating pain" (abdominal?) accompanied by vomiting and diarrhea as reported by Suetonius and Tacitus, fatal intoxication with some other, more caustic agent is a more likely cause of his death. If he recovered temporarily from his illness only to suffer a fatal relapse, as suggested by Suetonius and Tacitus, their theory that a second poison was administered because the first proved nonfatal is possible, though unlikely. Wasson[12] has suggested that colocynth was the second poison administered by Xenophon. However, because that toxin is lethal only in "larger doses" (Wasson's words), it is difficult to conceive of how a lethal dose of colocynth might have been delivered on the tip of a feather used to induced vomiting. In fact, no drug available to the ancients has been shown to kill in the minute quantity able to be delivered on the tip of a feather, and then partially expelled in the ensuing vomiting. A more plausible explanation for the fatal "relapse" is that it was actually an acute myocardial infarction or intestinal catastrophe precipitated by the effects of the poison on a cardiovascular system riddled with ateriosclerosis owing to Claudius' age, sedentary life-style and unhealthy diet.

If mushrooms themselves were the poison used to assassinate Claudius, the "death cap," *Amanita phalloides* (see Figure 5-3), and its close relatives, the "destroying angels," *A. verna* and *A. virosa,* are the ones most likely to have been employed.[12] *A. phalloides* is deadly and yet no less tasty than its edible counterparts. Moreover, it is the predominant poisonous mushroom of Europe. Even a small piece of its cap can kill a grown man. Thus, a small, finely minced amount of *A. phalloides* might have been used to poison an edible mushroom, or the cap of one of the deadly species of Amanita might have been hidden whole among nonpoisonous counterparts populating the dish that killed Claudius. *A. phalloides* is readily identified by its white gills, veil (or ring) and vulva[18] and easy to find in season, which in Rome includes October, the month in which Claudius

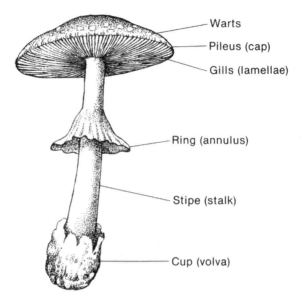

Warts
Pileus (cap)
Gills (lamellae)

Ring (annulus)

Stipe (stalk)

Cup (volva)

Basic structure of an *Amanita* mushroom.

FIGURE 5-3. Basic structure of an Amanita mushroom. From Ellenhorn MJ, Barcelaux DG. Medical Toxicology. Diagnoses and Treatment of Human Poisoning. New York: Elsevier: 1988, 1324-1351. Used with permission.

died. Many supposed experts have fallen victim to mushroom poisoning after having failed to distinguish poisonous from edible species.

Mushrooms were both feared and highly prized by Roman epicureans. Pliny, for example, wrote in his Book XXII that "Among all those things that are eaten with danger, I take the mushrooms may justly be ranged in the first and principal place; true it is that they have a most pleasant and delicate taste, but discredited much they are and brought to an ill name, by occasion of the poison which Agrippina the empress conveyed unto her husband, Tiberius Claudius...."[19] The prevailing notion at the time was that mushrooms became poisonous by absorbing toxins from earth contaminated by iron or rotten cloth or the presence of snakes in their vicinity.

Typically, the victim of Amanita poisoning is seized by sudden, appalling abdominal pain, followed shortly thereafter by vomiting and diarrhea.[18] The onset of symptoms is generally delayed until six to twenty-four hours after ingestion of the poisonous mushroom, owing to the time required for digestion and for the mushroom's toxin to be absorbed and to bind to its site of action within the nuclei of metabolically active cells. The diarrhea is generally watery and profuse, sometimes bloody. Although this initial phase of intoxication usually resolves within a day, occasionally it is accompanied by fever, a rapid pulse, dehydration and/or electrolyte abnormalities, any of which can prove fatal if the patient is old or otherwise debilitated. The gastrointestinal phase of the illness is followed by a latent period of some three to four days in which the patient appears to recover fully, only to be disabled by a final hepatorenal phase of intoxication, with mounting jaundice, delirium and confusion as the liver and kidneys fall victim to the evolving toxicity of the mushroom's poison. Today, between ten and forty percent of cases are fatal, depending on the amount of toxin ingested, the presence of underlying diseases and the patient's condition on admission to the hospital.

If Claudius was poisoned with *A. phalloides*, in view of the initial latent period of six to twenty-four hours required for the toxin to be absorbed and to bind to its site of action, he would have to have ingested the critical mushroom the day before, perhaps at the banquet he shared with priests on the Capital, rather than the day his fatal illness began. The abdominal pain, vomiting and diarrhea described by Suetonius and Tacitus are consistent with the gastrointestinal phase of Amanita poisoning. Moreover, owing to his age and underlying disabilities (see below) this initial phase of intoxication might well have proved fatal, even in the face of apparent resolution of his most distressing complaints.

Valente[20] has suggested that Lucusta might have chosen a different, and less toxic, species of *Amanita* to poison Claudius, *A. muscaria*. In contrast to the toxin of *A. phalloides*, its toxin is destroyed by cooking.[20] It works by stimulating the parasympathetic nervous system to cause a whole host of symptoms, including tearing, salivation, rhinorrhea (runny nose), diarrhea, abdominal pain, incontinence, wheezing, a slowing of the pulse and a drop in blood pressure.

Symptoms begin as early as thirty minutes after ingestion of *A. muscaria*. Thus, intoxication with this particular species of mushroom might well have caused an illness having both the character and tempo of that described by Claudius' biographers. Although *A. muscaria* intoxication is rarely fatal, Valente has suggested that Claudius' underlying dystonia (see below) could have combined with the toxic effects of the mushroom to produce the fatal outcome.

Claudius was sixty-four, sedentary, obese and chronically drunk when he died. Moreover, he had long suffered from a stable (or perhaps slowly progressive), non-familial, neurological disorder characterized by tics and jerks, stammering and shaking of his head, and deafness, hoarseness and a lame leg. The most likely explanation for these chronic disabilities is that he had a congenital dystonia, that is, a movement disorder that was a life-long legacy of his premature birth.[20] If Graves' information was correct, and Claudius was born nearly two months early, it is a wonder that he even survived beyond infancy. Having done so, he appears to have been less fortunate with regard to one of the potential complications of prematurity: damage to the basal ganglia, the region of the brain responsible for coordinating motor (muscle) activity. When the basal ganglia are damaged, as a result of the stresses of premature birth or some other disorder, the consequence is an incoordination of motor function (or dystonia) of the general character exhibited by Claudius.

Prematurity has other long-term consequences as well, which might have contributed to Claudius' death. As adults, premature babies of low birth weight have higher blood pressures, higher blood sugars and higher blood cholesterol levels than adults born after a normal gestation.[21] Thus, Claudius' premature birth, like his age, sedentary life-style, obesity and alcohol abuse, rendered him unusually prone to the ravages of atherosclerosis (hardening of the arteries) and atherosclerotic cardiovascular disease.

If Claudius was poisoned, Xenophon's attempt to evacuate undigested poison from the stomach by inducing vomiting was the standard medical practice of the day.[19] Moreover, some would suggest that the treatment of poisoning has changed little since that time.

Evacuating undigested poison by inducing vomiting and/or preventing its absorption with agents such as activated charcoal, which
bind poison within the intestine, are the first and most important
measures taken in cases of poisoning today.

In instances of A. *phalloides* intoxication, initial efforts are directed at restoring fluids and minerals lost as a result of the vomiting and diarrhea that characterize the initial, gastrointestinal phase
of the illness.[18] If the patient is obtunded, intravenous fluids and
glucose are administered. Vomiting is beneficial only if induced
within four hours of ingestion. After four hours, gastric contents
will have passed into the small intestine and are no longer subject to
regurgitation. Activated charcoal and cathartics are recommended
to bind and inactivate unabsorbed toxin in the intestine and acceler-
ate its transit through and elimination from the gastrointestinal
tract. Forced diuresis (promoting urination with fluids and diuretic
drugs) is also recommended to enhance the elimination of absorbed
toxin, since amatoxins (the technical name given to poisons derived
from A. *phalloides* and its close relatives) are filtered and eliminated
by the kidneys. Patients who present within twenty-four hours of
ingestion receive charcoal hemoperfusion (a type of artificial kidney
treatment) as another means of eliminating absorbed amatoxins.
Penicillin, which displaces amatoxin from the blood proteins to
which it binds and in this way promotes its excretion by the kidneys, is also recommended by some experts.

Claudius' congenital dystonia and unhealthy life style had more
than likely long been conspiring to end his "doddering life" before
the Parcae finally cut his mortal thread. Thus, even if he had not
been poisoned, as the circumstances surrounding his fatal illness and
its symptoms seem to indicate, he likely did not have much longer
to live. Perhaps he sensed this in marrying his niece, Agrippina, and
compromising his own son's claim to the throne by adopting Nero.
Whether he perceived some flaw in Britannicus' character which
made him less fit to rule than Nero or was secretly planning to name
him as his successor in his will, can never be known. Nero saw to
that at midday on October 13, 54 C.E., when the palace gates in

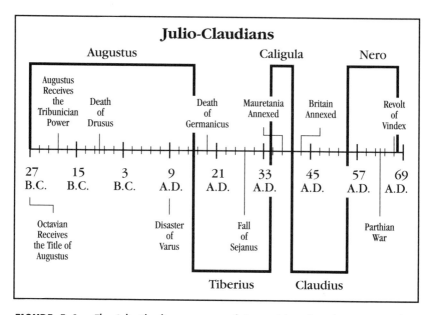

FIGURE 5-4. The Julio-Claudian emperors of Rome. Adapted, with permission, from http://www.umich.edu/~classics/programs/class/cc/372/sibyl/timeline/Julio-Claudians.html.

Rome were suddenly thrown open and he presented himself to the battalion then on duty. At a word from Sextus Afranius Burrus, commander of the Guard, the troops cheered and placed him in a litter. Although some of the men are said to have looked around hesitantly and asked where Britannicus was, as no answer was given, they accepted the choice offered them and conducted Nero to their camp. There, after saying a few words appropriate to the occasion, Nero was hailed as emperor. Claudius' will was not read (see Figure 5-4).[10]

Notes

1. "Caveat Cenans!" means "Banqueter Beware!"
2. According to Fagan, Claudius "displayed immediate understanding of the centrality of the military to his position and sought to create a military image for himself that his prior sheltered existence had denied him. Preparations got under way

soon after his accession for a major military expedition into Britain, perhaps sparked by an attempted revolt of the governor of Dalmatia, L. Arruntius Camillus Scribonianus, in 42 C.E. The invasion itself, spearheaded by four legions, commenced in the summer of 43 and was to last for decades, ultimately falling short of the annexation of the whole island (if indeed that was Claudius' final objective at the outset). This move marked the first major addition to the territory of the Roman empire since the reign of Augustus. Claudius himself took part in the campaign, arriving in the war zone with an entourage of ex-consuls in the late summer of 43 C.E. After a parade at Camulodunum (Colchester) to impress the natives, he returned to Rome to celebrate a triumph in 44 C.E." (Fagan GG. Roman Emperors: DIR Claudius [An Online Encyclopedia of Roman Emperors. 1998]).

3. Graves R. *I, Claudius.* New York: Vintage Books. 1961. Through his two novels, *I, Claudius* and *Claudius the God,* Graves did more to shape the modern perception of Claudius and other Julio-Claudians than, perhaps, any other historian. Although rooted in history, his two works are pastiches of fact and fiction, not readily differentiated one from another, because neither book is referenced. If Graves was correct, and Claudius did have "infantile paralysis" (another name for polio), then polio must be entertained as the cause of his shortened leg and permanent limp.

4. Graves R. *Claudius the God and his Wife Messalina.* New York: Vintage Books. 1962.

5. In 9 C.E., during the reign of Augustus, Arminius, chief of the Cherusci, brought together a coalition of German tribes united against Rome. He then lured three Roman legions under the command of Publius Quintilus Varus into the German wilderness where he annihilated them in what was one of Imperial Rome's greatest military catastrophes. Graves (in *Claudius the God*) credited Claudius with recovering the last two of the three imperial standards captured by Arminius in the engagement. Graves, unfortunately, does not give his source for this information.

6. Most of the ancient sources portrayed Claudius as a dupe of freedmen advisors and his wives. His reliance on freedmen (ex-slaves) as advisors is thought to have been a defensive reaction to the general hostility of his fellow aristocrats. For whatever reason, his was the first era of imperial freedmen, in which ex-slaves like Narcissus, Polybius and Pallas attained considerable power within the empire. Claudius' third and fourth wives, Messalina and Agrippina, were, likewise, portrayed as exercising influence that was both excessive and unhealthy.

7. Seneca. *Apocolocyntosis.* Sullivan JP, trans. Rev ed. London, United Kingdom: Penguin Books. 1986:209-42.

8. According to Dio, "[Claudius] received the state funeral and all the other honours accorded to Augustus. Agrippina and Nero made a show of mourning for their victim and they elevated to heaven the man they'd carried out from the banquet in a litter. This prompted Lucius Junius Gallio, Seneca's brother, to a very pungent witticism. Seneca himself had written a piece he called the *Apocolocyntosis*, playing on the word *Apotheosis*, and Gallio is credited with the following pithy remark. As the public executioners used to drag the bodies of those executed in prison to the Forum with large hooks and hauled them from there to the river, he commented that Claudius had been hauled into heaven on a hook." (*Dio's Roman History.* Cary, E. trans. Loeb Classical Library series; vol. 7 and 8. Cambridge, Massachusetts: Harvard University Press; 1914-1927.)

9. Suetonius. *The Twelve Ceasars.* Graves R, trans. Rev ed. New York, New York: Viking Press; 1979.

10. Tacitus. *The Annals of Imperial Rome.* Grant M., trans. Rev ed. New York, New York: Penguin Classics, 1989.

11. Grant M. *The Ancient Historians.* London: Weidenfeld and Nicolson. 1970:329-42.

12. Wasson RG. The death of Claudius or mushrooms for murderers. Botanical Museum Leaflets vol 23. Cambridge, Massachusetts: Harvard University Press;1972:101-28.

13. Barrett AA. *Agrippina.* Yale U. Press: New Haven. 1996:140-2.

14. Gallo MA. History and scope of toxicology. In Amdur MO, Doull J, Klaassen CD, eds. *Casarett and Doul's Toxicology. The Basic Science of Poisons.* 5th Ed. New York, New York: McGraw Hill;1996:3-11.

15. Meek WJ. The gentle art of poisoning. *Medico-Historical Papers.* Madison: University of Wisconsin, 1954; reprinted from *Phi Beta Pi Quarterly.* May 1928:1-11.

16. Gunther RT. *The Greek Herbal of Dioscorides.* New York: Oxford University Press, 1959.

17. According to Meek (Note 16), professional poisoners were attached to some of the royal Roman households. Lucusta was one such poisoner who served Livia (Claudius' grandmother and the wife of Caesar Augustus), Agrippina and Nero. She is believed to have provided the poison that killed not only Claudius, but also Britannicus, his natural son and possibly Caesar Augustus as well. She outlived her last patron, Nero, only to be executed by his successor, Galba, for her crimes.

18. The mushroom is the reproductive structure of the fungus that grows from an underground mycelium as a densely packed cap and stipe (stalk) of interwoven hyphal strands. This structure contains the spores that upon germination form new mycelia. Variation in size, shape, color, and spore and other microscopic structures aids in the identification of mushroom species. Frequently, the use of a microscope is necessary to identify species (see Figure 5-3).

19. Benjamin DR. *Mushrooms: Poisons and Panaceas. A Handbook for Naturalists, Mycologists, and Physicians.* New York: W.H. Freenan and Co. 1995.

20. Valente WA, Talbert RJA, Hallett JP, Mackowiak PA. Caveat Cenans! *Am J Med.* 2002; 112:392-8.

21. Irving J, Belton NR, Elton RA, Walker BR. Adult cardiovascular risk factors in premature babies. *Lancet.* 2002;355: 2135-6.

6 A CALL TO ARMS

In the 15th century everyone believed in saints and demons. Therefore, even normal people must have been inclined to interpret monitions of their consciences as external realities. But this patient's voices and visions were of a vividness and a purpose far surpassing the experiences of ordinary souls[1], so much so that her mental health has been a source of debate since her death, with some convinced that she was mad, and others that her hunger and thirst after righteousness had simply filled her with the spirit of God.

According to the patient, the voices first approached her when she was on the verge of womanhood. She was shepherding when they came to her with word of God's great pity for the people of France and His plan for her to go to their aid. She said she knew the voices by their speech, which was the language of angels.[2] Saint Catherine of Alexandria and St. Margaret of Antioch spoke to her, as did St. Michael the Archangel.[3] She also claimed often to have seen angels who came unseen (by others) among Christian people.[4] She later intimated that God himself, and not the individual saints, gave her her directives.[5] Some scholars have suggested that she might even have believed herself an angel,[6] one endowed with a personal knowledge of the mind of the Lord. After the advent of her voices, it was His will, and not her own, that determined her actions in her two brief years of public life.

Most of what we know about the patient's voices was revealed during her interrogation and trial by Burgundian clerics after her capture outside Compiègne in May of 1430. She testified that the voices commanded her to leave her village of Domrémy-Greux,

127

which was then on the far frontier, and travel to France.[7] She obeyed them, though she said she would rather have been torn apart by four horses than to have left her home for France had not God commanded her to do so.[8] Her voices sent her to Chinon imbued with the temerity to inform the dauphin, Charles de Valois, that she had been sent by God to champion his cause against the English invaders and their Burgundian allies. After three weeks of interrogation by Armagnac theologians, the dauphin allowed her to join his forces, then struggling to lift the siege of Orleans. Though his troops were demoralized and had long since given up hope of success, she rallied them, lifted the siege and inspired a chain of military and political victories that would culminate in the coronation of the dauphin as King Charles VII at Reims in July of 1429.[9] Her voices also told her she would be wounded in the battle for the bastide of the Tourelles and that she would be captured at Compiègne. Both came to pass, yet she never once wavered in her devotion to the cause or to her faith in the voices.[10]

Whatever the source of her inner strength, after answering her calling, the patient exhibited a boldness and a prowess of arms in the dauphin's service more characteristic of a fully grown man than a girl still in her teens.[11] Her success as a leader, however, lay not in her feats as a warrior or her skill as a strategist, but in her capacity to inspire confidence and idealism among the Armagnacs in their struggle against the English and their Burgundian allies during the Hundred Years' War. When she came to them, they were demoralized by repeated losses to the English forces, often despite numerical advantages on the field of battle. She transformed their self-doubt and discouragement into faith in the righteousness of Charles's claim to the throne and a belief in the inevitability of an Armagnac victory. She counterbalanced their perception of God's negative judgment, symbolized by a history of defeats, with her own vision of His will, first convincing the Armagnacs that she was His instrument, then reassuring them of the justice of their cause and giving them hope that, through her presence, their losses would be converted into victories.[12]

After a year of intermittent combat, the patient was captured by Burgundians outside the walls of Compiègne, where she was trying to rally the rear guard after the rest of her forces had retreated into the city. According to Georges Chastellain, a Burgundian chronicler,[11] a grizzled archer, enraged that "a woman....should be the *rebuttress* of so many valiant men," pulled her from her horse by her surcoat and took her prisoner. The Burgundians sold her to the English and transported her to Rouen, where her interrogation and trial for heresy took place.

Before her capture, the patient fought many battles for the dauphin in which she carried a standard displaying the image of her savior, sitting in judgment in the clouds of heaven with an angel holding in his hands a fleur-de-lis blessed by the image of her lord.[13] She claimed her voices gave her the design. The voices also told her where to find the sword Charlemagne's grandfather had buried at Sainte-Catherine-de-Fierbois,[14] the one he left as a trophy of his victory over the Muslims in 732 C.E.[15] Finding it was just one of many "miracles" for which she was later credited. Charlemagne's sword became part of her military equipment. However, her standard, not the sword, was her weapon. She took it in hand when leading an assault, both to rally her troops and "to avoid having to kill anyone."[16]

Not everything the patient claimed her voices told her came to pass. During the dark days of her imprisonment, Saint Catherine told her that she would be delivered from her tormentors, though perhaps no sooner than the very hour of her execution.[17] Help, however, never arrived. After her capture she struggled alone and in vain against those who persecuted her and delivered her to her personal Golgotha. Nevertheless, when it was over, and she was being consumed by the fires of her enemies, she found comfort in the knowledge that she would receive the keys to the kingdom of heaven.[18] The voices had told her so.

This was the manner of a woman, who in the words of her holy book, came to France "not to send peace, but a sword" (Mathew 10:34). If she is to be believed, she saw visions and heard voices that no one else saw or heard, and which came not from her own mind but from God.

There are additional reasons why some have questioned this patient's mental health. During her confinement in the castle of Beaurevoir, she threw herself from a tower window some sixty feet above the ground after briefly freeing herself.[19] There are those who believe it was a suicide attempt rather than an abortive escape, speculation she fueled by explaining that she jumped because "she had heard said that all those of Compiègne who had attained seven years of age were supposed to be put to death by fire and by sword, and she preferred to die than to live after such a destruction of good people," people she was struggling to liberate when captured.[20] She also said she leaped because she knew she had been sold to the English and would rather die than be placed in the hands of her English adversaries. Nevertheless, the patient also considered herself a prisoner of war and duty-bound to attempt escape. [21]

She had tried escaping once before, when confined at Beaulieu-lès-Fontaines. That time she somehow managed to lock her guard in the tower in which she was confined and would have escaped had not a porter suddenly arrived and stopped her.[22] Her jump from the tower at Beaurevoir was a rare instance of disobedience to her voices. As she later reported, not only had St. Catherine instructed her not to jump, she had also assured the patient that "God would aid [her] and also the people of Compiègne."[23]

During her crusade, the patient ignored the corporeal distinction between masculinity and femininity, assuming men's clothes and performing masculine deeds while never denying that she was a woman.[24] She wore men's clothes, she explained, because they were more appropriate for the work she performed among men-at-arms, and because she was compelled to do so by a higher force.[25] In the patient's time however, cross-dressing was viewed as a serious transgression. The book of Deuteronomy (22:5) warns that, "The woman shall not wear that which pertaineth unto a man, neither shall a man put on a woman's garment: for all that do so are abomination unto the LORD thy God," And some clerics of the patient's day interpreted the admonition literally. Of all the charges leveled against the patient, this was the one the Church settled on as justification for her execution.

During her trial, the patient's accusers tried to make much of a "Fairy tree" she visited as a child. Like the other girls in her village, she fashioned garlands and placed them on the tree and danced and sang in its vicinity. The clerics claimed that her garlands were actually offerings to "fairies" who inhabited the tree, and that her dancing, venerations and singing were incantations and spells. Whereas other village girls claimed to have seen fairy ladies about the tree, the patient never did. [26, 27]

Finally, shortly before her execution, nervous exhaustion briefly caused the patient to renounce her voices. Until this point, she had spoken only words of truth and soberness, with one exception. After Charles' coronation, when the patient was experiencing nearly constant waves of disillusionment following an unsuccessful effort to take Paris, she rode to Saint-Pierre-le-Moûtier to assist in a siege that was not going well. According to Jean d'Aulon, when asked why she did not withdraw like the others, she removed her helmet and answered that she was not alone but had come with fifty thousand of her men and would not depart from there until she had taken the city. In fact, she had only four or five men with her at the time. [28]

The nervous breakdown came after a year of imprisonment and five months of unrelenting interrogation and intimidation. From January 9 till the end of May, the patient's tormentors tried to confuse and entrap her; however, she held her own against the forty-four ecclesiastical scholars from the University of Paris, and the hostile presiding judge. [29] For five months, she held them at bay, defending herself without counsel of any kind. Pierre Cauchon, formerly rector of the University and bishop of Beauvais, who presided over the proceedings as chief judge, was single-minded and tireless in his efforts to see her executed for heresy. Such was his zeal that he overlooked several procedural flaws, which later made the trial easy to nullify. [29]

The Burgundian clerics spied on her through the floor of her cell and threatened and insulted her. They assigned five English "abusers" of the lowest rank to guard her and to spare her no humiliation. Three spent the night in her cell and two outside at the door. They placed her in irons, forcing her to sleep with two pairs of irons on her legs, attached by a chain to another chain connected to the foot of her bed, itself anchored by a large piece of wood five or six feet long.[30] Twice they subjected her to an examination of virginity, finding to their disappointment that she was a virgin. They tried to violate her and she resisted. They challenged her, many all at once, in a nightmarish interrogation of ecclesiastical ambiguities,[31] all of this in the absence of a formal charge.[32] Their intent was to confuse and trap her through the answers she gave to their myriad questions.[33] Convinced that she could not be tricked into heresy, they settled on cross-dressing as the visible basis for their accusations,[34] thus failing in their intention to condemn her in a way that would bring dishonor and discredit to both her and her king.[35] And through it all, Charles, the dauphin whose forces she had rallied to make him king, took no action; although deeply indebted to the patient for his crown, he made no effort to ransom her or to provide any other assistance after her capture.[36]

The patient wept during her imprisonment and interrogation, but at no time could she be separated from her love of God. Nevertheless, just before her captors killed her, her burning and shining light flickered, if just for an instant. It happened in the aftermath of a period of accelerated and intense interrogation in which she was taken to the great tower of the castle and threatened with torture. When she could not be broken, her captors led her to the Old Marketplace, in the shadow of the Saint-Ouen cemetery where she was to be burned. As she looked out over the crowd that had gathered, including the forty or so clerics assembled on a platform opposite her, she could see another solitary platform meant for her, with firewood beneath it and a stake above. In a final ejaculation of bitterness and iniquity, a spokesman for her accusers railed "O Royal House of France! You have never known a monster until now! But now behold yourself dishonored in placing your trust in this woman, this magician, heretical and superstitious."[37]

Only then did the patient give evidence of the transformation the clerics had long sought. First, she began to blame herself for the transgressions of which she had been accused. Then she renounced her mission and the voices that had inspired it. Several times in the presence of the assembly of her accusers, she admitted that her apparitions and revelations could not be supported nor believed, nor did she want to support them any longer herself; in all things she now deferred to the holy mother, the Catholic church and the clerics who were her judges.[38] Saved from the stake by this statement of abjuration attesting to her submission to the Church Militant,[39] she was consigned, as a penance, to prison for the rest of her days.[40] Four days later, however, she renounced her abjuration, "shift[ing] her positions from one remark to the next throughout this exchange, as if she were no longer sure what positions she wanted to assume."[41] Was she mad? Save for the voices, there seems to be little about the patient that could be posited as abnormal. Those who knew her as a child growing up in the village of Domrémy-Greux testified at the nullification trial[42] a quarter century after her death that she was "just like everyone else" before she left on her mission.[43] Like her mother, "she spun very well, indeed,"[44] and "was a good and simple girl, pious, well-raised, fearing God, such as had no equal in the village; she confessed her sins often, and ....if [she] had any money of her own, she would give some to her parish priest to have masses said...every day he celebrated mass, she was there.... She led a simple life, marked only by piety that astonished and even disconcerted her group ...[In short, she was] "Like the others."[44] From one deposition to the other, this phrase recurs, almost irritating in its monotony: "She was just like everybody, she did everything like everybody else, and, except for her notable piety, she rarely distinguished herself from her group."[45] The patient was as ordinary in her youth as her later speech and deeds were extraordinary.

At age sixteen or seventeen, however, the patient underwent a striking transformation in personality and character. Her great piety, humility and simplicity persisted.[46] However, the peasant girl, who did her mother's chores and tended her father's flock so willingly and so well, vanished. That girl was replaced by a one who rode like a man-at-arms, discussed theology on a par with St. Catherine and argued with barons and knights so persuasively that they thought her miraculous.[47] She was focused, intense and impatient, but also endowed with a robust humor that even the clerics at her condemnation trial could not extinguish.[48] She was gallant and a virgin.[49] Though uneducated, she learned to write during the course of her mission[50] and spoke with such passion and simple eloquence that "Her words put [her followers] on fire, inspiring in [them] a love for her that was [believed to be] divine."[51]

The patient was the youngest of five children of a family of devout Catholics. Although in a fit of belated gratitude Charles ennobled them all, they were ordinary folk. They belonged to the peasant class and were neither rich nor poor. The patient's father, who was elected docent of the village of Domrèmy, promulgated decrees of the village council, supervised the collection of taxes, rents and dues, and monitored weights and measures and the production of bread and wine.[52] Not much is known of her mother, except that she too is believed to have been an intensely pious woman, who transmitted her faith in God to her daughter.[53] There were three brothers, two of whom accompanied the patient on her mission. An older sister died at a young age of unknown cause. No family member is known to have heard voices or seen visions, nor to have suffered from mental illness.

The patient had an exceptionally robust constitution. She had no known illnesses or injuries of any consequence before her mission and became seriously ill only once afterward, despite wounds (to the head and thigh[54]), injuries sustained following her jump from the tower at Beaurevoir, and the fatigue and extreme stress of her campaigns and imprisonment. Her sole serious illness occurred a little more than a month before her execution and caused the Church Militant not a little concern that a natural death would rob it of an apostate it hoped to cleanse by fire. The illness, which was marked by fever and much vomiting, followed a meal of carp provided by Cauchon, the bishop of Beauvais. The patient was convinced she had been poisoned. A physician took her pulse in order to discern the cause of her illness and asked her what she felt and where she hurt. He palpated her on the right side, found her feverish, and decided to bleed her, which relieved her immediately.[55] She relapsed once and then recovered.[56]

The patient's life ended a little more than a month later before a crowd of clerics and other onlookers on the morning of May 30, 1431 on a platform near the butchers' market hall at the Vieux Marché. Nicolas Midi began the process of her execution with a sermon based on First Corinthians 12:26, in which he admonished her to reflect upon the salvation of her soul, to repent her misdeeds and to accept the counsel of the clergy who had condemned her. She listened calmly to the sermon but then began to weep as she forgave her accusers for what they were about to do and asked them to pray for her. Some of the onlookers also wept openly. A few soldiers, however, became impatient and yelled for the executioner to do his duty. When the patient was tied to the pillar, she pleaded for a crucifix, which was brought from the nearby church and held before her during her immolation. Several eye witnesses later recalled that until the very moment of her death, she called out through the flames without ceasing to Jesus and to the saints of paradise for assistance.[57]

If the patient's story were not so extraordinarily beautiful and terrible, questions concerning her mental health would have attracted little attention. Indeed, the era in which she lived was replete with women of extraordinary powers who became saints.[58] Unlike many of those saints, however, many of whom are now all but forgotten, the patient earned for herself a crown of glory that has not faded away. In death, she became the embodiment of everything good about the soul of France, a symbol of fierce resistance to oppression and patriarchal violence, the archetypal political prisoner.[59] In life, she was Jeanne La Pucelle (Joan the Maid), Joan of Arc (see Figures 6-1 and 6-2).

FIGURE 6-1. Portrait of Joan of Arc (the "Echevins" portrait). Anonymous, 16th century. Musee Historique et Archeologique, Orleans, France. Photo Credit : Snark/Art Resource, NY.

***

Joan of Arc's voices and, to a lesser extent, her visions are the essence of a case for mental illness, just as they are for one of divine inspiration. Except for these, what we know of her thought processes and beliefs (and we know a great deal thanks to the transcripts of her interrogation and the nullification trial convened twenty-four years after her death,[42]) give no hint of delirium, dementia, periodic or episodic confusion, or, for that matter, signs of

FIGURE 6-2. Sketch by Clément de Fauquembergue in the register for the Parlement of Paris. de Fauquembergue never saw Joan, but this is the only surviving image of her that was made during her lifetime. Public Domain.

epilepsy, with the possible exception of a bright light she perceived during an early visitation.[1]

Her personality was strong. Her mental and social development was normal, although culminating in exceptional intelligence, drive, leadership and charisma. She exhibited no impairment of cognitive function or disorganization of thought, except under the extreme stress of the later stages of her interrogation and, perhaps, at the time she arrived at the siege of Saint-Pierre-le-Moûtier with four or five men, rather than the fifty thousand she claimed to have with her. She was never clinically depressed, even during the darkest days of her interrogation. Her grandiosity buoyed her during both good times and bad: grandiosity as evidenced by her belief that, of the many called, God had chosen her;[60] by her presumption that she, a young woman without rank, training or experience, was fit to command the armies of a nation; and by her self-appointment as the savior of France and its king. Although these manifestations of her grandiosity suggest a diagnosis of manic psychosis, Joan gave no evidence of pressured speech (speech so rapid and disorganized it is almost impossible to follow), disturbed sleep, irritability or grandiosity unrelated to her special mission, all of which would have been expected if she had been truly manic. Moreover, she had no exalted expectations of recognition or reward, which, coupled with her basic humility and simplicity, all but exclude manic psychosis from consideration.[61]

If Joan's purity in heart did not actually enable her to see God through his messengers, how might one explain her voices and her visions? One possibility is that she fabricated them in order to influence the future Charles VII and/or the court that tried her for heresy. This seems unlikely, at least with respect to the latter objective, because it was before her capture that she had begun discussing her voices with persons having no subsequent input into the condemnation trial. Moreover, it is difficult to reconcile her creating such a myth for personal gain given her humility and her simple desire (her reward, if you will) to return to her family after accomplishing God's mission. It is even more difficult to reconcile her fabricating her voices to influence the outcome of the condemnation trial with her failure to sustain her recantation of the "myth" once it became clear that its "reward" was to be immolation in the courtyard of the church of Saint Ouen.[61]

Could she have had schizophrenia, a mental disorder noted for its auditory hallucinations? Although the diagnosis must be considered, schizophrenia is typically a devastating mental disorder, manifested not just by hallucinations, but also by bizarre behavior and significant impairment of social and occupational skills. All forms of schizophrenia, except the paranoid type, are also characterized by cognitive impairment, negative symptoms (that is, symptoms reflecting abnormally low emotion, spontaneity, curiosity and gratification in social or occupational functions), and disorganized thought. Joan had none of these symptoms. In the paranoid type of schizophrenia, delusions are persecutory in character and bizarre: her voices and visions were not persecutory, nor were they bizarre, at least not by fifteenth-century, Catholic standards, when "communication with saints" occurred with some regularity among the faithful.[61]

Epilepsy involving the temporal lobe (the area of the brain abutting the temples) is another cause of hallucinations.[62] The most constant features of this particular form of epilepsy (temporal lobe epilepsy) are disturbances of the content of consciousness (such as smell or taste, as well as more elaborate sensations such as remembered visions or musical tones), disordered perceptions (especially of the size or proximity of objects or of one's own body), *déjà vu* phenomena (a feeling that what is happening at the time has happened before) and vivid revivals of past memories and abnormal emotions (especially intense fear or depression). Abnormal motor activities frequently accompany temporal lobe seizures, during which patients appear dazed and unresponsive, while performing highly organized functions such as dressing or undressing. Temporal lobe epilepsy might explain Joan's voices and visions but would be unusual in the absence of the other equally prominent features of the disorder.

During the early Middle Ages, outbreaks of mass poisonings caused by *ergot*, a fungal contaminant of rye and other grains, were occasionally associated with hallucinations.[63] When ingested in sufficient quantities, usually in bread made from contaminated rye, the fungus produced a disorder now known as *ergotism*. Thousands were affected, some with a gangrenous variant of the disorder and others with a convulsive variant. Patients with the former variant experienced nausea, pains in the arms and legs and, quite often, gangrene of the limbs, all caused by a vasoconstrictive chemical produced by the fungus. Those with the convulsive type of ergotism experienced bizarre convulsions, ravenous appetites, retching, tongue biting and unusual breathing patterns. A less common form of the disorder, *hallucinogenic ergotism,* produced vivid hallucinations, nervous excitement, insomnia and disorientation, much like that induced by modern psychedelic drugs. Could Joan's voices and visions have been manifestations of ergotism? Although the intoxication can cause hallucinations, Joan had none of the other symptoms characteristic of the complex clinical syndrome.

If Joan's voices and visions were not real, that is, if they were not actually generated by angels, saints or God, then they can only be explained on the basis of a "delusional disorder." The essential feature of the disorder as defined by the American Psychiatric Association's *Diagnostic and Statistical Manual of Mental Disorders*[64] is "the presence of one or more non-bizarre delusions that persist for at least one month." Although today auditory or visual hallucinations are not usually a prominent feature of delusional disorder, they were likely more so during Joan's era, when women visionaries were at the height of their influence in religious life. According to Sullivan,[58] the percentage of women among those canonized doubled from 11.8 to 22.6 percent between the twelfth and thirteenth centuries and then stabilized at 23 to 25 percent during the fourteenth and fifteenth centuries. These changes came about because of a shift in the identification of sanctity with persons exhibiting holiness in ruling an outer kingdom, bishopric or monastery, who were normally upper-class and male, to those exhibiting holiness in ruling an inner self, who were more likely middle- or lower-class and female. As inner experience became an ever more important determinant of saintliness, supernatural states of mind, including the hearing of voices and the seeing of visions, increased in religious value. A recent survey found that female saints living between 1000 and 1700 C.E. were twice as likely to be credited with these sorts of extraordinary powers as their male counterparts.

Apart from the direct impact of delusions on a patient's behavior, they typically do not markedly impair psychosocial functioning nor are they associated with behavior that is obviously odd or bizarre. A diagnosis of "delusional disorder" is only appropriate if the delusions are not a consequence of the direct physiologic effects of a drug or toxin (for example, ergot) or a general medical condition (for example, temporal lobe epilepsy). The determination of whether delusions are bizarre is critical in differentiating delusional disorder from schizophrenia. In schizophrenia delusions are bizarre, whereas in delusional disorder they are not. In categorizing delusions, it must be remembered that *bizarre* is a relative concept that varies across different cultures and different eras. Delusions are deemed not to be bizarre if they are both understandable and plausible within the culture and era in which they occur (as for example, visitations of fifteenth-century French peasants by saints), even though as in Joan's case, they cause social, marital or professional difficulties of varying severity.

There are seven basic subtypes of delusional disorder based on the predominant delusional theme: erotomanic (central theme involves love with an individual), grandiose, jealous, persecutory, somatic (central theme involves bodily functions or sensations), mixed and unspecified. Of these, the grandiose type is the one most consistent with Joan's condition. This subtype applies when "the central theme of the delusion is the conviction of having some great (but unrecognized) talent or insight or having made some important discovery."[64]

Psychiatry is the youngest branch of medicine and one concerned with perhaps the profession's most difficult pathophysiological concepts, those related to the body-mind relationship. The criteria by which society judges a person to be mentally ill are not primarily a function of the presence of certain unvarying and universally accepted symptoms but have to do with the capacity of the individual to adapt and to function at some minimal level within that society. Moreover, such criteria are relative, even within a given society. If, for example, an illiterate peasant believes in the evil eye, one cannot assume *a priori* that he/she is mentally ill. If, however, the same belief is held by a university professor, the assumption is inescapable. This is not to say that behind the varied symptoms of mental illness there might not be some common or essential biological predisposition to disease operating in all societies. The problem is that no absolute biological criteria yet exist for diagnosing and classifying even the most florid and pervasive mental disorders. For this reason, even today, when diagnosing mental disorders, we must rely primarily on symptoms and how they affect persons' capacities to conform to the societies in which they live.[65]

During the medieval period, mental disorders were generally attributed to one of three conditions: *melancholie, phrenitis* and *mania.*[66] Melancholie was marked by the absence of fever and was thought to be due to an excess of black bile, in accordance with Galen's interpretation of the humoral theory of the Hippocratic School (see Chapter 2). Its most common symptoms were sadness, fear and anxiety. Occasionally, the disorder was accompanied by delusions, and, when persistent, these led to a diagnosis of "insania." If the person claimed to be possessed by divine influence and the gift of prophecy, they were given the distinctly uncommon diagnosis of "possession." Phrenitis was differentiated from melancholie by the presence of fever and by its cause, an excess of yellow bile. Mania, which was characterized by restlessness, wildness and excitement in the absence of fever, was also thought to be due to an imbalance of yellow bile. Thus, of the three major mental disorders recognized by medieval physicians, both melancholie (with features of insania and possession) and mania had features similar to Joan of Arc's mental condition as reflected in the transcripts of her interrogation and condemnation trial of 1431.

If Joan had been examined by a physician and a diagnosis of *insania* or *possession* had been made, based on her claim of being possessed by divine influence, any treatment given would have conformed to Hippocratic tradition.[66] Accordingly, she likely would have been confined to a light, warm and airy room, with windows high enough to prevent her from jumping out. The attendants might have entered into a few of her delusions while rejecting others. Warm poultices of oil might have been applied to her head and careful blood-letting performed (recall this was the treatment given for her episode of food poisoning[67]). She also might have had her head shaved and been treated with cupping, leeches and/or scarification. Passive exercise (such as rocking) and a special diet devoid of wine would have been prescribed. Most important, attempts would have been made to strengthen her "reasoning powers" by asking her questions and having her analyze texts containing false statements. Apart from this, her time would have been spent in light reading (Joan, who was just learning to read and write, would have required help with this measure), play acting (in plays intended to be therapeutic) and delivering speeches to a friendly audience. Chess and travel might also have been recommended. Drug therapy, if given, would have consisted of an emetic such as hellebore.[66]

Note the similarities between these treatments and those recommended today for patients like Joan with delusional disorders. According to the *Textbook of Clinical Psychiatry*:

> Because there are no systematic data comparing treatments in delusional disorder, recommendations are based on clinical observation, not empirical evidence.... Most patients have little insight about their illness and refuse to acknowledge a problem, so an initial obstacle is getting the patient to the physician.... The potential for violence may exist because some patients will act on their delusions.... Thus, a clinician caring for a patient [like Joan] with delusional disorder must carefully assess potential for harm to self or others. Tact and skill are necessary to help persuade a delusional disorder patient to accept treatment.... Once a therapeutic relationship is established, a clinician can begin to gently challenge the delusional beliefs [Joan's voices and visions] by showing how they interfere with the patient's life [In Joan's case, today's clinicians might try to show her how her voices and visions were responsible for her religious and secular difficulties.], but must neither condemn nor collude in the beliefs. The patient should be assured of privacy, and the physician should take care not to discuss confidential matters with the patient's family without the patient's consent.... Because delusional disorder is relatively uncommon, its treatment with antipsychotic medication has never been properly evaluated; anecdotal evidence suggests that response is poor.[68]

Thus, Joan (or a patient like her) would be no more likely to be medicated for her delusions today than at the time of her incarceration over six hundred years ago.

Although long dead, death has not diminished the impact of Joan of Arc. If anything, her legend has grown, enhanced by myth-making that began almost immediately after her sudden assault on the European consciousness in 1429. Before Compiègne, the belief was almost universal that she could not be captured or kept in captivity, her power being so great that God would help her to escape.[69] After she died, rumors circulated that although her body had been reduced to ashes, her heart remained intact.[70]

The similarities between Joan's life story and that of her Savior are striking.[71] How much of it was distorted by the failing memories and growing devotion of converts who testified at the nullification trial can only be guessed. Had she lived today rather than over six hundred years ago, it is not likely that any physician would seriously consider that her voices and visions were those of angels or saints. Instead, she would be given a diagnosis of delusional disorder, even though the voices and visions, and the deeds they inspired, are why, for many, "the maid is not dead, but sleepeth" (Matthew 9:24).[72]

Notes

1. Morey-Kyrle. A psycho-analytic study of the voices of Joan of Arc. *Br J Med Psychol*. 1933;13:63-81.
2. Sullivan K. *The Interrogation of Joan of Arc*. University of Minnesota Press. Minneapolis: 1999, p. 40.
3. Saint Catherine and Saint Margaret were among the most popular saints of the Middle Ages and were often paired together. As of the 14th century, Saint Catherine was viewed as one of the most powerful intercessors with God after the Virgin Mary and, along with John The Baptist, was one of the most popular subjects of religious statues. There was a church dedicated to Saint

Catherine in Maxey, a village just across the river from Joan's village of Domremy, and a statue of Saint Margaret, extant today, more than likely was present in Domremy during Joan's lifetime. (Ibid p. 163.)

4. Pernoud R, Clin M-V. *Joan of Arc. Her Story.* Translated by Adams J. St. Martin's Press. New York: 1998, p 121.

5. Op cit (Sullivan) p. 24.

6. Martin Lavenu, one of the clerics who met with Joan in her cell for a final interview on the day of her execution attested that:

> spontaneously, without being constrained to do it, she said and confessed that, whatever she had said and boasted about this angel, there had been no angel who brought the crown [meant for Charles VII], but, rather, Joan herself had been the angel who said and had promised to him who she calls her king that, if he put her to work, she would crown him at Reims. (Ibid p. 74)

7. Op cit (Pernoud and Clin) p. 15.

8. Ibid p. 114.

9. Ibid p. 21, 55, 78.

10. Ibid p. 89-90.

11. Op cit (Sullivan) p. 50-1.

12. Ibid p. 78-9.

13. Op cit (Pernoud and Clin) p. 37.

14. Ibid p. 114.

15. Ibid p. 16.

16. Ibid p. 36.

17. Op cit (Sullivan) p. 141.

18. Op cit (Sullivan) p. 107.

19. Op Cit (Sullivan) p. 116.

20. Joan was captured during a skirmish outside Compiegne in May 1430 and felt a deep sense of obligation to the people of Compiegne [Op cit (Sullivan) p. 113-4].

21. Op cit (Sullivan) p. 112-115.

22. Op cit (Pernoud and Clin) p. 92.

23. Op cit (Pernoud and Clin) p. 96.

24. Op cit (Sullivan) p. 42.

25. Op cit (Sullivan) p. 55.

26. Op cit (Pernoud and Clin) p. 112-113.

27. Op cit (Sullivan) p. 13.

28. Op cit (Pernoud and Clin) p. 80.

29. Op cit (Pernoud and Clin) p. xv, 89, 103.

30. Op cit (Pernoud and Clin) p. 104.

31. Op cit (Sullivan) p. 89-90.

32. Op cit (Pernoud and Clin) p. 108.

33. Op cit (Sullivan) p. 87.

34. Op cit (Pernoud and Clin) p. 117.

35. Op cit (Pernoud and Clin) p. 126.

36. Op cit (Pernoud and Clin) p. 106.

37. Op cit (Pernoud and Clin) p. 130.

38. Op cit (Pernoud and Clin) p. 131.

39. At the time of Joan's trial, Catholic clerics promulgated a complex vision of the church. The "Church Militant" was the Catholic church on earth. It was distinguished from the "Church Triumphant," which was the church in heaven. There was also a "Church Suffering" composed of members of the church in purgatory. This was just one of many abstract concepts, unfamiliar to Joan, which were used to develop a case for heresy based on inadequate submission to the Church Militant. [Op cit (Pernoud and Clin) p. 122]. Joan viewed the church as a single entity, and although she confessed frequently and ardently, she rejected the Burgundian clerics who tried her as intermediaries between herself and God. On the contrary, because of her Voices and Visions, she viewed herself as their intermediary with God. [Op cit (Sullivan) p. 128].

40. Op cit (Sullivan) p. 131.

41. Op cit (Sullivan) p. 132-3.

42. On May 30, 1431 C.E., Joan was convicted of heresy based on her refusal to submit to the Church Militant by continuing to wear men's clothes. In 1449 C.E., Charles VII petitioned the pope to authorize a new trial, which convened in November 1455 C.E. and concluded its deliberations on July 7, 1456

C.E., after lengthy interrogation of one hundred fifteen witnesses, many of whom were involved in the original trial. The second (nullification) trial declared the original (condemnation) trial to have been procedurally flawed and therefore nullified. [Op cit (Pernoud and Clin) p. 139].

43. Op cit (Pernoud and Clin) p. 159.

44. Op cit (Pernoud and Clin) p. 20.

45. Op cit (Pernoud and Clin) p. 159-60.

46. Op cit (Pernoud and Clin) p. 22.

47. Op cit (Pernoud and Clin) p. 54.

48. Op cit (Pernoud and Clin) p. 116.

49. Joan vowed in the presence of her Voices to retain her virginity forever (Note #1). Prior to her "mission," she appears to have rejected a betrothal arranged by her parents and had to defend herself in a breach-of-promise suit in ecclesiastical court. [Op cit (Pernoud and Clin) p. 119].

50. Op cit (Pernoud and Clin) p. 81-3.

51. Op cit (Pernoud and Clin) p. 21.

52. Op cit (Pernoud and Clin) p. 221-2.

53. Op cit (Pernoud and Clin) p. 36.

54. Op cit (Pernoud and Clin) p. 60, 77.

55. Physicians of the late Medieval period continued to subscribe to Hippocratic concepts of medicine as interpreted and expanded by Galen and, in the latter part of the 12th century, by Maimonides, all of whom promoted bleeding as a means of correcting humoral imbalances. In a compendium of medicine written between 1187 C.E. and 1190 C.E., Maimonides expounded on physiology, anatomy, therapy and hygiene. He used as his form of presentation, the aphorism, after the model of Hippocrates. Although he offered several new prescriptions derived from his own research, his work, like that of Galen, was mainly a refresher course in Hippocratic Theory (see Chapter 2). (Heschel AJ. *Maimonides. A Biography.* [Translated from German by Neugroschel J.] Farra, Strauss. Giroux. New York: 1982, p. 213-15.

56. Op cit (Pernoud and Clin) p. 125.

57. Op cit (Sullivan) p. 147-8.

58. Op cit (Sullivan) p. 21.

59. Op cit (Pernoud and Clin) p. xix.

60. According to Joan, she was chosen because: "It pleased God to do so through a simple maiden, to humble the king's enemies" [Op cit (Pernoud and Clin) p. 118].

61. The assessment of Dr. William T. Carpenter, Professor of Psychiatry at the University of Maryland School of Medicine and Director of the Maryland Psychiatric Research Center, who in 2002 testified for the defense in a mock trial of Joan of Arc hosted by the VA Maryland Health Care System and the Alumni Association of the University of Maryland School of Medicine. The purpose of the trial was to determine if Joan would be found criminally responsible for her actions in a 21st century C.E., Maryland Court of Law. By a vote of one hundred thirteen to seventy-six, the jury (the audience at the mock trial) found Joan not responsible under the indictment of 1431 C.E. (Sullivan K, Rappeport J, Carpenter WT, et al. *A medico-legal re-examination of the Maid of Orleans. Was Joan of Arc criminally responsible for her alleged acts of heresy?* The Pharos. 2004; 67:4-11.)

62. Brain L. *Clinical Neurology.* 2nd ed. Oxford U. Press. London:1964, p. 131-2.

63. http://ou066065.otago.ac.nz/edmedia/HxPharmacy/Overviews/ergotism_o.htm.

64. *Diagnostic and Statistical Manual of Mental Disorders.* 4th ed. American Psychiatric Association. Washington, DC: 2000. p. 323-9.

65. Ackerknecht EH. *A Short History of Psychiatry.* (Translated from German by S. Wolff.) Hafner Publishing Co. New York: 1968. p. vii-xii, 1-27.

66. Howells JG. Schizophrenia in the medieval period. In Howells JG. Ed. *The Concept of Schizophrenia: Historical Perspectives.* American Psychiatric Press, Inc. Washington, DC: 1991, p. 29-46.

67. Bloodletting continued to be prescribed for various illnesses until the early part of the 19th century. In the 1830s, P.C.A.

Louis provided the first scientific data discrediting the treatment in a carefully conducted investigation showing that early bloodletting increased mortality in patients with pneumonia. (Morabia A. PCA Louis and the birth of clinical epidemiology. *J Clin Epidemiol.* 1996;49:1327-33.)

68. Hales RE, Yudofsky SC. Eds. *Textbook of Clinical Psychiatry.* 4th ed. American Psychiatric Publishing, Inc. Washington, DC: 2000, p. 426.

69. Op cit (Pernoud and Clin) p. 99.

70. Op cit (Pernoud and Clin) p. 137.

71. One can only wonder how the striking parallels between Joan's life story and that of Jesus Christ might have influenced the attitudes and testimonies of those who participated in the nullification trial:

   • Joan's Story/Christ's Story
   • Marie Avignon/John The Baptist
   • Domremy/Bethlehem
   • Examination at Poitier/Examination by the Rabbis
   • Entrance into Orleans/Palm Sunday
   • Guillaume de Flavy/Judas Iscariot
   • Pierre Cauchon/Caiaphas
   • 10,000 livres tournois/30 pieces of silver
   • Immolation/Crucifixion
   • People of France/Mankind

72. Although Joan is largely remembered for her Voices and the deeds they inspired, her canonization in May of 1920 C.E. was based on her "heroic virtues" and not on an acknowledgement by the Church that she had communicated directly with the heavenly host [Op cit (Pernoud and Clin) p. 245].

CRIPPLED DOVE

7

Give me a spirit that on life's rough sea
Loves t'have his sails filled with a lusty wind,
Even till his sail yards tremble, his masts crack,
And his rapt ship run on her side so low
That she drinks water, and her keel plows air.
—*George Chapman (1559-1634)*
The Conspiracy of Charles, Duke of Byron

This patient was the first and possibly greatest mariner of the Age of Discovery, one so skilled in the business of sailing, it was as if he could see the wind. It has been said of him that his discovery was "one of the most important events in the history of humanity.... second only to the birth of Christ in beneficial results."[1] It has also been said that he was an arch-villain who brought genocide and pollution to the pristine New World paradise he discovered.[2] Whether despoiler or saint, he inaugurated an age of exploration and conquest that for a considerable period gave Europe hegemony over the entire globe.

Except for his medical history, every facet of the patient's story is so familiar it hardly needs retelling, yet it is a story riddled with inconsistencies and contradictions. According to the standard account most of us learned in grammar school, the patient was born in Genoa, was a Christian, and wandered much of his life, until finally given the opportunity by King Ferdinand and Queen Isabella of Spain to pursue his dream of discovering a western route to the orient. Some have argued, alternately, that he made his historic voyage to prove the Earth round, but this view seems to be repudiated by a letter the patient wrote to his sovereigns in 1498:

> I have always read that the world, both land and water, was spherical, as the authority and researches of Ptolemy and all the others who have written on the subject demonstrate and prove, as do the eclipses of the moon and other experiments that are made from east to west, and the elevation of the North Star from north to south.[4]

On August 3, 1492, the patient began the historic voyage beyond the western horizon that would bring unimagined wealth and power to the kingdom that sponsored him. He made four voyages to the New World. At the very end of the first, he contracted an arthritis that would cripple him, just one of many hardships he would endure before he died. The arthritis began suddenly during a violent storm off the Iberian coast. Until then, the patient had enjoyed excellent health and was all the more surprised and dismayed by his symptoms because during the entire voyage no one else had taken to his bed due to illness, except for one old man who suffered the pain of kidney stones, an affliction he had had his entire life, and even he was well at the end of two days. No one else had so much as complained of a headache.[5,6] The nature of the patient's disease is only partially known but seems to have consisted of an intermittent, though relentlessly progressive, arthritis which, at least initially, affected his legs more than his arms or hands. Recurrent attacks, like the first, seemed to coincide with periods of privation, stress and violent weather, in which he was exposed to cold and water, deprived of sleep, and ate little.[7]

The patient was forty-one years old when his arthritis first flared. He had a younger sister and three younger brothers, one of whom died at an early age of unknown cause. He came from a respectable, though lower middle class family of wool carders, and he had little if any formal education. A more recent account of his origins, one supported by considerable circumstantial evidence, maintains that the patient concealed his true heritage and was actually the scion of a prominent Catalan family from the region of Barcelona, whose mother was a *converso,* a converted Jew. This account also posits that the patient was nearly fifty when he experienced his initial attack of arthritis on returning from his first voyage to the New World.[8] The controversy over his origin is relevant to his illness, in that if the latter account is true, and he was a native of the Barcelona region, he would have been nearly twice as likely to have had a genetic predisposition to arthritis than if he had come from Genoa.

Contemporary biographers diagnosed the patient's illness as *gotte,* "the gout." However, at that time, *gotte* was a generic term for arthritis and not necessarily indicative of the disorder of uric acid metabolism we call "gout" today. Although no other member of the patient's family is known to have had symptoms of *gotte,* postmortem examination of remains believed to be those of his brother demonstrated fusion of the fourth and fifth vertebrae of the lower back (the area known as the lumbar region), which might have been due to arthritis of the spine, and incomplete spina bifida (a congenital abnormality resulting in incomplete closure of the spine). Identical abnormalities have also been detected in the remains of one of the patient's sons,[9] suggesting that a predisposition to diseases of the joints and bones was an inherited family trait.

The patient's formative years are shrouded in mystery. His writings demonstrate a fluency in Latin, as well as considerable knowledge of the works of Aristotle, Ptolemy, Marinus of Tyre, Strabo, Pliny and Marco Polo.[10] Thus, it seems that contrary to the standard account of his life, he was well-educated, although neither the source nor the extent of his formal education (if any) is known.

He married Doña Felipa Perestrello e Moniz, a Portuguese noblewoman who bore him a son. After six years of marriage, she died of unknown cause. The patient then took a mistress, a poor but well-connected commoner named Beatriz Enríquez de Harana, with whom he had a second son. Some believe he had at least one other mistress, Doña Beatriz de Peraza, who, like his wife, was a noblewoman. He visited her in the Canary Islands at the beginning of his first voyage of discovery. It was the only time he is known to have veered, even briefly, from his single-minded pursuit of his destiny.[11]

When he and his men first reached the New World, they encountered an innocent and compliant people, whose women were beautiful, naked and "completely promiscuous."[12] After two cramped and uncertain months at sea, his men disembarked hungry and unruly. Sexual orgies ensued, which were all the more unrestrained because of his men's belief that the only appropriate relationship with the native peoples was that of master to slave, and also because, at least initially, the natives regarded the patient and his crew as "men from Heaven."[13] Many of the patient's men and the early explorers who followed contracted syphilis from native women, which they carried home with them at the cost of massive outbreaks of a deadly disease not previously encountered by residents of the Old World (see Chapter 9).

Whether the patient was party to the sexual promiscuity rampant among the men who served under him is not known; he mentioned nothing of the subject in his log, which was intended for the eyes of his modest queen, and there is no direct evidence that he ever engaged in sexual relationships with native women. If his son Ferdinand's account of the patient's piety can be trusted, he may well have abstained:

> [He was] so strict in matters of religion that for fasting and saying prayers he might have been taken for a member of a religious order. He was so great an enemy of swearing and blasphemy that I give my word I never heard him utter any other oath than 'by St. Ferdinand!'....If he had to write anything, he always began by writing these words *IESUS cum MARIA sit nobis in via*.[14]

Prior to the onset of his arthritis, the patient's only recorded medical problem was a wound of unknown location and severity that he received during a battle at sea when he was in his mid-thirties.[15] Details of the battle are sketchy and of uncertain veracity. However, according to his son, the patient's ship was sunk during the engagement, forcing him to swim two leagues to safety on the nearby coast. When he reached shore, his legs were temporarily "crippled by the wetness of the water."[15] This was over a decade and a half before his first attack of *gotte*.

Physically, the patient was a well-built man with long face, high cheek bones and well-proportioned body. He had an aquiline nose and light-colored eyes. His complexion was light and tending to bright red. As a youth his hair was blonde, but by the time he reached the age of thirty it had all turned white.[14]

In eating and drinking and in his manner of dress he was moderate, even modest. He was affable in conversation with strangers and pleasant to members of his household, though he conducted himself with a certain gravity.[14]

The patient never really recovered fully from his initial attack of *gotte*. In December of the year following that attack, while on his second voyage to the New World, he and many of his men contracted an influenza-like illness.[16] Whereas the others recovered quickly, the patient developed unspecified complications that troubled him for four months before finally resolving, though he was then only fifty years of age. While sailing in the vicinity of Puerto Rico during that voyage, he again became ill, this time with fever, delirium and impaired vision. Another attack of *gotte* ensued, this one so severe he was nearly completely incapacitated for more than five months.[9] When at last the patient returned to Spain, he donned the habit of a Dominican friar and sought solace in religious mysticism as both his health and his celebrity began to ebb.

There were repeated exacerbations and remissions of the disorder over the ensuing years. One attack, six years after the onset of the illness when the patient was in his mid-fifties, was particularly severe, causing excruciating pain in the leg and four days of high fever. It struck him during a disastrous third voyage to the New World, one that ended in charges of criminal misconduct over his inability to control the excesses of an unruly crew and growing hostility of an increasingly restive native population. The attack lingered for months and before ending was accompanied by a painful, bleeding inflammation of the eyes, which temporarily all but blinded him. At that time, his letters were rambling and incoherent, suggesting that the disorder had effected his mind as well as his body.[17] A prolonged period of enforced rest temporarily restored his health. As he approached his seventh decade, however, repeated attacks of his illness left him an aged man before his time.[18]

During a fourth and final voyage of discovery, the patient continued to search the Caribbean in vain for *Cipangu* (Japan), driven by faulty calculations as to the width of the single, vast "Ocean Sea" then believed to separate Europe from China and its neighboring islands.[19] He was then in his mid-sixties and so incapacitated by his *gotte* that he was forced to command his flag ship from a bed placed in a dog house-like structure he had constructed on the poop deck. In the midst of his deteriorating health, worms destroyed his ships, marooning him on the island of Jamaica for an exhausting and humiliating year.[20] Starving, shaken by malaria and so crippled by his arthritis he could no longer stand, he somehow found the strength to maintain order among a mutinous crew until help arrived. Following his rescue and return to Spain, a period of rest brought him little relief from the agony of his *gotte*. By then, the disorder had determined that he would never again return to the sea in search of new lands. That work would have to be carried on by Juan de la Cosa, Peralono Niño, Vincet Yáñez Pinzón, Alonso de Hojeda and the other great Spanish navigators he had trained. Fourteen years had passed since the onset of his illness during his historic first voyage of discovery, some sixty to seventy years since his birth.

The patient spent his last year confined to bed. Cold, damp weather, as before, brought on his most intense suffering. Although his mind and his will remained strong to the last, the *gotte* eventually found his hands, causing pain so intense he could no longer write. On May, 20, 1506, his agony ended. Cristóbal Colon, Christopher Columbus (see Figure 7-1), Admiral of the Ocean Sea, was dead.[21]

***

The controversy surrounding the life and death of Columbus has many voices. They question, among other things, the etiology of his

156

FIGURE 7-1. Portrait of Columbus by Ghirlandaio (1483-1561). Museo Navale di Pegli, Genoa, Italy. Photo Credit: Scala/Art Resource, NY.

progressive and ultimately fatal arthritis, his true origin, the nature and extent of his formal education, his concept of the earth's shape, the degree to which he participated personally in the early excesses of the European entrada and the full spectrum of his sexual liaisons. With regard to his arthritis, most medical authorities conclude that it represented some form of "post-infectious [or reactive]" arthritis, also known as Reiter syndrome.[8] This being the case, the questions remain: what was the particular infection that caused Columbus' immunological defenses to turn on him causing a *reactive* arthritis in its wake, and why was he the only one of the crew so afflicted?

Although gout can produce many of the features of Columbus' illness, it leaves much to be desired as his diagnosis. It is a cause of recurrent, incapacitating arthritis in men in their fifth and sixth decades, one that affects joints of the lower extremities earlier and more often than the hands or arms. In its early stages, the arthritis is episodic and sometimes accompanied by high fever. Moreover, in the absence of effective treatment, it tends to become polyarticular, involving multiple joints, especially those of the hands, the late targets of Columbus' arthritis. Gout, however, tends to be a disorder most often attacking obese persons, especially those with a penchant for purine-rich foods and alcohol. Columbus was never obese and was "moderate, even modest" in eating and drinking. What is more, his acute attacks of arthritis lasted weeks to months. Acute attacks of gout typically last no longer than seven to ten days. Perhaps most important, gout does not cause painful, bleeding eyes or temporary blindness.[8]

Could Columbus have had rheumatoid arthritis, a crippling arthritis afflicting an estimated 1% of the world's population today?[8] Rheumatoid arthritis is a systemic immunological disorder with a particular predilection for the joints of the hands but also other organs such as the membrane surrounding the heart (pericardium), lungs and eyes. The arthritis is typically episodic and occasionally complicated by inflamed, even bleeding, eyes. The first clear description of rheumatoid arthritis in Europe, however, was not published until 1800,[22] leading some authorities to conclude that it did not reach that continent until several centuries after the time of Columbus. Recent evidence of its existence in pre-Columbian America raises the possibility that, like syphilis, it was one of only a few diseases transported from the New World to the old, although in what manner (e.g., as an infection or a genetic trait) has yet to be determined, since its cause is still unknown.[23] Even if it was a New World disorder, it is unlikely that Columbus' was the first case in a European. For one thing, the pain of rheumatoid arthritis is not typically excruciating. Furthermore, the hands are almost always involved early in the course of the arthritis; its course tends to be unremitting; and fever, particularly high fever, is unusual.[8]

Scurvy, vitamin C deficiency, also occasionally causes arthritis and was rampant among sailors throughout the Age of Discovery.[24] Many crews of that era, in fact, were so devastated by the disorder they were barely able to man the ships that carried them to new lands. As vitamin C deficiency intensified among crews of sailing ships owing to lack of fresh vegetables and fruit, men's teeth began to fall out, hemorrhaging into the skin occurred and, in the most severe cases, victims descended into a state of lethargy and died. In some cases, hemorrhaging into the joints and eyes caused symptoms similar to those reported by Columbus. However, Columbus had none of the other classic features of scurvy, nor did any member of his crew at the time he experienced his first attack of arthritis.

Of all the causes of arthritis, one now known as "reactive arthritis" is the one most likely responsible for Columbus' long agony and death. The cardinal features of the disorder are inflammation of joints (arthritis), inflammation of the outer membrane of the eyes and eyelids (conjunctivitis) and inflammation of the urethra (urethritis).[8] Uveitis (inflammation of various structures of the inner eye) also occurs and can produce ocular complaints identical to those of Columbus. The arthritis and other abnormalities develop because of an overly zealous immune system, which attacks both the microbe responsible for the inciting infection and various host tissues (joints, for example) having molecular compositions similar to those of the invading microbe. The arthritis has been designated a *reactive* arthritis, because it develops as a consequence of an excessive immunological *reaction* to certain infections. Although formerly it was assumed that such arthritis was due entirely to the abnormal immunological response (specifically, antibodies initially produced against the inciting microbe which cross-react with host tissues), fragments of inciting microbes have recently been detected in the joints of patients with the arthritis, indicating that, strictly speaking, reactive arthritis is not a sterile arthritis, but one resulting from actual invasion of joints by the inciting microbe.[8]

Prior to the advent of AIDS, reactive arthritis was the most common arthritis among young men serving in the U.S. military and one of the most common in the general population as well.[8] The infections most often inducing the disorder were sexually transmitted ones, particularly non-gonococcal urethritis, a sexually transmitted infection of the urethra caused by highly specialized bacteria belonging to the genus *Chlamydia*. Food-borne infections caused by pathogenic bacteria such as shigella, salmonella and the like have also been important causes.

A famous outbreak of reactive arthritis after an epidemic of food poisoning on a U.S. naval vessel in 1962 is instructive because of a number of potentially important parallels with Columbus' case history. The outbreak involved over six hundred cases of shigellosis (an invasive infection of the colon caused by bacteria belonging to the genus *Shigella*) after a picnic prepared for the crew celebrating the ship's anniversary.[25] Nine cases of reactive arthritis developed in the aftermath of the outbreak two to five weeks after the onset of the inciting shigella infection. Arthritis developed only among shigella-infected crew members and attacked the joints of the lower extremities and spine three times as often as those of the upper extremities. Eight of the cases of reactive arthritis had associated conjunctivitis. Five of the original cases were evaluated thirteen years later.[26] One had minimal disease and remained symptom free after his initial attack. The other four patients had chronic, persistent arthritis; one was blind in one eye and had blurred vision in the other due to recurrent occular inflammation and hemorrhage. All four of the latter patients tested positive for HLA-B27, a genetic marker associated with various forms of arthritis (see below). Based on the results of this investigation, it was estimated that the risk of developing reactive arthritis in the aftermath of shigellosis is less than one in fifty. However, in persons positive for HLA-B27, the risk may be as high as one in three. Although there is no record of outbreaks of shigellosis or other forms of dysentery (invasive infections of the colon) on Columbus' ships during the two- to five-week period preceding his first attack of arthritis, the close quarters and poor sanitation aboard vessels of that age provided all of the necessary ingredients for such outbreaks and may well have been so commonplace as not to have merited comment in a captain's log. If Columbus was the only member of his crew to develop reactive arthritis in the aftermath of such an outbreak, it might have been because he was one of the few who was HLA-B27-positive (see below).

If Columbus' disorder was reactive arthritis, what might have been the inciting infection? Aside from shigellosis, those worthy of consideration include a sexually transmitted infection; some other food-borne illness, such as brucellosis; and psittacosis, an acute respiratory infection acquired from birds, especially psittacine birds, such as parrots.

With regard to the first possibility, sexual promiscuity was epidemic among the men who served under Columbus, and it would be naïve to dismiss out of hand the possibility that he too succumbed to carnal temptations presented by scores of naked, comely, native women, over whom he came to exercise absolute authority. Could he have contracted non-gonococcal urethritis as a result of sexual intercourse with native women?

At the time of his first voyage, during which the inciting infection responsible for his reactive arthritis would have been acquired, Columbus was relatively young, ruggedly handsome and had already had an extramarital affair (with Beatriz Enríquez de Harana, the mother of his second son) and, likely, at least one other (with Doña Beatriz de Peraza, the wife of the lord of La Gomera, whom he first met during the wars of Malaga and Granada [1486-1492]). Even so, as we have heard from his son, Columbus was an extremely pious man, driven by an unshakable will and weighted down by ineffably heavy responsibilities. Thus, it is not beyond the realm of possibility that he was simply too preoccupied with his responsibilities as admiral of a fleet never entirely free from danger or that his devotion to his god was so intense that he had neither the time nor the inclination to join the orgies of his men. With regard to the former possibility, Morison, Columbus' principal American biographer, says: "He watched and figured while others slept; he was the kind of officer who woke instantly with a change of the wind or of course, and came on deck to see what was up and log it. The ill health from which he suffered in his later voyages, the arthritis that tortured him, was mostly due to lack of sleep and to exposure in the line of duty."[27]

The most persuasive argument against Columbus' having yielded to the sexual temptations of Caribbean women is that if he had, like many of his men, he would almost certainly have contracted not non-gonococcal urethritis, but syphilis. Although syphilis, "the great imitator," has many forms, Columbus' illness does not look like any of those existing now or during his time (see Chapter 9).

Could he have developed reactive arthritis as a consequence of brucellosis, a systemic infection frequently acquired from goats? Goats were an important source of animal protein for the early Spanish explorers and were among the cargo carried by Columbus on his second voyage to the New World.[28] Although ship manifests from the first voyage no longer exist, it is likely goats were among the cargo of that voyage as well. If so, brucellosis (see Chapter 11), a sometimes virulent and at others a chronic progressive infection, must be included among those likely to have been responsible for Columbus' reactive arthritis. Brucellosis infects bones and joints directly and can also damage them indirectly by causing reactive arthritis, chronic sacroiliitis and chronic inflammation of the spine (spondylitis), in short, all of the recorded features of Columbus' fatal disorder.

What of psittacosis, like influenza, an infection occasionally transmitted by birds to humans? One of the many wonders encountered by Columbus in the New World were flocks of parrots so numerous that according to 19th-century American writer Washington Irving,[29] "they occasionally obscured the sun." So impressed was Columbus by these birds, so different from any native to his home, he carried several varieties back to Spain, which he presented to his sovereigns as proof of the existence and the wonder of the new land he had discovered. Parrots, it turns out, harbor a specialized bacterium called *Chlamydia psittaci* (members of the same family of specialized bacteria responsible for non-gonococcal urethritis), which causes a highly variable, acute, febrile illness in humans, not unlike acute influenza. In rare instances, the illness is complicated by reactive arthritis.[30] Although psittacine birds (parrots, cockatoos and the like) are the most common source of such infections, human cases have been traced to contact with many other varieties of birds as well. The agent, *C. psittaci*, is present in nasal secretions, excreta, tissues and feathers of infected birds and is almost always transmitted to humans by the respiratory route. It is possible that Columbus and other crew members contracted the infection from infected parrots carried home on the first voyage in extremely cramped quarters conducive to air-borne spread of the avian pathogen. If so, Columbus might have been the only one among his crew unfortunate enough to develop reactive arthritis because the birds were housed in his quarters during the return voyage to Spain and/or he was the only one on board (or at least one of a very few) with the arthritis-associated protein, HLA-B27, on his cell surfaces. Given the latter possibility, what is HLA-B27, and how might it have been involved in the pathogenesis of Columbus' arthritis?

The surfaces of human cells are studded with specialized proteins (or "antigens"), known as major histocompatibility complex (MHC) antigens which play a fundamental role in allowing the immune system to distinguish "self" from "non-self."[31] Such proteins were originally called "transplantation antigens" because of their importance in determining whether transplanted tissues are accepted or rejected. When functioning properly, non-self intruders, like bacteria and other microorganisms, are eliminated by the immune system through a process called immunity. When this process fails to eliminate invading microbes, infection ensues. In rare instances, intruding microbes pervert the host's recognition of self, causing it to attack its own tissues in a process known as autoimmunity. Such autoimmune reactions are especially problematic for persons inheriting the MHC antigen known as HLA-B27. Whereas only a few percent of the general population carry HLA-B27 on their cell surfaces, seventy-five percent of patients diagnosed with reactive arthritis have cell surfaces studded with HLA-B27. Moreover, virtually all cases of the chronic, progressive form of reactive arthritis and those with associated inflammation of the eyes (Columbus' form of reactive arthritis) are HLA-B27-positive. HLA-B27, in fact, predisposes those who carry it on their cell surfaces to a whole family of chronic arthritides referred to as "spondyloarthritis." One such spondyloarthritis, ankylosing spondylitis, causes fusion of vertebral bodies similar to that identified in the remains of both Columbus' brother and son.

How HLA-B27 predisposes to reactive arthritis is not clear. It might have a special affinity for peptides produced by the bacteria that cause reactive arthritis, interacting with them in some mysterious way to activate the inflammatory cascade. It has also been speculated that HLA-B27 impairs the ability of lymphocytes to eliminate these same bacteria and, by promoting persistent infections, simultaneously encourages the development of reactive arthritis.[8]

The frequency of HLA-B27 among Europeans today, and presumably also at the time of Columbus, varies according to region, increasing gradually as one travels north within the continent[8]. Its frequency among residents of Barcelona (nine percent) is nearly twice that among residents of Genoa (five percent). This being the case, the controversy surrounding the true origin of Columbus has potential clinical and historical implications, in that if he came from Barcelona, rather than Genoa, he would have been almost twice as likely to have had a genetic predisposition to severe reactive arthritis.

Aside from Columbus' physical appearance (tall, fair-skinned, light hair and eyes), suggesting a northern European ancestry, an argosy of other circumstantial evidence has been offered by those doubting the standard account of his life to support their belief that he came from the region of Barcelona and was of Catalan stock.[8] For one thing, in over five hundred thirty-six existing pages of Columbus' letters and documents, not once does he claim to have come from Genoa, or anywhere else for that matter.[32] Moreover, all of these documents, including letters to his brothers and ones to Genoese and other Italians are in Spanish or Latin, none in Italian. In official Castilian documents in which his origin should have been specified if he had been from Genoa, he is simply referred to as "Cristóbal de Colomo, foreigner" or "Xrobal Coloma" with no qualifying adjective. By contrast, other foreign mariners were invariably identified in royal documents as to their place of origin: "Fernando Magallanes, Portuguese," for example, and "Amerigo Vespucci, Florentine." Also curious is that ambassadors from Genoa to the court of Ferdinand and Isabella, at the time of Columbus' return from his first voyage to the New World in 1493, said not a word about his being one of their countrymen in letters they wrote home.[8]

Cristoforo Colombo, the man from Genoa the standard account maintains was the very same master mariner who discovered America, was born in 1451. He was the grandson of Giovani Colombo and son of Susanna and Dominico Colombo and entered adulthood as a wool carder like his father. No record exists of his having been to sea before 1478, when existing documents indicate he traveled to Madeira to purchase sugar, presumably by boat. The lack of evidence of early sailing experience is especially troubling to those who doubt this standard account because of the extraordinary nautical skill exhibited by Columbus in voyages beginning in 1492 (see Figure 7-2).[8]

The man who arrived in the kingdom of Castile in 1485 proposing to find a western route to the Indies was called Cristóbal Colon. Neither he nor anyone acquainted with him ever referred to him as *Cristoforo Colombo*. His surname was always given as *Colón, Colom* (a Catalan surname) or *Colomo*, all of which mean "dove." This same *Cristóbal Colon* was addressed as *don*, had his own coat-of-arms and married a Portuguese noblewoman, all before his historic voyage of 1492-1493. Some scholars believe this could only have been possible in the rigidly class-conscious Iberian society of the 15th century if he were of noble birth himself, completely out of the question if he had been the son of a humble wool carder from Genoa.[8]

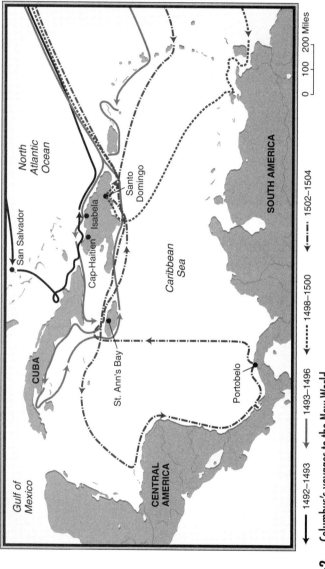

FIGURE 7-2. Columbus's voyages to the New World.

If Columbus did conceal his true origin, he most likely did so because he had fought against Ferdinand's cousin, King Ferrante of Naples in the Catalan civil war of 1462-1472, when circumstantial evidence indicates he was a captain in the navy of Rene d'Anjou, king of the rebellious Catalans, then at war with Ferdinand's father.[8] Many Portuguese fought on the Catalan side in that war, including Peter of Portugal, close relative of the Portuguese king. If this story is true, it explains how Columbus happened to be involved in a sea battle when wounded in his mid-thirties, where he honed his nautical skills, how he might have been introduced to the Portuguese noblewoman he married, and why he would have concealed his (Catalan) heritage from the royal couple who sponsored his voyages of discovery.

Whether or not Columbus began life as a privileged member of Iberian society, he was clearly one by the time he returned from his first voyage to America. As such, he would have had access to the very best medical care available when his arthritis first flared. Unfortunately, even the most skilled physicians of his day had little to offer patients with reactive arthritis.

Columbus' son, and apparently Columbus himself, believed his symptoms were the result of "always being exposed to cold and water and from eating (and sleeping) little."[7] There is no record of Columbus having been examined or treated by a physician. During his lifetime, medicine, like all of the sciences, was enjoying a period of revival and reformation known as the Renaissance, in which medical humanists struggled to reconcile Hellenist with Arabist doctrine.[33] The Aphorisms of Hippocrates were revived with the publication of several accurate Latin translations of the works of Galen. Therefore, it is likely that if Columbus had been attended by a physician, his symptoms would have been explained in humoralist terms and treated accordingly (see Chapter 2). Although clinicians had taken advantage of the anti-inflammatory properties of salicylate-containing plants to treat illnesses similar to Columbus for millennia (see Chapter 8), and, in the late 15th century, botanist commentators were beginning to lay the foundation for a *materia medica*, there is no evidence that Columbus received any treatment for his symptoms other than rest.

If Columbus had been treated by inhabitants of the islands he discovered, in keeping with their medical practices as described by his son, Ferdinand,[34] he would have been taken to the *buhuitihu* (doctor), who would have approached the illness by observing a diet just like the patient and assuming the same suffering expression. He would have purged himself along with the patient by sniffing a mysterious powder called "cohoba." The powder produced a disorienting intoxication in which the senseless things said were thought to come from "cemies" (the bones of ancestors) and to contain clues to the cause of the illness. As far as we know, Columbus received no such treatment.

Today, the symptoms of reactive arthritis are treated with anti-inflammatory drugs like indomethacin (indocin).[35] Aspirin, prednisone and most of the other drugs used to treat rheumatoid arthritis are ineffective. Although modern treatment provides symptomatic relief, it is no more effective in curing the disorder than those that might have been offered to Columbus five hundred years ago. In most cases the condition is self-limited, lasting no more than three months to a year. However, relapses occur in up to a third of patients, and in fifteen to twenty percent of cases the arthritis is both persistent and progressive.

When Columbus could no longer answer the call of the running tide because of his reactive arthritis, he asked to be "judged as a captain who went from Spain to the Indies to conquer a people numerous and warlike....whereby Spain, which was reckoned poor, is become the richest of countries."[36] He is remembered, of course, for a great deal more.

Notes

1. de Ybarra AMF. The medical history of Christopher Columbus. *JAMA*. 1894:22:647-54.
2. Shreve J. Christopher Columbus: a biographic voyage. *Choice.* 1991;29:703-11.
3. Letter to the Sovereigns written on October 18, 1498 during the third voyage to the New World.
4. Columbus, in fact, concluded from several faulty calculations that the earth "is not round in the form they [Ptolemy, etc.] describe, but that it is in the shape of a pear which is round everywhere but where the stalk is, for there it is higher; or that it is a very round ball, on one part of which is something like a woman's breast, and that this part of the stalk is the highest and nearest the heavens...." (Morison SE. *Admiral of the Ocean Sea. A Life of Christopher Columbus.* Vol 1&2, Little, Brown and Company, Boston: 1942, p. 284 [Vol 2]).
5. Entry in Columbus' journal during a delay at Baracoa on returning from his first voyage of discovery [Morrison 364].
6. Martin Alonso Pinzó, who commanded the *Pinta* during the first voyage of discovery, died shortly after returning from the New World. Although Columbus' son, Ferdinand, attributed his death to grief he experienced when denied the honor of presenting his account of the voyage to Ferdinand and Isabella, one wonders if he was actually the index case of the epidemic of syphilis that began ravaging Europe almost immediately upon his return (see Chapter 9). (Columbus, F. *The Life of the Admiral Christopher Columbus by His Son Ferdinand.* Translated and annotated by B. Keen. Greenwood Press, Westport, Conn: 1959, p. 101.)
7. Ibid p. 93.
8. The date of Columbus' birth is uncertain. According to the traditional account of his life, he was forty-one when he discovered America and only fifty-five when he died. However, recent

evidence reviewed later in this chapter suggests that he actually lived to be sixty to seventy years of age. Ages given in this chapter, which reflect the latter chronology, are eight years higher than those given in the traditional account of his life. (Arnett FC, Merrill C, Albardaner F, Mackowiak PA. A mariner with crippling arthritis and bleeding eyes. *Am J Med Sci.* 2006; 332:123-30.

9. Hoenig LJ. The arthritis of Christopher Columbus. *Arch Intern Med.* 1992;152:274-7.
10. Op cit (Morison) p. 79.
11. Op cit (Morison) p. 214-5.
12. Op cit (Morison) p. 340.
13. Op cit (Morison) p. 371
14. Op cit (Morison) p. 9.
15. Op cit (Morison) p. 32.
16. Op cit (Morison) p. 121-2.
17. Op cit (Morison) p. 299.
18. Op cit (Morison) p. 319.
19. Op cit (Morison) p. 140.
20. Op cit (Morison) p. 387-406.
21. Op cit (Morison) p. 407-20.
22. Landu-Beauvais AJ. Doit-on admettre une novelle espece de goutte sous la denomination de goutte primitive asthenique? *These de Paris.* 1800.
23. Buchanan WW. Rheumatoid arthritis: another New World disease? *Semin Arthritis Rheum.* 1994; 23:289-94.
24. Hough R. *Captain James Cook. A Biography.* W.W. Norton & Co. New York: 1994, p. 15-16.
25. Noer H.R. An "experimental" epidemic of Reiter's syndrome. *JAMA.* 1966;197:693-8.
26. Calin A, Fries JF. An "experimental" epidemic of Reiter's syndrome revisited. Follow-up evidence on genetic and environmental factors. *Ann Intern Med.* 1976;84:864-6.
27. Op cit (Morison) p. 253.
28. Albardaner F (personal communication).

29. Irving W. *The Life and Voyages of Christopher Columbus.* G.P. Putnam's Sons. New York: 1893, p. 184.

30. Cooper SM, Ferriss JA. Reactive arthritis and psittacosis. *Am J Med.* 1986;81:555-7.

31. Winchester RJ. Immunogenetics and the initiation of the immune response. In Kelly WN. *Textbook of Internal Medicine.* 2nd ed. J.B. Lippincott Co. Philadelphia: 1992, p. 874-80.

32. Colón, C. *Textos y Documentos Completos. Nuevas Cartas.* 2nd ed. Varela C and Gil J Eds. Alianza. Madrid: 1992.

33. Garrison FH. *An Introduction to the History of Medicine with Medical Chronology, Suggestions for Study and Bibliographic Data.* 4th ed. W.B. Saunders Co. Philadelphia: 1929, p. 193-201.

34. Op cit (Morison) p. 159.

35. Arnett FC. Spondyloarthropathies. In Kelly WN. *Textbook of Internal Medicine.* 2nd ed. J.B. Lippincott Co. Philadelphia: 1992, p. 923-6.

36. Letter to Doña Juana de Tores, October 1500.

SURELY THE GREATEST TRAGEDY IN THE HISTORY OF MUSIC

This patient was born on January 27, 1756, in the Austrian provincial city of Salzburg. His extraordinary talent was evident almost before he could walk. By the time he was three, he was already playing the harpsichord; at four he was composing minuets; and at seven violin sonatas. During his brief life, he produced six hundred twenty-six works in all, including twenty-two operas, twenty-seven string quartets, forty violin sonatas, fifty symphonies, twenty-eight piano concertos and seventeen masses. As he approached his thirty-sixth birthday, he was preoccupied with his last major work, a mysteriously commissioned Requiem that would prove to be an omen of his own impending death from a strange illness, the exact nature of which has been debated by biographers and historians for over 200 years.

Its official diagnosis was *hitziges Frieselfieber*, "acute miliary fever," which implies that the dominant features of the fatal disorder were fever and a rash.[1] Rash, however, was never mentioned in eyewitness accounts of the patient's final illness, and fever was referred to only tangentially.[2]

In many ways, his last illness was simply the finale of a life-long fugue of pernicious disorders that began at birth. His parents, who knew little of the nutritional requirements of infants, believed that simple barley water was the only proper food for babies, and of their seven children, only the patient and his older sister, Nannerl, survived infancy.

Toward the end of his sixth year, when the patient was already a musical sensation, he came down with "catarrh" (an upper respiratory infection) during a journey on the Danube from Linz. At the time he was giving harpsichord recitals in one of many exhausting tours organized by his ambitious father. Seventeen days later, while performing in Vienna, he developed an attack of fever accompanied by a few painful, tender, very red and slightly raised spots, the size of an old English penny, which were distributed over his shins, elbows and buttocks. Over a period of about a week, the spots increased in size but not in number. Today, physicians have a name for the condition, erythema nodosum, but little understanding of why it develops. The spots kept the patient in bed for eleven days and although treated with medicinal powders of uncertain composition, most likely disappeared on their own.[3]

A month later, the patient was ill again, this time with fever and rheumatism in his feet so severe he was unable to stand. Two months passed before he recovered sufficiently to resume his performances. He had identical attacks of fever and intense pain in his toes, feet and knees when he was seven and ten years of age (generally believed to have been episodes of acute rheumatic fever).

In 1765, when he was nine, the patient and his sister, Nannerl, were both stricken by a serious fever, now thought to have been either typhus or typhoid. They were visiting The Hague in the Netherlands in mid-September when Nannerl first became ill with a "cold." Although her symptoms improved after a few days, she then came down with chills, fever and an inflamed throat. After putting her to bed, her father called a Dr. Haymann, who bled her and was encouraged by an improvement in her pulse. Her fever persisted, however, and soon she became delirious. Fearing her lost, her father summoned a priest and then a Professor Thomas Schwenke, who noted a rash and offered a diagnosis of "pocks on the lungs."[4] To her parents' relief, she finally began to improve, and by mid-November was out of danger.

The patient came down with the same illness just as his sister began her recovery. According to their father, his son's case was so severe that during the month after Nannerl's recovery, the patient was reduced to "skin and his little bones."[5] Most of the time his tongue was dry and dirty and had to be moistened constantly. Three times his lips became hard and black after losing their covering. He was too weak to walk without assistance until the middle of January, when he finally recovered.

The patient also had recurrent episodes of "strep throat" during his early years, the first attack occurring when he was eight. According to his father, he was ill in bed for four days at that time with a sore throat and a very high fever. At one point, he appeared to be in danger of choking, which suggests that his throat infection might have been complicated by an abscessed tonsil. He was again treated with medicinal powders, violet juice and tamarind water and recovered.

The patient had smallpox when he was eleven, and when he was sixteen, shortly after completing his symphony in A major (K114), he had an episode of jaundice. He then enjoyed reasonably good health until age twenty-six, when he developed sweats, abdominal pain and vomiting, most likely due to exposure to a communicable virus or bacterium.[6]

In his thirties, the patient complained of headaches, inflamed tonsils and joints, stomach cramps and toothaches. These were especially troublesome during his thirty-fourth year, at least in part because his finances were in disarray, and his wife was away most of that year being treated for inflamed varicose veins. The patient sought relief in a variety of medications, but what they were, exactly, we have no way of knowing. All in all, these complaints were relatively minor when compared with those of his youth, and during his final year, except for two brief illnesses, he felt surprisingly well.

His sister, Nannerl, was five years older than the patient and far healthier. His mother lived to be fifty-seven but then developed a fever accompanied by a variety of symptoms, including headache, shaking chills, diarrhea, hoarseness, deafness and cough. Within a month she slipped into a coma and died. His father died at age seventy-nine. The old man had long suffered with rheumatism; however, what actually killed him is not known.

The patient was born with an oddly-shaped ear, but blessed with perfect pitch. His external ear lacked a lobe, and its helix (the fold forming the outer border) was unusually flat and smooth (see Figure 8-1). One of his sons had the same odd ear. His internal ear, however, was so finely tuned it could distinguish differences of just one-eighth of a tone.[7] A Salzburg neighbor, a professional musician named Johann Andreas Schachtner, recalled that one day when the patient was a young boy, he paid a visit and amused himself by playing on the neighbor's violin. A day or two later, when the neighbor dropped by to see the patient's family, the boy was playing his own violin and remarked offhandedly: "Your violin is tuned half a quarter tone lower than mine, if you left it tuned as it was last time I played it." This so astounded the neighbor that he fetched his violin immediately and discovered that the child's memory was correct.[8]

The patient was a small, kind-hearted man, very thin and pale, with a large head and an enormous nose inherited from his mother. His eyes were myopic. His plump hands were constantly in motion. His blondish hair was thick and it is said that he dressed it carefully, eschewing a wig as was then fashionable, to cover his abnormal ear.

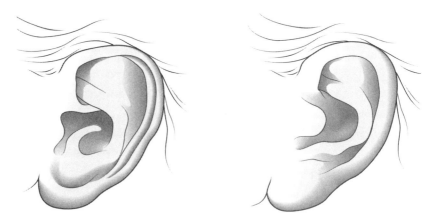

FIGURE 8-1. The patient's son's ear (left) compared with a normal ear (right).[35]

He was married and had two healthy sons. He drank wine and beer in moderation, though he was quite fond of punch. He delighted in billiards and dancing and occasionally smoked a pipe. He traveled extensively, but only throughout Europe, and had two pets, a canary and a dog. He loved to hear the former sing, but, oddly, as he lay dying, he asked that the bird be removed from his room.[9]

The patient's final illness apparently struck suddenly and was marked by a foul odor and progressive swelling of the entire body, which eventually became so pronounced the patient could barely move. In addition, he acquired such a foul odor that his wife, Constanze, and sister-in-law, Sophie Haibel, made him a special gown, one that opened in the back much like today's hospital gowns, in order to change him more easily.

In spite of his increasingly desperate condition, the patient remained alert; however, the illness moved swiftly. In just a few days, his appearance became greatly distorted by his crescendoing edema and he was barely recognizable. On the fourteenth day of his illness, his condition deteriorated sharply with the first signs of delirium. An urgent call went out to his family physician, Dr. Nickolaus Closset, who was at the theater and waited until the play he was watching was over before coming. When he finally arrived, Closset bled the patient in a futile attempt to reverse the progression of the disorder and then had cold compresses applied to the patient's head. Shortly thereafter, on the fifteenth day of the illness, December 5, 1791, the patient shuddered, vomited a great brown arch, and died.[10] He was seven weeks shy of his thirty-sixth birthday.

Two days later, the body of Wolfgang Amadeus Mozart was taken to a cemetery in the village of St. Marx, some five kilometers outside of Vienna. In accordance with edicts promulgated by a Hapsburg monarchy appalled by the cost of lavish funerals, the body was interred in a common grave, doused with quicklime to hasten decomposition and covered with earth. No permanent marker was erected to commemorate the site (see Figure 8-2).

FIGURE 8-2. Wolfgang Amadeus Mozart in Verona, January 1770. Saverio della Rosa. Oil on canvas. Mozart House, Salzburg, Austria. Photo Credit: Erich Lessing/Art Resource, NY.

***

In the two centuries since Mozart's death, many theories have been offered to explain his final illness. They have varied from homicide to acute rheumatic fever. None has settled the controversy, in no small part because of limitations of the medical record. What we have by way of a case history consists mainly of reminiscences of family members unsophisticated in medical concepts or terminology, composed decades after the event, and almost certainly corrupted by faltering memories and hidden agendas.

Little remains of the observations or conclusions of Mozart's physicians, and those terse recollections that do exist add little to the lay accounts. Moreover, time transforms the medical concepts and terminology that determine what clinicians see and how they describe their findings, in many cases to the extent that today's clinicians are hard-pressed to interpret conclusions reached by colleagues of only a few generations earlier. Even terminology preserved from one generation to the next poses potential problems in interpretation. Today, for example, the term "syphilis" is applied narrowly to infections caused by the bacterium, *Treponema pallidum*. In Mozart's day, syphilis was a generic diagnosis applied broadly to a range of venereal infections, including *Treponema pallidum* infection, but also gonorrhea and other sexually transmitted diseases.[11] Consequently, one cannot assume that a diagnosis of "miliary fever," rendered over two hundred years ago, necessarily corresponds to the condition such terminology evokes in the mind of today's clinicians: fever accompanied by a diffuse rash composed of spots the size of millet seeds.

There is also the problem of evolution. Diseases, like the animals they attack, evolve over time. Syphilis, again, is a case in point. Five hundred years ago, during epidemics that ravaged Europe just after Columbus' return from the New World (see Chapter 7), syphilis was a rapidly progressive and frequently fatal disorder. Today it is a much less aggressive infection, which kills only rarely and, even then, *sotto voce* over many decades, presumably because five hundred years of evolution have created both a less aggressive *T. pallidum* and a more resistant human host.

Additional problems arise because only recently have clinicians had access to diagnostic tools now regarded as fundamental to clinical examinations. For example, the stethoscope was not introduced into clinical practice until 1819, some twenty-eight years after Mozart's death.[12] Prior to that time, clinicians had no effective means of evaluating the heart or the lungs. Similarly, although crude thermometers were used in medical experiments as early as the 16th century, measurements of body temperature did not become routine in the clinical setting until 1868, when Carl Reinhold August Wunderlich published his seminal work, *Das Verhalten der Eigenwärm in Krankheiten (The Course of Temperature in Diseases)*.[13] Likewise, the sphygmomanometer, which is used to measure blood pressure, was not available to clinicians until the late 19th century. Thus, even if they had recorded their observations for posterity, Mozart's physicians lacked the necessary clinical tools to provide even the most basic data from which a modern clinician might glean a correct diagnosis.

These limitations of the clinical record aside, there are certain features of Mozart's final illness that seem reasonably certain. His illness was acute, and it began suddenly and killed him quickly. Although Mozart was sickly most of his life, he was uncharacteristically fit during the year preceding his final illness. To be sure, he seems to have worked to the point of nervous exhaustion that final year. However, he did not exhibit signs of unrelenting ill health, as some biographers have suggested.[14] In July 1791, four months before he died, for example, he wrote, "as to my health, I feel pretty well."[15] In October, his appetite was hearty enough for him to write to Constanze of the arrival of his valet with pork cutlets for his supper, exclaiming *"Che gusto!"* (How delicious!) The very next evening, he exhibited sufficient vigor and youthful zest to play a practical joke on his partner, Shikaneder, by banging a glockenspiel off stage while Shikaneder was performing the part of Papageno in *The Magic Flute*. Later that evening he ate sturgeon, exclaiming "as I have a rather voracious appetite today, I have sent [my valet] out to fetch some more."[15] The next day Mozart slept well and thoroughly enjoyed half a capon for breakfast. On October 15 he again wrote animatedly about arrangements for his supper, as well as of the good health and future education of his elder son, whom he had just taken to see *The Magic Flute*.[15]

A further indication of Mozart's vigor during the year or so preceding his final illness is that he remained sufficiently potent to father his last child, conceived less than fourteen months before he died. Moreover, his productivity at that time can only be described as prodigious. He composed virtually all of his opera, *La Clemenza di Tito*, for the coronation of Emperor Leopold II in an astonishingly short eighteen days;[16] and, in his final ten weeks, he completed *The Magic Flute*, and a clarinet concerto, composed a cantata for his Masonic Lodge and began work on his Requiem Mass (see Figure 8-3).

FIGURE 8-3. Mozart's last work, "The Requiem," was not finished when he died. This original shows his last notes. Oesterreichische Nationalbibliothek, Vienna, Austria. Photo Credit: Erich Lessing/Art Resource, NY.

Although the official diagnosis suggests otherwise, aside from its fatal outcome, the most striking feature of Mozart's last illness was edema, edema so pronounced that according to his son, Carl Thomas: "a few days before [he] died, his whole body became so swollen that he was unable to make the smallest movement...." Carl Thomas also described a "stench, which reflected an internal disintegration and after death increased to the extent that an autopsy was rendered impossible."[17]

Mozart was far from the only resident of Vienna taken by the illness. According to Dr. Eduard Vincent Guldener von Lobes, who was consulted by the clinicians caring for the composer during his final illness: "A great number of the inhabitants of Vienna were at this time laboring under the same complaint, and the number of cases which terminated fatally, like that of Mozart's, was considerable. I saw the body after death, and it exhibited no appearances beyond those usual in such cases."[18]

What is less certain about Mozart's final illness, the official diagnosis notwithstanding, is whether fever or rash or pain (due to inflamed muscles or joints) were prominent features. Each of these complaints has been critical to one or more of the most popular theories as to the cause of his fatal disorder. Yet, the written record does not mention a rash (except in the form of the official diagnosis) and offers only scant evidence of the existence of either fever or painful joints or muscles.

With respect to fever, we cannot ignore the official diagnosis, *hitziges frieselfieber* (acute miliary fever), which suggests that the illness was a febrile disorder. And yet, Mozart's sister-in-law, Sophie Haibel, does not mention fever in her account except to say that her brother-in-law's family physician, Dr. Nickolaus Closset, "ordered cold poultices to be placed on Mozart's *burning* head" just before he died.[2] She never mentions fever, per se, nor is there specific mention of it in other references to Mozart's illness. Nevertheless, in view of Haibel's statement regarding Mozart's "burning head" and the official diagnosis ("acute military fever"), it must be assumed that fever was present during the final illness. However, because fever is mentioned only tangentially in eyewitness descriptions, it was not likely a dominant feature of the illness, and might well have been limited to its terminal phase.

Several authorities have suggested that Mozart's inability to turn in bed was not so much a consequence of his edema as the result of painful joints or muscles. His sister-in-law, however, was clear on this matter, stating that "...on account of his swollen condition he was unable to turn in bed."[2] This is why she and Constanze made Mozart a night-jacket, which opened at the back to make it easier to change.

In an autobiographical note for the *Allegemeine Musikalische Zeitung*, Joseph Eybler, a protégé of Mozart and a member of the "Requiem team," refers to Mozart's "painful last illness," again implying that pain might have been a feature of that illness.[19] Likewise, Vincent and Mary Novello, an English music publisher and wife, who wrote a biography of Mozart based on interviews with Constanze, described the composer's limbs as "much inflamed and swollen."[20] Although these two statements imply that Mozart might have been in pain during his final illness, the former does not necessarily imply *physical* pain, nor does it indicate the location of such pain, if, in fact, it was physical. Moreover, the latter statement might simply have been a tautology, in which the Novellos were equating swelling with inflammation. In view of Haibel's failure to mention pain in her account, it seems likely that Mozart was not in great physical pain during his final illness, or that his pain, if it existed, was present only terminally.

Thus, the limited historical record describes an acute illness having a *tempo agitato* and massive edema as its most striking features. The illness appears to have simultaneously attacked other residents of Vienna. It was a malodorous and most likely febrile disorder. Possibly, it also caused muscle or joint pains. What could it have been?

A systematic approach to diagnostic conundrums generally begins with a distillation of the clinical history, physical examination and preliminary laboratory data into an inventory of essential elements similar to the one provided above. Next, the distillate is scrutinized for evidence pointing to a specific organ or organ system as the disorder's primary target. And finally, a prioritized list is generated of those diseases most often attacking the organ or organ system identified and producing the essential signs and symptoms exhibited by the illness in question.

The second phase of this clinical problem-solving technique, that is, the phase in which an attempt is made to identify the disorder's primary target, must take into account that diseases, like symphonic compositions, are complex entities. Some take the form of concertos in which the disability of a single organ plays the dominant part. Endocarditis is an example. It is primarily a bacterial infection of heart valves. However, secondary spread of the infection to other organs brings them into the pathological composition as well, albeit in supporting roles. Occasionally, diseases assume the form of concerto grossos in which multiple organs become involved simultaneously in a cacophony of disordered function. Bacterial sepsis and leukemias are examples of such diseases.

With regard to Mozart's terminal illness, three organs deserve special attention in the search for a primary target: the heart, the liver and the kidneys, for diseases targeting these three organs are the ones most often causing edema of the magnitude and distribution of that described by Haibel.

When the heart fails, because of disordered valves or cardiac muscle, diminished blood flow to vital organs such as the liver and kidneys causes a cascade of compensatory hemodynamic and hormonal mechanisms to be activated which directs the kidneys to reduce their excretion of salt and water. The net effect is an accumulation of salt and water, which in time manifests as edema. If the primary defect is with the muscle or valves of the left side of the heart, the side which siphons oxygen-enriched blood from the pulmonary vessels and delivers it to oxygen-hungry tissues throughout the body, the edema accumulates first and most strikingly in the lungs (see Chapter 4). In such cases, shortness of breath is the earliest and the most prominent symptom. If the defect is with the right side of the heart, the side which returns oxygen-depleted blood from peripheral veins to the pulmonary circulation for reoxygenation, dependent edema, primarily of the legs, is the most prominent symptom. Mozart exhibited the latter, but not the former type of edema. Thus, if his final illness was one primarily attacking the heart, its specific target would have to have been the right side of the heart.

Peripheral edema is also a complication of cirrhosis of the liver. In patients with cirrhosis, edema is characteristically a late manifestation of an illness, such as alcoholic or viral hepatitis, which has droned on for years. The mechanisms responsible for the edema of cirrhosis are similar to those of edema due to heart failure. In cirrhosis, however, reduced blood flow to vital organs is the result of a low blood *volume* rather than inadequate blood *flow* due to pump failure. Nevertheless, the net effect is the same. Activation of hemodynamic and hormonal responses again causes the kidneys to retain salt and water, which accumulate in the form of edema. Initially, the excess edema fluid oozes into the abdominal cavity from abdominal veins engorged with blood no longer able to pass through the fibrotic liver. For this reason, edema in patients with cirrhosis tends to be most pronounced in the abdomen.

Of all the diseases producing edema, those attacking the kidneys (especially those that attack the kidneys' microscopic filters, the *glomeruli*) are the ones most often causing generalized edema of the magnitude described by Sophie Haibel. The glomeruli filter water, salt and waste products from the blood and deliver them to a series of collecting ducts in which they are processed into urine. When glomeruli are damaged, blood proteins (albumin, in particular) leak through these microscopic filters into the collecting ducts and are lost in the urine. Because such proteins have a magnetic (osmotic) effect on water, when their concentration in the blood falls (as, for example, because of glomerulonephritis) salt, water and waste products begin to escape from porous capillaries throughout the body into surrounding tissues to create generalized edema. This activates the same compensatory mechanisms described above, leading to a vicious cycle of salt and water retention and progressive edema formation, which over time, creates an edema so massive and so generalized, that modern clinicians have given it its own name: "anasarca."

Thus, Mozart's generalized edema, his *anasarca*, points to his kidneys as the most likely primary target of his final illness. As the most striking feature of that illness, the anasarca suggests further that the glomerulus was the specific structure within the kidney attacked. Of the long list of disorders of glomeruli, only a few merit consideration given Mozart's clinical history.

Could Mozart's glomeruli have been damaged by a poison? It is a possibility worth considering, if for no other reason than the suddenness of Mozart's death immediately gave rise to rumors of poisoning.[21] In her interview with the Novello's, Constanze fanned the flames of such rumors by reporting that some six months before he died, Mozart exclaimed "I know I must die, someone has given me acqua toffana (arsenic) and has calculated the precise time of my death, for which they have ordered a *Requiem*, it is myself I am writing this."[22]

Antonio Salieri, Mozart's rival and the tortured narrator of the movie, *Amadeus*, was an initial suspect, as were the Freemasons of Vienna. Salieri's purported motive was professional jealously. The fact that after Emperor Joseph II's death Mozart received no further commissions to write operas for the Viennese court where Salieri was *Kapellmeister* suggests that Salieri might indeed have been a thorn in Mozart's side for at least a decade before he died. Moreover, Beethoven's conversation books (see Chapter 9) are redolent with references to supposed fantasies of Salieri that he had poisoned Mozart.[23] However, in October 1823, Ignaz Moscheles, one of Beethoven's pupils, visited Salieri in the General Hospital in the Vienna suburb of Alservorstadt and was told by the dying composer:

> Although this is my last illness, I can assure you on my word of honour that there is no truth in that absurd rumour; you know that I am supposed to have poisoned Mozart. But no, it's malice, pure malice, tell the world, dear Moscheles, old Salieri, who will soon die, has told you.[23]

If the Freemasons had murdered Mozart, their motive would have been retribution for having revealed the secrets of the order's sacred symbolism in *The Magic Flute* through a whole series of hints that would have been obvious to Masons in the audience. The symbolic figure three, for example, dominates the entire work: three flats in the signature of the principal key (E flat major), three boys, three ladies. There is also the character of Tamino, who is shown initially as a 'profane' (i.e., non-Mason), then a 'seeker,' a young Mason, a second-degree, Fellow Craft and finally a third-degree Master Mason.[24]

Speculation that Mozart was murdered by the Masons emerged immediately after his death, waned for a time and then reemerged in 1971 with the publication of a book titled *Mozart's Tod*, in which three German physicians theorized that his lodge was not only guilty of the crime but committed it as a "ritual murder." Several facts, however, render their theory highly improbable. First, Emanuel Schikaneder for whom Mozart wrote the opera, and was thus just as responsible for betraying the Masonic secrets, was not killed. In fact, he lived another twenty years after Mozart's death. In addition, Mozart's own (Masonic) lodge held a *Lodge of Sorrows* for the dead composer, published the ceremony's main speech, printed the cantata (K.623) he had composed for them just before he died and also supported his wife in the aftermath of his tragic death.[25]

In the unlikely event that Mozart was poisoned, mercury would almost certainly have been the agent used. Not only had it been used medicinally for centuries, and was thus readily available in 1791 to would-be assassins, it is also toxic to the kidneys. Even if Salieri and the Masons were innocent of the crime, as most scholars now believe, Mozart might yet have poisoned himself with either mercury or some other nephrotoxic medication taken to relieve his myriad physical ailments. In fact, of Mozart's outstanding debts of 918Fl.16kr at the time of his death, 170 Fl.83kr (an amount slightly less than the annual stipend paid to Mozart by Archbishop Heironymus during his days in Salzburg) were owed to apothecaries, suggesting that he was, indeed, consuming large quantities of medications when he became ill for the last time.[26] Nevertheless, although mercury damages the kidneys, it poisons the kidneys' collecting tubules to a much greater extent than its glomeruli. Tubular damage causes relatively modest urinary protein losses and is, thus, not an important cause of anasarca. More important, neither mercury intoxication nor, for that matter, intoxication with any other poison, would explain the epidemic nature of Mozart's illness.

In the *Journal of the Royal Society of Medicine*, Peter J. Davies[3] has proposed another renal disorder, Henoch-Schonlein syndrome, as the cause of Mozart's final illness. Henoch-Schonlein syndrome is a mysterious disorder, sometimes preceded by an acute streptococcal infection. Although the precise triggering mechanism of the disorder is unknown, the syndrome's fundamental problem is one of a host of abnormal immunological reactions acting in concert to produce a generalized allergic inflammation of small blood vessels. Davies has suggested that streptococcal infections contracted earlier in life triggered prior episodes of the syndrome and in the process sensitized Mozart to the lethal effects of a particularly severe terminal episode of the disorder. By damaging small vessels throughout the body, Henoch-Schonlein syndrome produces bowel symptoms (such as abdominal pain and diarrhea), joint pains and rash. It also damages the glomeruli. Thus, it could explain many of the features of Mozart's final illness. However, it is uncommon after the age of twenty-one (Mozart was almost thirty-six when he died), does not occur in epidemics and is rarely fatal.[27]

Mozart's early episodes of rheumatic fever have suggested to some that he might have had rheumatic heart disease. It has even been proposed that his final illness was a fulminant episode of acute rheumatic fever, another immunological disorder triggered by streptococcal infections.[7] Acute rheumatic fever is a clinical diagnosis based on criteria proposed by T. Duckett Jones in 1948. To qualify as acute rheumatic fever, an illness must exhibit two of Jones' major criteria or one major and two minor criteria in conjunction with evidence of a preceding streptococcal infection (one caused by streptococci belonging to Lancefield group A). Jones' major criteria consist of inflammation of the heart (carditis), an incapacitating arthritis involving several joints, bizarre spasms of the limbs and facial muscles (chorea) and an unusual rash known as "erythema marginatum." The minor criteria include a history of previous rheumatic fever or rheumatic heart disease, painful joints, fever and a number of abnormal but nonspecific laboratory test results. It is doubtful that Mozart exhibited any of Jones' major criteria. The official diagnosis ("acute miliary fever") suggests he had a rash, but not likely the particular one seen in patients with acute rheumatic fever, *erythema marginatum* (an evanescent, red and serpiginous rash involving the trunk, upper arms and legs). If he had arthritis, as suggested by the Novellos' reference to his "inflamed and swollen" limbs, there is no evidence that it was the peculiar type of migratory arthritis of acute rheumatic fever which moves in a characteristic fashion from one joint to another. With respect to minor Jones criteria, Mozart had only those of prior episodes of rheumatic fever as a child and, perhaps, a fever during his final illness.

Thus, it would be difficult to incriminate acute rheumatic fever as the cause of Mozart's final illness. It can cause edema by impairing cardiac function. However, because rheumatic fever attacks the left side of the heart, its edema almost always accumulates first in the lungs, thereby causing severe shortness of breath (see above). The absence of respiratory distress from Mozart's clinical record, therefore, argues against acute rheumatic fever as the cause of his final illness. Moreover, acute rheumatic fever is a disease primarily of children. Even persons who have had attacks early in life rarely suffer recurrences as adults. When rheumatic fever does attack adults, it tends to settle in joints rather than in the heart.

If acute rheumatic fever didn't kill Mozart directly, it might yet have done so indirectly by damaging heart valves during childhood, thereby rendering them susceptible to bacterial attack later in life. Such infections are known as *bacterial endocarditis*. They are typically febrile and, although originating on heart valves, tend to disseminate via the bloodstream throughout the body. With dissemination to the skin, a pleomorphic rash develops, sometimes in the form of a *miliary* eruption (i.e., one with spots the size of *millet* seeds) of tiny red or blue spots involving the arms and legs. Joints may become inflamed, either because of direct invasion by bacteria or as a result of the action of antibodies generated in response to the infection which attack joint tissues as well as the bacteria against which they have been generated. The glomeruli may become inflamed for similar reasons, producing anasarca through mechanisms outlined above. Thus, bacterial endocarditis might have caused all of the reported features of Mozart's terminal illness. Bacterial endocarditis, however, is not an epidemic disorder and thus, could not explain the many other cases of disease identical to Mozart's diagnosed in Vienna by Dr. von Lobes the year the composer died.

Shortly after Mozart's death, stories of extramarital affairs began to circulate.[28] He was, after all, a bona fide celebrity in the prime of life, who spent much of his final year separated from his wife. Moreover, many composers of his era had mistresses. Salieri, for example, had the singer, Caterina Cavalieri. Hayden had Luigia Polzelli. Mozart entertained Salieri and Cavalieri only months before he died.[28] Could his final illness have been syphilis contracted in the course of similar extra-marital dalliances?

Syphilis, long referred to as the "great pox," is an epidemic disorder sometimes accompanied by low-grade fever and noted for its protean rash (see Chapter 9). Thus it was in 1791, as it is today, a cause of "epidemic miliary fever." It also attacks glomeruli and is thus a potential cause of anasarca. Moreover, in Mozart's day, it was frequently treated with mercury,[29] which, as already mentioned, is toxic to the kidneys. Add to this Mozart's outstanding apothecary bills, and one must wonder if "the great pox" was not his undoing, either in the form of malignant syphilis or a complication of its treatment. Today, as noted above, syphilis is a chronic rather than an acute infection. Nevertheless, as recently as the turn of the last century, Osler described an acute, febrile form of syphilis involving the kidneys, which "proved rapidly fatal in a fortnight or three weeks,"[30] precisely the time course of Mozart's final illness. Such fulminant courses, however, were rare even in Osler's day. Moreover, Mozart's work habits were not conducive to dalliance. He habitually worked from early morning until ten at night when he took his only meal of the day, and he loved his wife dearly, dedicating many (unfinished) compositions to her. There is no credible evidence that Mozart was ever unfaithful to Constanze, or for that matter, she to him.

Dr. Jan Hirshmann has offered one of the most recent and innovative theories to explain Mozart's final illness.[31] He believes that Mozart died of trichinosis, which the composer contracted from the pork cutlet he raved about a little over a month before he died (see above), a cutlet Hirschmann believes was infested with larvae of *Trichina spiralis*, a parasitic worm of muscles. In fatal cases of trichinosis, larvae released from infested meat during digestion penetrate the intestinal wall, enter the bloodstream and attack tissues indiscriminately. Although any tissue is a potential target, the larvae of *T. spiralis* attack muscles with particular ferocity. Thus, the most striking feature of trichinosis, even the most severe cases, is muscle pain. One can also see puffiness around the eyes and swelling of affected muscle groups. However, massive edema (anasarca) would be unusual. Moreover, if Mozart died of fulminant trichinosis, his inflamed muscles would have caused pain so extreme that even after twenty-eight years, his sister-in-law would have remembered pain as the most striking and terrifying feature of the illness, not swelling massive enough to prevent him from turning in bed.

Could Mozart have had a congenital (hereditary) disorder of glomeruli, one responsible for his fragile health as a child, which took thirty-six years to kill him? Alport's syndrome is a congenital kidney disorder with a number of features compatible with Mozart's various illnesses.[32] It is a disorder marked by progressive inflammation of the glomeruli (a condition we now refer to as *glomerulonephritis*) and abnormal ears. It affects approximately one in five thousand persons, males as well as females, although it is substantially more severe in males. In the adult form of the disorder, men characteristically develop renal failure at precisely the age Mozart died, thirty-five. However, bloody urine (hematuria) is common; the "ear abnormality" is progressive deafness, not a deformed external ear; and the disorder does not occur in epidemics.

What then could have been the cause of Mozart's final illness? It would have to have been a disorder capable of producing an acute, most likely febrile, inflammatory derangement of glomeruli (a glomerulonephritis) having the potential to dispatch its victim swiftly. It would have to have been an epidemic form of glomerulonephritis capable of affecting substantial numbers of persons simultaneously, and, possibly, one capable of inflaming muscles or joints.

Acute post-streptococcal glomerulonephritis is just such a disorder. It is an inflammatory disorder of glomeruli. It is an acute illness, which occasionally appears in epidemics. One of its most striking and consistent features is generalized edema. Fever is less common but develops in approximately half the cases. However, muscle and joint pains are not prominent. Moreover, classical post-streptococcal glomerulonephritis (glomerulonephritis caused by *Streptococcus pyogenes* [the streptococcus responsible for "strep throat," belonging to the group of streptococci known as *Lancefield group A*]) is a disease primarily of children between the ages of two and ten years. Fewer than ten percent of cases are older than thirty years of age. Moreover, classical post-streptococcal glomerulonephritis is typically an acute but reversible condition in which patients normally recover fully within two to four weeks.

There is, however, another form of post-streptococcal glomerulonephritis which does attack adults, sometimes with fatal consequences. This type of glomerulonephritis is caused by streptococci belonging to a different Lancefield group, group C. The particular species of streptococcus responsible for such epidemics is one called *Streptococcus equi*. It primarily attacks horses, in which it causes *strangles*, a highly contagious disorder characterized by fever, inflamed lymph nodes (lymphadenitis) and abcesses of the head and neck. It is one of the most widespread and costly infections of horses worldwide.[33] It also infects cows. In rare instances in which humans are infected, generally after consuming milk or milk products contaminated with *S. equi*, the illness that follows is one characterized initially by fever, headache and muscle aches[34] and then, in a week or so, by bloody urine, kidney failure and anasarca. Rash is uncommon. Over ninety percent of the time the victim is an adult. One in fifty dies, even with the best care available today. One in twenty patients requires renal dialysis and, presumably, would have died in Mozart's time because such treatment was not available.

Thus, epidemic, acute post-streptococcal glomerulonephritis caused by milk or cheese contaminated with S. *equi* is a final and, in many respects, best explanation for Mozart's terminal illness. It would explain Mozart's edema, his fever, his pain and the epidemic nature of his illness. It would also explain his death, as well as the specific means by which his death came about. If Mozart did die of glomerulonephritis induced by S. *equi*, as the character of his illness suggests, his end might have been brought about by either fatal uremia (i.e., accumulation of metabolic waste products in his blood) or a cerebral hemorrhage due to malignant hypertension (see Chapter 12), which occurs in approximately a third of such patients. It would not explain Mozart's rash, if, indeed, he had one. However, it might explain the stench that so repulsed his son, Carl Thomas. When the kidneys fail, waste products of metabolism accumulate in the bloodstream, and then in sweat, saliva and other secretions, until the body reeks of urine. Modern day physicians call this stench of renal failure "uremic fetor."

Modern science has developed tools such as DNA hybridization, which when applied to historical specimens allow investigators to reach back in time to confirm or refute theories concerning the etiology of ancient diseases. Unfortunately, for those who would use such techniques to discover the cause of "the greatest tragedy in the history of music,"[35] the precise whereabouts of Mozart's remains are not likely ever to be known. Mozart was buried in a common grave (in accordance with edicts promulgated by the Hapsburg monarchy) in the cemetery of St. Marx, outside of Vienna. None of the funeral party, of whose identity we are ignorant, accompanied the corpse, and for years no one cared to discover where Mozart was buried.[36] One of many myths arising in the aftermath of his death is that Joseph Rothmayer, Sexton of St. Marx, marked the corpse so that it might be retrieved at a later date. Rothmayer did retrieve a skull, reportedly ten years after the fact in 1801, which eventually made its way to the Mozarteum in Salzburg where it now resides. The skull shows evidence of a calcified, chronic extradural hematoma arising from a linear fracture of the left temple. Unfortunately for the Mozarteum, Mozart had no history of head trauma,[37] suggesting that the skull in the museum's possession is that of some other departed soul.

It has been said of the 18th century in which Mozart lived that aside from the work of a few original spirits, it was essentially an age of theorists and system makers who adhered to a tedious and platitudinous philosophy of exaggerated sobriety and apparent contentment with the old order of things.[38] Nevertheless, as Mozart's century drew to a close a revolutionary era was awakening, one marked by spiritual and intellectual freedom and the birth of modern medicine, unfortunately too late to help Mozart. In 1761, for example, Leopold Auenbrugger (1722-1809 C.E.) introduced clinicians to the diagnostic value of percussion in his *Inventum Novum*.[39] His work went unnoticed, however, until taken up by Jean-Nicolas Corvisart (1755-1821) in 1808, just a year before Auenbrugger's death.[40] In 1785, William Withering (1741-1799) launched the modern age of therapeutics with his demonstration of the salutory effect of foxglove (digitalis) on dropsy (edema).[41] At the time, dropsy was thought to be a disease itself, rather than a manifestation of an underlying disorder. Thus, no distinction was made between edema of cardiac origin and that due to kidney failure until the work of Richard Bright (1789-1858) some half century later.[42] Mozart's dropsy, which was most likely renal in origin, would not have responded to foxglove because the drug is effective only against edema caused by heart failure. On May 14, 1796, Edward Jenner (1749-1823) introduced vaccination to the world and launched the golden age of preventive medicine. That was the day he successfully immunized a country boy by the name of James Phipps against smallpox using material from the arm of Sarah Nelmes, a milkmaid infected with cowpox.[43] His work, as well, was too late for Mozart, who had contracted smallpox as a child.

Thus, regardless of the cause of his final illness, Mozart's treatment would have been largely supportive, although in the final phase of his illness, he was bled in the hope of reversing his inexorable decline. At best, phlebotomy was ineffective; at worst it was an intervention that hastened death. If his illness had been acute rheumatic fever, he might have received salicylates (in the form of extracts of willow bark), as their salutory effect on inflammatory disorders was known as early as the Sumerian period.[44] Moreover, scientific proof of the anti-inflammatory property of salicylates entered the medical literature nearly thirty years before Mozart's death.[45] Unfortunately, the special capacity of salicylates to reverse the uncontrolled inflammation of acute rheumatic fever was not appreciated until 1876.[46]

If Mozart had been attended by modern day physicians, they would have given him antibiotics if endocarditis or syphilis were suspected. If his illness was diagnosed as acute rheumatic fever, salicylates in the form of high-dose aspirin would have been his treatment.[47] If aspirin produced intolerable gastric irritation or other toxicity, or if it failed to control the inflammatory process, corticosteroids would have been administered. Such therapy has proved highly effective in alleviating acute rheumatic carditis. However, neither salicylates nor corticosteroids prevents the development of chronic rheumatic heart disease.

Even today, little can be done for post-streptococcal glomerulonephritis. Its treatment is supportive, consisting of short-term management of fluid overload and hypertension with diuretics and other antihypertensive medications. In cases of glomerulonephritis induced by *S. equi*, dialysis may be life-saving. Such treatments obviously were not available in 1791, and, sadly, no physician of Mozart's era would have been able to prevent, "Surely the greatest tragedy in the history of music."[35]

Notes

1. "Friesel" (German for "milliaria") refers to a skin eruption of distinct, small nodules (papules) or blisters (vesicles) the size of millet seeds from which the name is derived.

2. The most extensive account of Mozart's final illness, unfortunately not produced until almost thirty-four years after the fact, was given by Sophie Haibel, Mozart's sister-in-law, in a letter to George Nicholaus Nissen to be included in his biography of Mozart. In the letter, she wrote:

> ....Now, when [he] fell ill, we both made him a night-jacket which he could put on frontways, since on account of his swollen condition he was unable to turn in bed. Then, as we didn't know how seriously ill he was, we also made him a quilted dressing-gown (though indeed his dear wife, my sister, had given us the materials for both garments), so that when he got up he should have everything he needed. We often visited him and he seemed to be really looking forward to wearing his dressing-gown. I used to go into town every day to see him. Well, one Saturday [3 December] when I was with him, [he] said to me: 'Dear Sophie, do tell Mamma that I am fairly well and that I shall be able to go and congratulate her on the octave of her name-day.' Who could have been more delighted than I to bring such cheerful news to my mother, who was ever anxious to hear how he was? I hurried home therefore to comfort her, the more so as he himself really seemed to be bright and happy. The following day [4 December] was a Sunday. I was young then and rather vain, I confess, and liked to dress up. But I never cared to go out walking from our suburb into town in my fine clothes, and I had no money for a drive. So I said to our good mother: 'Dear Mamma, I'm not going to see [him] today. He was so well yesterday that surely he will be much better this morning, and one day more or less won't make much difference.' Well, my mother said: 'Listen to this. Make a cup of coffee and then I'll tell you what you ought to do.' She was rather inclined to keep me at home; and indeed my sister knows how much I had to be with her. I went into the kitchen. The fire was out. I had to light the lamp and make a fire. All the time I was thinking of [him]. I had made the coffee and the lamp was still burning. Then I noticed how wasteful I had been with my lamp, I mean, that I had burned so

much oil. It was still burning brightly. I stared into the flame and thought to myself, 'How I should love to know how [he] is.' While I was thinking and gazing at the flame, it went out, as completely as if the lamp had never been burning. Not a spark remained on the main wick and yet there wasn't the slightest draught — that I can swear to. A horrible feeling came over me. I ran to our mother and told her all. She said: 'Well, take off your fine clothes and go into town and bring me back news of him at once. But be sure not to delay.' I hurried along as fast as I could. Alas, how frightened I was when my sister, who was almost despairing and yet trying to keep calm, came out to me, saying: 'Thank God that you have come, dear Sophie. Last night he was so ill that I thought he would not be alive this morning. Do stay with me today, for if he had another bad turn, he will pass away tonight. Go in to him for a little while and see how he is.' I tried to control myself and went to his bedside. He immediately called me to him and said: 'Ah, dear Sophie, how glad I am that you have come. You must stay here tonight and see me die.' I tried hard to be brave and to persuade him to the contrary. But to all my attempts he only replied: 'Why, I already have the taste of death on my tongue. And, if you do not stay, who will support my dearest Constanze when I am gone?' 'Yes, yes dear [.....], 'I assured him,' but I must first go back to our mother and tell her that you would like me to stay with you today. Otherwise she will think that some misfortune has befallen you.' 'Yes, do so,' said [he], 'but be sure and come back soon.' Good God, how distressed I felt! My poor sister followed me to the door and begged me for Heaven's sake to go to the priests at St Peter's and implore one of them to come to [him] – a chance call, as it were. I did so, but for a long time they refused to come and I had a great deal of trouble to persuade one of those clerical brutes to go to him. Then I ran off to my mother who was anxiously awaiting me. It was already dark. Poor soul, how shocked she was! I persuaded her to go and spend the night with her eldest daughter, the late Josepha Hofer. I then ran back as fast as I could to my distracted sister. Süssmayr was at [his] bedside. The well-known Requiem lay on the quilt and [he] was explaining to him how, in his opinion, he ought to finish it, when he was gone. Further, he urged his wife to keep his death a secret until she should have informed Albrechtsberger, who was in charge of all the services [at St Stephen's Cathedral]. A long search was made for Dr Closset, who was found at the theatre, but who had to wait for the end of the play. He came and ordered cold poultices to be placed on [his] burning head, which, however, affected him to such an extent that he became unconscious and remained so until he died. His last moment was an attempt to express with his mouth the drum passages in the Requiem. That I can still hear. Müller [21] from the Art Gallery came and took a cast of his pale, dead face. Words fail me, dearest brother, to describe how his devoted wife in her utter misery threw herself on her knees and implored the Almighty for His aid. She simply could not tear herself away from [him], however much I begged her to do so. If it was possible to increase her sorrow, this was done on the day after that dreadful night, when crowds of people walked past his corpse and wept and wailed for him.... (Robbins Landon, HC. 1791. Mozart's Last Year. New York: Thames and Hudson, 1999; p. 165-8).

3. Davies PJ. Mozart's illnesses and death. *J Roy Soc Med.* 1983; 76:776-85.

'Erythema nodosum' is a descriptive term which refers to multiple red, tender nodules appearing principally on the anterior aspects of the legs and occasionally the arms and face. The condition is associated with a number of unrelated disorders and, hence, not diagnostic of any particular disease.

4. Ibid

5. Ibid

6. Outlaw, KK, O'Leary, JP. Wolfgang Amadeus Mozart 1756-1791: a mysterious death. American Surgeon 1995; 61: 1025-7

7. In psychoacoustical terms, *half a quarter tone* is a difference of 25 *cents,* cents being a logarithmic scale used to measure dis-

tances between pitches, in which 100 cents equal the distance between any two adjacent semitones as found, for instance, on the modern piano. Because the "just noticeable difference" (JND), of human pitch perception is around half a cent, a difference of 25 cents can readily be perceived when confronted with the two pitches in close juxtaposition, but can only be recalled by someone who has well-developed absolute pitch, that is, the ability to recognize or produce any musical pitch in the absence of other pitches. Some absolute pitch is found in fewer than 1% of the general population. The patient was gifted, although not extraordinarily so, for 15% to 17% of musicians are similarly blessed. (Fitzgerald FT, Zaslaw N, Mackowiak PA: Noble heart. *Am J Med.* 2001;110:633- 40.)

8. Ibid.
9. Ibid.
10. Case history derived from the following sources:
    (a.) Deutsch OE. *Mozart. A Documentary Biography.* 2nd ed. London: Adam & Charles Black, 1966.
    (b.) Anderson E. *The Letters of Mozart and His Family.* 3rd ed. New York: St. Martin's Press. 1985.
    (c.) Haibel S. *Memoirs 1828. A Documentary Biography.* Stanford, Calif: Stanford University Press; 1967.
    (d.) Jenkins JS. The medical history and death of Mozart. *JR Coll Phys London.* 1991;25:351-2.
    (e.) Carp L. Mozart: his tragic life and controversial death. *Bull NY Acad Med.* 1970;46:267-80.
    (f.) Davies PJ. Mozart's illness and death. *J Roy Soc Med.* 1983;76:776-85.
    (g.) Sakula A. The death of Mozart: a bicentenary medical review. *Tans Med Soc London.* 1991;107:21-6.
    (h.) Treves R. Mozart's death. *Ann Rheum Dis.* 1991;50:963-4.
    (i.) Kubba AK, Young M. Wolfgang Amadeus Mozart. A case report. *J R Coll Surg Edinburgh.* 1996;41:44-7.
11. In 1767, John Hunter (1728-1793), the foremost surgical investigator of his age, conducted experiments to determine

whether syphilis and gonorrhea are one in the same or different diseases. Unfortunately, the experiment involved inoculation of pus obtained from a patient suffering with both syphilis and gonorrhea. The experimental subject who some believe was Hunter himself, developed both infections, leading Hunter to conclude that gonorrhea and syphilis were the same disease, thus perpetuating a misconception that was to persist for another century. Hunter J. A treatise on the venereal disease. In Major RM. *Classic Descriptions of Disease.* Charles C. Thomas, Publisher. Springfield:1995, p. 45-6. London, Sherwood, Neely and Jones, 1818. p. 449 9. Tramont EC: Treponema pallidum (syphilis). In Mandell GL, Bennett JE, Dolin R, Eds. *Principles and Practice of Infectious Diseases.* Churchill Livingstone. Philadelphia: 2000, p. 2474.

12. Laennec, R-T-H. *A Treatise on the Diseases of the Chest and on Mediate Auscultation.* Translated by John Forbes, Samuel Wood and Sons. New York:1830; p. 339.

13. Mackowiak PA. Carl Reinhold August Wunderlich and the evolution of clinical thermometry. *Clin Infect Dis.* 1994;18: 458-67.

14. Jenkins JS: The medical history and death of Mozart. *J Roy Coll Phys.* London 1991;25:351-3.

15. Op cit (Anderson) p. 659;967-71.

16. Robbins Landon, HC. *1791: Mozart's Last Year.* New York: Thames and Hudson, 1999; p. 99.

17. Op Cit (Robbins Landon) p. 159.

18. Op Cit (Robbins Landon) p. 175.

19. Joseph Eybler, a friend of Hayden's and a protégé of Mozart's, was the third member of the "Requiem Team" recruited by Constanze Mozart to complete her husband's unfinished Requiem mass. The other two members of the team were Franz Xaver Süssmayr and F. J. Freystädtler. Süssmayr, whose handwriting was the most like Mozart's, was the main copyist. He was also chosen to falsify Mozart's signature on the first page: 'di me W:A:Mozart mpria.' 792 [Op Cit (London) p. 161].

20. Vincent Novello was a British composer and publisher. In 1829 C.E., he and his wife Marg traveled to Salzburg to present to Mozart's aged and invalid sister a modest sum of money for materials they intended to use in a biography of the composer. They succeeded in obtaining an audience with Constanze and recorded their numerous conversations with her in diaries which have been invaluable to students of Mozart's life. [Op Cit (London) p 154].

21. Op Cit (Robbins Landon) p. 172.

22. Novello V, Novello M. *A Mozart Pilgrimage. Being the Travel Diaries of Vincent and Mary Novello in the Year 1829.* Maignano N, Hughes R, Eds. London: Novello & Co. 1955.

23. Op cit (Robbins Landon) p. 172-3.

24. Ibid p.129.

25. Ibid p.132.

26. Ibid p. 30.

27. Mills JA, Michel BA, Bloch DA, et al. The American College of Rheumatology 1990 criteria for the classification of Henoch-Schönlein purpura. *Arthritis Rheum.* 1990;33:1114-21.

28. Op Cit (Robbins Landon) p. 138, 144, 180.

29. Duncan A. *The Edinburgh New Dispensary.* T. Dobson, Philadelphia: 1790; p. 434.

30. Osler W. *The Principles and Practice of Medicine.* D. Appleton and Co. New York: 1905, p. 277.

31. Hirschmann JV. What killed Mozart? *Arch Intern Med.* 2001; 161:1381-89.

32. Gregory MC, Atkin CL. Hereditary nephropathies. Alport's syndrome. In *Textbook of Internal Medicine.* 2nd ed. Kelley WN, Ed. JB lippincott Co. Philadelphia: 1992. p. 737-8.

33. Harrington DJ, Sutcliffe IC, Chanter N. The molecular basis of *Streptococcus equi* infection and disease. *Microbes Infect.* 2002; 4:501-10.

34. Balter S, Benin A, Pinto SWL, et al. Epidemic nephritis in Nova Serrana, Brazil. *Lancet.* 2000;355:1776-80.

35. Op cit (Robbins Landon) p. 147.

36. Op Cit (Robbins Landon) p. 170.

37. Sakula A. The death of Mozart: a bicentenary medical review. *Trans Med Soc London.* 1991;107:21-6.

38. Garrison FH. *An Introduction to the History of Medicine.* 4th ed. W. B. Saunders Co. Philadelphia:1929, p. 310.

39. Ibid p 352-3.

40. Ibid p 414.

41. Ibid p 356-357.

42. Ibid p 421.

43. Ibid p 372-5.

44. Mackowiak PA. Brief history of antipyretic therapy. *Clin Infect Dis.* 2000;31(S5):s154-6.

45. Stone E. An account of the success of the bark of the willow in the cure of agues. *Philos Trans R Soc London.* 1763;53:195-200.

46. MacLagan TJ. The treatment of rheumatism by salicin and salicylic acid. *Lancet.* 1876;I:342.

47. Bisno AL. Nonsuppurative post streptococcal sequellae: rheumatic fever and glomerulonephritis. In Mandell GL, Bennett JE, Dolin R, Eds. *Principles and Practice of Infectious Diseases.* 5th ed. Philadelphia: Churchill Livingstone;2000:2121-2.

48. Adapted from a lithograph from Georg Nikolaus von Nissen, *Biographie W. A. Mozart's. Nach Originalbriefen, Sammlungen alles über ihn Geschriebenen, mit vielen neuen Beylagen, Steindrücken, Musikblättern und einem Facsimile,* Leipzig, 1828.

9

THE SOUND THAT FAILED

Sound first began to fail this patient when he was twenty-six. It was then that he began to lose his capacity to hear the majestic creations that were his gift to mankind and the inspiration for the Romantic Age of musical composition. Initially, he thought the problem was transient and reversible; it was barely noticeable the first two years and progressed little for nearly five. By his thirty-first year, however, his deafness was certain. In its early phase, the disorder produced loud, intermittent humming, ringing, buzzing and other discordant sounds and also intense pain in response to high frequency or loud noises.[1]

The patient's doctors advised him to spare his hearing as much as possible[2] and prescribed ear drops, tonics, herbs and "vesicatories" of bark placed on both arms.[3] When these proved useless, he consulted Pater Weiss, a priest familiar with the physiology of the ear, who was reputed to have cured many such cases using simple remedies.[4] Weiss' treatments proved no more effective than those of the physicians. Although cotton in his ears gave the patient temporary relief from the unpleasant buzzing, his hearing defect progressed in an uneven fashion to total deafness in the his sixth and final decade.

Neither the patient nor his friends or physicians - nor, for that matter, scores of modern medical investigators - ever determined for certain the cause of his deafness. He had a chronic and violent digestive disorder most of his life, and some thought this affected his ears as well. At one time, the patient was convinced that a "frightful attack of typhus" at age twenty-six planted the germ that destroyed his hearing.[5] Later, as his evolving deafness drove him ever deeper into paranoia, he suspected that he had induced the problem himself by raging uncontrollably at a *primo tenore* who he imagined was persecuting him. Others blamed his lost hearing on such varied causes as having been drenched while composing music outdoors, exposure to a draft one hot summer day, rheumatism, and even on a congenital weakness of his auditory canals (see Figure 9-1).[6]

The patient's reaction to his disability and its effect on his work are a source of pathos, awe and much speculation. He was by nature gay and lively, fond of a jest, an inveterate though not always happy punster and a great lover of wit and humor.[7] These qualities endowed him with an elasticity of spirit that kept him from brooding in solitude for long over his misfortune. When he first understood that he was going deaf, he became anxious. Fortunately, his left ear was less affected, and this sustained him for a time. However, as the disorder evolved and its course became clear, grief bordering on despair set in. That was when he vented thoughts of suicide in his Heiligenstadt testament, a self-justifying essay he wrote to convince the world that it was the suffering and anguish of his illness that

FIGURE 9-1. An assortment of ear trumpets (hörrohre) used by the patient.

caused him to appear "malevolent, stubborn or misanthropic."[8] Happily for mankind, he came to terms with his fate, submitting to it, accepting it and, ultimately, triumphing over it.

If the patient had belonged to another profession, it would have been easier for him to have accepted his handicap. He was a virtuoso and a composer,[9] an heir to Handel, Bach, Hayden and Mozart.[10] Although his works are all the more astonishing because of his handicap, he is not the only composer to surmount deafness in pursuing his art. Smetana, Fauré and Franz did likewise. Their collective accomplishments have led to speculation that the intimate relationship between the senses provides compensation for the absence of one sense, such as sound, through some kind of ill-defined, central sensory mechanism.[9]

Early in the course of his deafness, the patient avoided almost all social gatherings to conceal his evolving disability. When he did attend concerts, he had to sit close to the orchestra to hear any of the high tones of either the instruments or the singers. When someone spoke softly, he could hear tones but not words, but if they shouted, he experienced great pain.[11]

When his hearing was gone, he became a tragic and a comic figure, hurrying through the open fields from which he drew his inspiration, gesticulating with his hands, and muttering and singing loudly to himself some new melody heard only in his mind.[12] When conducting, he looked bewildered, his eyes appearing almost unearthly, as he waved his baton back and forth with violent motions in the midst of the performers. If *piano* was called for, he crouched down almost under the conductor's desk, and if he wanted *forte*, he jumped up with the strangest gestures while uttering the weirdest sounds.[13] Some found it difficult to accept these idiosyncrasies, which seemed to grow *pari passu* with his deafness. They dismissed the patient as a misanthrope, a recluse and a lunatic because of his rages, uncontrolled emotional states and increasing obsession with feelings of persecution.[14]

The effect of the patient's deafness on the character of his work is a source of ongoing debate. Clearly, he did not need to hear what he composed to create some of his most innovative works, for example, his late quartets, which Stravinsky rated as "beyond the impudence of praise."[9] In fact, some believe the patient's deficit actually might have enhanced his abilities as a composer by destroying the piano virtuoso in him that competed for his creative energy. It has even been speculated that his auditory seclusion excluded intrusive sounds that otherwise might have distracted him from previously undreamed-of forms and structures.[15] Perhaps he sensed this, for when he was forty-seven and already quite deaf, he advised Cipriani Potter (a minor British composer who had hoped to become the patient's pupil) never to write in a room with a piano lest he be tempted to consult it, but rather to try out the finished work on it later.[9]

Deafness, however, was but one element of the *sturm und drang* of the patient's ill health. He had many disabilities. Some believe they were inherited, others that they had been caused by social indiscretions.

The patient was the product of a marriage marked by "a little joy, and then a chain of sorrows."[16] His father, a court tenor and music teacher of modest talent, was an alcoholic[17] who recognized his son's gift early and conducted his musical education brutally and willfully.[18] He died of heart failure at age fifty-two when the patient was twenty-seven. The patient's paternal grandmother was also an alcoholic.[19] His grandfather, however, was not; he died of a stroke when he was sixty-one. Like the patient, he was short and muscular and of dark complexion.[20]

The patient's mother, who had been married once before, died of tuberculosis when she was forty and he was sixteen. She was an upright, brave and stable woman, unlike her own mother, who had been feebleminded and prone to psychological breakdown.[21]

There were six siblings, only two of whom survived beyond early childhood. The patient became the eldest when a brother of the same name died in infancy a year before his own birth. Another brother, four years his junior, died of tuberculosis at age forty-one. That brother had a son over whom the patient assumed sole guardianship in what proved to be a tumultuous relationship.[22] The patient's youngest brother, an apothecary, was physically robust and outlived him by many years.[23]

The patient never married, and there are those who claim that "he was above the more obvious frailties of the flesh."[24] Although his habits were irregular, he was as temperate in eating and drinking as the society in which he lived allowed, at least during his younger years. He did not engage in games of chance. In fact, he didn't even appear to know one playing card from another. On cursory examination, he seems to have hungered only for music, books, and conversation with men and women of taste and intelligence.[25]

On closer scrutiny, however, the patient's appetites were not nearly so discriminating. He was, after all, the product of a society in which gratifying one's sexual desires was no more discountenanced than the satisfying of any other appetite.[25] In fact, he had many love affairs and proposed marriage to the object of his affection on more than one occasion. In every instance, however, he was rejected by the woman or withdrew from the relationship in anticipation of a rebuff.[26] His fate was to be attracted to women already firmly attached to other men, perhaps because he regarded love relationships as impediments to his creative mission.[27] This might explain why later in life he turned to prostitutes for sexual gratification.

The patient's conversation books (books that visitors wrote in to communicate with him after he was completely deaf) remove any doubt of such liaisons. They speak of prostitutes from the district near Haarmarket and identify Janitschek and Karl Peters as procurers of prostitutes and other willing women. When the patient began to indulge in such sexual favors and what effect they had on his health is uncertain. An indication that his interest in the latter issue was more than theoretical is reflected by reference to a book entitled, *On the Art of Recognizing and Curing All Forms of Venereal Diseases*, in a Conversation Book used when he was forty-nine.[28]

The patient's use of alcohol, though not as great as his father's or maternal grandmother's, grew with the passing years. In later decades, he drank a great deal of wine at the table, and although he could stand a great deal he sometimes drank to the point of inebriation.[29] Toward the end, his liver began to fail, and many have wondered about the extent to which alcohol was responsible.

The patient was born in Bonn (Germany) and lived there until age twenty-one, when he moved to Vienna. Although Vienna would be his principal residence for the rest of his life, he craved the tranquility and seclusion of the countryside and contact with nature, which he worshiped almost as a religion.[30] Whether peregrinations in the countryside exposed him to the germ that blossomed into his illness is not known. The patient was born Catholic, but there is no evidence he practiced his religion, at least until the very end, when he permitted a priest to be summoned and seemed to derive comfort and edification from the sacred function he received.[31]

Since his youth he was prone to gastrointestinal complaints, with recurrent bouts of diarrhea, abdominal pain, and associated weakness. Over the years these were treated with "strengthening medicine," cold baths and stomach pills. Tepid baths alone seemed to help but only temporarily. Because his abdominal complaints were particularly severe when the deafness began, the intestinal condition was one of the early suspects considered by the patient in his vain attempt to identify the source of his lost hearing.[32]

The patient had smallpox as a child, and this scarred his face and weakened his eyes, compelling him even in his early youth to use concave, very strong (highly magnifying) spectacles.[33] The illness that would take his life, however, did not begin to reveal itself in all its variations until his fourth decade.

When he was thirty-three and working on his "Eroica" symphony, the patient developed an obstinate, intermittent fever,[34] which recurred later that same decade.[35] When he was thirty-seven and finishing his fifth and sixth symphonies, he nearly lost a finger because of a felon (a closed-space infection of the fingertip pulp). Fortunately, the infection responded to surgical removal of the affected finger nail.[36]

The patient's forties were marked by further episodes of "feverish catarrhs and tormenting headaches," which confined him to bed for long periods and were refractory to the powders and teas, and the volatile salve and tincture his doctor prescribed.[37] In October of his forty-sixth year, he developed "chest problems" and a "rheumatic seizure." The following year he had attacks of "rheumatism" and recurrent bronchitis. By then, he was nearly totally deaf but continued to compose. As his fifth decade drew to a close, persistent ill health and anxiety over the care of his nephew kept him in bed much of the time.

When he was fifty, the patient had his first attack of jaundice,[38] which was accompanied by the earaches that had long plagued him.[39] The following year an attack of "gout in the chest" sent him to bed for six weeks.[40] When he was fifty-two, a painful inflammation of the eye forced him to spend long periods in a darkened room, sometimes with eyes bandaged, before he was able to tolerate light.[41] When his intestinal disorder again flared, his doctor gave him "a powder" and insisted on a diet free from wine, coffee, spirits and spices.[42] He also sought relief, as he had done many times before, at spas, such as the one in Baden.[43] He felt old, though he was still young[44] and complained of "catarrhal trouble" and nose bleeds. When he was fifty-four, he wrote of spitting up "rather a lot of blood, apparently only from the windpipe. But often it streams out of my nose."[45] He had had similar episodes the previous winter, though not as severe, and began to wonder if "the man with a scythe [would give him] much more time."[46]

In spite of his many ailments, the patient's creative energy never flagged, but seemed to surge in a final cadenza of transfigured emotion and imagination.[47] He completed the last and, in the minds of many, greatest of his string quartets, the one in C-sharp minor, Op.131, even as his health began its final downward spiral.

His old abdominal complaint flared once more as prelude to the mortal crisis of his last year. He began to have difficulty ambulating, and his eye problem returned. When these were accompanied by back pain, he suspected he was having an attack of either "rheumatism or gout." Soups and small doses of quinine gave him temporary relief.[47]

The disease's final phase began at his brother's country estate in Gneixendorf, a little village near Krems on a high plateau above the Danube. The patient had resisted repeated prior invitations,[48] perhaps sensing that this was to be his last pastoral excursion. Although not fully recovered from his illness of earlier that year, he made it his custom once he had settled there to arise at half-past five o'clock in the morning, seat himself at a table and write while singing and beating time with his hands and feet. After breakfast at half-past seven o'clock, he would hurry out into the open air, shouting and waving his arms as he rambled through the fields, sometimes stopping to write notes in a pocketbook. The peasants thought him a madman and kept out of his way.[48]

At first the fresh air seemed beneficial. The patient's eyes, at least, improved. However, his diarrhea worsened, his brother believed because of the wine he was consuming in great quantities. When his belly began to swell, the patient bandaged it but gained little relief. His appetite failed even as his thirst increased. Finally, in early December, he could bear his illness no longer and left Gneixendorf for treatment in Vienna.[49]

The patient traveled in an open air carriage in weather that was raw, damp and frosty while suffering greatly with serious symptoms, suggesting an inflammation of the lungs. When he finally reached Vienna, his face was flushed; he was spitting up blood and appeared to be on the verge of suffocating. He also complained of a painful stitch in the side, which made lying on his back a torment. An anti-inflammatory treatment of uncertain composition brought gradual relief, so that by the fifth day after his return, he was able to sit up, and by the seventh day he was well enough to get out of bed, walk about, read and write.[50]

On examining the patient the next morning, however, his doctor was alarmed by how much his condition had deteriorated over night. The patient was jaundiced, trembling and doubled over with sharp pains in the right upper abdomen in the area of his liver, which was hard and nodular. His feet, which had previously been puffy, were now so swollen the physician in attendance diagnosed *dropsy*, a term then used for massive edema. The patient's urinary output fell, even as his jaundice increased in intensity. By the third week after his return to Vienna, he was having incidents of "nocturnal suffocation," and his abdomen was so distended with (ascetic) fluid, his physicians feared it would burst unless they immediately performed an operation to relieve the pressure.[51]

Dr. Johann Seibert, principal surgeon, performed the operation on December 20. When Seibert made the incision and inserted a tube into the abdomen, water spurted out, causing the patient, who even then had not lost his sense of humor, to quip, "Professor, you remind me of Moses striking the rock with his staff."[51] The patient subsequently received Almond milk and enemas, and on January 8 underwent a second operation, which produced water that was clearer and which flowed more freely than the first time, suggesting that there had been an inflammation of the abdominal cavity that was resolving at the time of the second operation. During the second surgery, "ten measures [probably 10 pints of fluid] were drawn off."[52]

Following the surgeries, his physicians prescribed frozen fruit punch containing spirituous liquor, and this so refreshed the patient that he began to perspire profusely and for the first time since his return slept quietly through the night. His apparent improvement did not last long, however. He began to consume the frozen punch in ever greater amounts and grew progressively lethargic; his breathing became stertorous, like that of an intoxicated person; and his speech began to wander. He became unruly. By the time his physicians finally discontinued the intoxicating punch, his colic and diarrhea had returned.[52] The patient then received repeated doses of a host of medicines, including almond milk, salep[53] and various powders.

When two more operations had to be performed to remove additional abdominal fluid (the last on February 27), both the patient and his physicians realized that the case was hopeless. All restrictions, including those on frozen punch, were removed.[52] The patient's mind began to wander.

In healthier days, the patient had been powerfully built, with wide shoulders, strong hands overgrown with hair and short thick fingers. He was short of stature, with a large head, bushy eyebrows and thick bristly hair framing a pockmarked and ruddy face. To some the patient had been ugly, even repulsive.[54] Now, he looked "more

FIGURE 9-2. Neugass, Isidor (c.1780-1847?). Portrait of the young Beethoven. Private collection. Photo Credit: Bridgeman-Giraudon/Art Resource, NY.

like a skeleton than a living being,"[55] emaciated and unshaven, with thick half-gray hair hanging in disorder over his temples.[56]

As his condition worsened, the patient lay in bed in obvious pain, groaning intermittently, speaking only in faint and disconnected phrases, sweat visible on his forehead. Realizing that he was near death, he looked to his physician and muttered: *"Plaudite amici, comoedia finita est!"* ("Applaud friends, the comedy is over !").[57] A priest administered the viaticum. "I thank you, ghostly sir," the patient mumbled, "You have brought me comfort."[58]

As evening approached on March 24, the patient lost consciousness, and the death struggle began in earnest. It ended for Ludwig van Beethoven on March 26, 1827 (see Figs. 9-2 and 9-3).

***

The autopsy performed following Beethoven's death[59] should have eliminated any doubt as to the cause of his illness.[60] It had much to tell about the anatomy of his disabilities, but not the etiol-

FIGURE 9-3. Schimon, Ferdinand (1797-1852). Portrait of Kudwig van Beethoven, 1819. Beethoven House, Bonn, Germany. Photo Credit: Snark/Art Resource, NY.

ogy. The ears, as expected, were abnormal, as were the skull, the brain and several other organs. The official report reads as follows:

> The Eustachian tube [tube connecting the inner ear to the posterior nasal cavity] was much thickened, its mucous lining swollen somewhat contracted....the auditory nerves.... shriveled and destitute of neurina [nerve fibers]; the accompanying arteries were dilated to more than the size of a crow quill and cartiloginous. The left auditory nerve much the thinnest, arose by three very thin greyish striae, the right by one strong clearer stria from the substance of the fourth ventricle [posterior-most chamber of a system of communicating cavities within the brain's interior]....The convolutions of the brain [irregular ridges on the brain's surface] were full of water, and remarkably white; they appeared very much deeper, wider, and more numerous than ordinary. The Calvarium

[skull] exhibited throughout great density and a thickness amounting to about half an inch. The cavity of the Chest, together with the organs within it, was in the normal condition. In the cavity of the abdomen four quarts of a greyish-brown, turbid fluid were effused. The liver appeared shrunk up to half its proper volume, of a leathery consistence and greyish-blue color, and was beset with knots, the size of a bean, on its tuberculated [lumpy] surface, as well as in its substance.... The spleen was found to be double its proper size, dark-colored and firm. The pancreas was equally hard and firm, its excretory duct being as wide as a goosequill.... Both kidneys were invested by cellular membrane of an inch thick, and infiltrated with a brown turbid fluid.... Every one of their calices [funnel-shaped structures in the interior of the kidney where the collecting tubes converge before emptying into the ureters] was occupied by a calcareous concretion [calcium deposit] of a wart-like shape and as large as a split pea.[60]

Shortly after Beethoven died Johnanna van Beethoven, the wife of Beethoven's brother, Carl Caspar, removed a lock of his hair and gave it to Anselm Hüttenbrenner, who was in attendance.[61] Chemical analysis of eight strands of that hair one hundred seventy-three years later found concentrations of lead one hundred times higher than normal.[62] No mercury was detected.

Thus, much is known of the character and the anatomy of Beethoven's illness, yet its name has never been confirmed. The signs and symptoms of his protracted illness are catalogued in considerable detail in one hundred thirty-seven conversation books containing uncensored personal conversations between Beethoven and his associates during his final decade, in several other documents such as the Heiligenstadt Testament, written by the composer when he was thirty-one, and in his Tagebuch (diary) of 1812-18.[63] These describe a protracted and multi-system disorder (or disorders), beginning in the patient's early twenties and culminating in his death at age fifty-six. For him the most distressing feature of the illness was its effect on the auditory nerves, which it left shrunken and useless after years of pain and ringing in the ears (tinnitus). The disorder's most lethal effect, however, was its destruction of the liver, which it rendered fibrotic and riddled with nodules visible to the naked eye (a condition now referred to as *macronodular cirrhosis*), causing secondary ascites, an enlarged spleen, nose bleeds and bleeding esophageal varices. These were its dominant features. However, myriad, contrapuntal features have complicated efforts at a unified diagnosis. There were the decades of intestinal complaints characterized by recurrent abdominal pain and diarrhea; the pulmonary attacks of bronchitis and feverish catarrhs (with no gross, post-mortem evidence of pulmonary pathology); the repeated episodes of rheumatism/gout; the "tormenting headaches"; and the post-mortem abnormalities of the brain, pancreas and kidneys. There were also possible episodes of smallpox and typhus, heavy alcohol consumption, a family history of alcoholism, sexual promiscuity (at least late in life) and high levels of lead detected in samples of hair analyzed over a century and a half after the composer's death.

Clinicians have long pondered the question of the cause of Beethoven's many disabilities and produced an array of diagnoses, ranging from lead poisoning to syphilis (see Table 9-1).[64] Ockham's razor[65] has been applied liberally in these dialectics in the hope of uncovering a single diagnosis which might explain all of the improvisations of Beethoven's complex illness.

If Beethoven's years of suffering were the work not of a single disease but of several, what might they have been? He is said to have had smallpox, which could account for his pock-marked face but not his many other disabilities. He is also reported to have had typhus, which seems to have coincided with the onset of his auditory complaints. Typhus (see Chapter 2), at least in some reports, has been associated with prominent auditory symptoms, including deafness, tinnitus and vertigo.[66] However, typhus is an acute disorder, in which auditory symptoms develop only occasionally. Although relapses (usually milder than the initial attack of the infection) occur, a chronic progressive form of the illness has not been described.

The high-lead level detected in the sample of the composer's hair raises the possibility that at least some of his complaints were due to

TABLE 9-1 Beethoven's Diseases

Organ System	Symptoms	Pathologic Findings	Suggested Diagnoses
Neurologic	Progressive hearing loss and tinnitus, chronic headaches, depression, social isolation, and personal neglect	Scaly external auditory canal; thickened Eustachian tube; shriveled auditory nerves with associated dilated and "cartilaginous" arteries; cerebral convolutions full of water, remarkably white, and deeper, wider, and more numerous than ordinary	Syphilis, otosclerosis, sarcoidosis, Paget's disease, typhus, measles, scarlatina, Whipple's disease, systemic lupus erythematosus
Gastrointestinal	Chronic, intermittent, abdominal pain; diarrhea and constipation; jaundice, ascites, edema, and coagulopathy	Stomach and bowels greatly distended with air; macronodular cirrhosis; greyish-brown, turbid, ascitic fluid; splenomegaly; hard pancreas with a dilated duct	Irritable bowel syndrome, inflammatory bowel disease, autointoxication, Whipple's disease, sarcoidosis, typhus, syphilis, hemochromatosis, Laennec's cirrhosis, viral hepatitis, primary sclerosing cholangitis, alcoholic pancreatitis, diabetes mellitus
Renal	Terminal anuria; recurrent abdominal pain	Thickened Gerota's capsule, calcareous caliceal concretions	Analgesic nephropathy, papillary necrosis, Whipple's disease, sarcoidosis, Paget's disease, inflammatory bowel disease
Pulmonary	"Asthma"; terminal fever, dyspnea, and hemoptysis	Chest cavity and organs "in normal condition"	Syphilis, systemic lupus erythematous, Whipple's disease, sarcoidosis, inflammatory bowel disease
Ocular	Painful eye attack	Not stated	Syphilis, Whipple's disease, systemic lupus erythematous, sarcoidosis, Paget's disease, inflammatory bowel disease
Articular	Recurrent attacks of "gout/rheumatism"	Not stated	Syphilis, Whipple's disease, systemic lupus erythematous, sarcoidosis, Paget's disease, inflammatory bowel disease

(From Donnenberg MS, Collins MT, Benitez RM, Mackowiak PA. The sound that failed. AM J Med 2000;108:475-80.)

216

plumbism, chronic lead intoxication. Lead damages several organ systems, including the gastrointestinal tract, liver, kidneys and nervous system,[67] all of which were perturbed in Beethoven. Colic, one of plumbism's most prominent symptoms, manifests as abdominal pain, cramps, nausea, vomiting, anorexia (loss of appetite) and *constipation,* not diarrhea, which was one of Beethoven's most persistent complaints. Lead is also toxic to nerves, impairing their ability to conduct the electrical impulses that stimulate muscles to contract. Weakness is the usual result. The acoustic nerves can be injured but are typically spared. While lead damages both the liver and kidneys, mild hepatitis, not macronodular cirrhosis, and progressive kidney fibrosis, not papillary necrosis (the condition most consistent with the "calcareous concretions" found in Beethoven's kidneys postmortem) are the typical hepatic and renal abnormalities seen in cases of chronic lead intoxication.[68]

If some of Beethoven's complaints were, indeed, due to plumbism, as the results of the analysis of his hair suggests, the question remains, what was the source of the lead responsible for his intoxication? Today, most cases of inorganic lead poisoning arise from two sources of chronic exposure: inhalation of lead fumes or ingestion of lead particles by adults in the workplace, and ingestion of lead particles (usually lead-based paint) by children in the home. In Beethoven's day, wine was the principal source of lead in cases of chronic intoxication. By some accounts, such intoxication was epidemic among the upper class of 18th and 19th century Europe, owing to the consumption of wine contaminated with the metal. Fortified wines were a particularly important source of lead with concentrations of 300 to 1900 μgm per liter having been detected recently in wines bottled between 1770 C.E. and 1820 C.E. Lead pipes, pewter pots and pans, unglazed pottery and some sauces used in dainty dishes were other sources of lead possibly consumed by Beethoven.[68]

Beethoven's deafness, which was as mysterious as it was ironic, had a course and associated abnormalities of the acoustic nerves that are not typical of any disease encountered today. Moreover,

Beethoven's case does not bring to mind any patient encountered in the author's three decades of clinical practice nor any patient encountered by several prominent neurologists and ear specialists interviewed by the author. Thus, current clinical experience would seem to be of little help in identifying the etiology of Beethoven's deafness. What of the clinical experiences of earlier generations of physicians? Those who practiced in the pre-antibiotic era saw many such cases of slowly progressive, bilateral destruction of the acoustic nerves. More often than not, the cause was syphilis.

What of Beethoven's fibrosis of the liver (cirrhosis)? The two commonest causes of cirrhosis today are chronic alcoholism and viral hepatitis, both of which destroy normal liver cells, though through different mechanisms, causing them to be replaced by fibrotic scar tissue.[69] Cirrhosis caused by alcohol is usually micronodular, that is, it is characterized by tiny (in many cases microscopic) fibrotic nodules rather than the large (macroscopic) fibrotic nodules found postmortem in Beethoven's liver. The cirrhosis of chronic viral hepatitis, which alcohol potentiates, is more commonly macronodular. Thus, a contemporary patient with Beethoven's social history and liver abnormalities would most likely have cirrhosis due to a combination of viral hepatitis and chronic alcohol abuse. Although viral hepatitis (in particular, hepatitis caused by the hepatitis C virus) is the most common cause of cirrhosis in Europe today, injection drug abuse, a modern blight, is the principal risk factor for the infection.[70] Because injection drug abuse did not exist in Beethoven's day, viral hepatitis was probably not an important cause of macronodular cirrhosis. Moreover, cirrhosis due to a combination of viral hepatitis and alcohol would not explain Beethoven's deafness, attacks of rheumatism, his ocular problems, or his renal abnormalities.

We know little of Beethoven's recurrent episodes of rheumatism/gout other than these complaints began at a relatively young age and were therefore not likely caused by the degenerative effects of aging on his joints. Rather, he appears to have had one of the acquired forms of arthritis, of which there are many and at least some of which are associated with abnormalities of organ systems other than the joints. Gout, for example, sometimes affects the kidneys as well as the joints, especially when it is a complication of lead intoxication (see above). Lyme disease, one of today's most important causes of chronic arthritis, occasionally attacks the facial nerve and sometimes the auditory nerve as well. In view of Beethoven's love of nature and probable exposure to ticks carrying the bacterium responsible for Lyme disease (*Borrelia burgdorferi*), the disorder should be included among the many possible etiologies of his rheumatism/gout and deafness.

Beethoven's eye disorder is, likewise, poorly characterized in the existing clinical record. It is clear from his letters that it was episodic, painful and aggravated by light. If he had interstitial keratitis, or uveitis (see below), which seems likely based on his symptoms,[71] his ocular complaints could have been due to any number of diseases. Formerly, congenital syphilis was the most common cause of interstitial keratitis.[72] Today it is usually the result of a herpes simplex infection. Less commonly it is part of a syndrome of unknown etiology, called Cogan's syndrome, or a complication of a systemic disease such as leprosy or tuberculosis. Uveitis has similar symptoms and is caused by syphilis and the herpes simplex virus, but also by a variety of immunological disorders such as rheumatoid arthritis and sarcoidosis.

The pancreas and the kidney are yet two other organs that appear to have been entangled in the complex skein of ill health that took Beethoven's life. His autopsy report describes a distorted and fibrotic pancreas that is "hard and firm...[with an excretory duct] as wide as a goose quill." The most likely explanation for this finding is chronic pancreatitis. Based on Beethoven's social history, his pancreatitis might well have developed as a consequence of alcohol abuse. Chronic pancreatitis is associated with recurrent attacks of excruciating abdominal pain of the kind Beethoven suffered with most of his life. Chronic pancreatitis is not associated with deafness or interstitial keratitis or arthritis or renal abnormalities. Moreover, Beethoven developed abdominal pains (and diarrhea) well before he began to abuse alcohol.

Beethoven's kidneys, it will be recalled, were "invested by a cellular membrane of an inch thick, and infiltrated with a brown turbid fluid.....Every one of their calices were occupied by a calcareous concretion of a wart-like shape...as large as a split pea." The most reasonable explanation for these abnormalities is that he had a kidney disorder now called "papillary necrosis." Because papillary necrosis is most often the result of chronic analgesic abuse, it has been suggested that Beethoven's abnormal kidneys might have been due to large doses of salicin (a precursor of aspirin) he obtained from his brother, Johann, an apothecary,[73] and consumed in the form of powdered, dry willow bark for his abdominal pains, rheumatism and headaches.[74] Such drugs also cause fibrosis of tissues surrounding the kidneys, which might explain the thickened cellular membrane found at autopsy. Syphilis is another cause of a thickened renal capsule with an associated "brown turbid fluid."

If Beethoven's various disabilities were the result of single disease, rather than an unfortunate congregation of many diseases, no disorder offers a better explanation for the character, course and social milieu of his illness than syphilis. Syphilis, the "great imitator," has clinical manifestations so protean, Sir William Osler was moved to remark that, "He who knows syphilis, knows medicine."[75] It is a systemic infection caused by a corkscrew-shaped bacterium called *Treponema pallidum*. In its advanced stage, which may take decades to reach its climax, it can inflict heavy damage on all of the organs affected by Beethoven's illness. The full spectrum of disabilities orchestrated by the infection has largely been forgotten, thanks to the advent of penicillin, which is spectacularly effective in curing the disorder. However, if one examines the extensive literature devoted to syphilis prior to the antibiotic era, the disorder emerges as a highly satisfactory explanation for virtually all of Beethoven's ailments.

Earlier generations of clinicians were all too familiar with the vulnerability of the nervous system to the destructive effects of syphilis. *T. pallidum* attacks its vessels, its membranes, its supporting tissues (glia), as well as nerve cells themselves.[76] The net result is a wide range of potential neurological abnormalities, the character of which is dictated in any given patient by various parasite and host factors (e.g., age, co-morbid conditions, immunity, etc.), only some of which are understood.

Destruction of the acoustic nerve occurs in less than one in a thousand cases of untreated syphilis but in as many as two to three percent of those who exhibit evidence of neurosyphilis. In such cases, deafness is frequently accompanied by tinnitus, which Beethoven complained of, but also vertigo, which he did not. Acoustic nerve deafness is particularly common in cases of congenital syphilis, in which it develops in as many as ten percent of untreated cases.[77] Interestingly, the onset of such deafness is generally delayed until after puberty and is always bilateral.[78]

Meningeal syphilis (syphilis involving the membranes encasing the brain and spinal chord [the meninges]), is the source of some of the earliest symptoms of neurosyphilis.[75] Headache, which Beethoven suffered greatly,[79] is particularly common, so much so that in earlier times, many patients with late meningovascular neurosyphilis underwent years of treatment for migraines.[80] Vascular abnormalities frequently accompany the meningeal inflammation,[75] which might explain the condition of the arteries adjacent to Beethoven's acoustic nerves (which "were dilated to more than the size of a crow quill and cartilaginous") and the "superficial substance surrounding the fourth ventricle (one of the internal cavities of the brain)...[which] was much denser in consistency and more vascular than these nerves which arose from it." The vascular abnormalities might also explain the condition of the brain itself, the exaggerated convolutions and excess water which suggest that in spite of Beethoven's unflagging productivity as a composer, his disease had produced some degree of brain atrophy by the time he died.

The eye is another target of late syphilis. The infection, in fact, is responsible for an array of eye abnormalities, with names such as *interstitial keratitis*, *uveitis*, *keratovitritis*, *neuroretinitis*, *chorioretinitis* and *optic atrophy*.[79] In congenital syphilis, interstitial or parenchymatous keratitis is the most frequent ocular lesion[81] and the one most consistent with Beethoven's symptoms of eye pain and photo-phobia in the absence of any apparent discharge from the eye. Children with congenital syphilis, like adults with the acquired form of the infection, sometimes do well for decades before developing eye problems.

Chronic inflammation of the liver sometimes leading to cirrhosis is another complication of both acquired and congenital syphilis.[82] In advanced cases, the liver is riddled with discrete inflammatory tumors called *gummas* of varying size and intervening fibrosis. According to early 20th century syphilologists, the combination of a generalized hepatitis and localized gummas with inflammatory extensions in patients like Beethoven (assuming he did have untreated syphilis) can imitate every imaginable clinical entity, medical and surgical, in which the liver may be involved,[83] including those of an enlarged spleen (splenomegaly) and ascites. Alcohol potentiates the toxicity of syphilis for the liver.[84] Long-standing syphilis is also a cause of fibrosis and gummas of the pancreas.[85] Thus, chronic syphilis in conjunction with many years of heavy alcohol consumption might explain Beethoven's macronodular cirrhosis, his ascites, his splenomegaly and his abnormal pancreas.

"Stomach trouble" is a common complaint for which, even today, an organic explanation is all too often lacking. In some cases, it can be a nonspecific reaction to a systemic disorder in which no structural abnormality of the gastrointestinal tract can be found. Syphilis is one such systemic disorder. Estimates derived during the pre-antibiotic era indicate that although fewer than five percent of cases of "syphilis of the gastro-intestinal tract" were due to direct invasion by *T. pallidumm*,[86] nearly one third of patients with untreated early syphilis reported gastric complaints at least as a minor element of their illness. In untreated cases of late syphilis, "stomach trouble" was even more common, and when present was the "chief symptom" ninety percent of the time.[85] Patients with neurosyphilis seemed to have had the most gastric complaints; these complaints were thought to be due to malfunction of the neural plexus supplying the gastrointestinal tract (the vagus nerve).[85] Painful attacks simulating chronic conditions of the gallbladder and appendix, pancreatitis and peptic ulcers were the most frequent manifestations and led to many unnecessary exploratory abdominal operations.

The two other organ systems entangled in the complex web of Beethoven's multi-system disorder were the musculoskeletal and genitourinary systems. Both are also potential targets of the chronic phase of acquired and congenital syphilis. Clinical experience before the advent of penicillin showed that most patients with untreated syphilis had musculoskeletal complaints at some time during the course of their infection.[87] Inflammation of the bones of the skull was particularly common and produced thickening and increased density of bone[88] reminiscent of "the great density and....thickness amounting to about half an inch" exhibited by Beethoven's skull on post-mortem examination. "Rheumatism" (pain and swelling of the joints) was a chief complaint in eight percent of cases of untreated syphilis,[89] and, like Beethoven's rheumatism, was characterized by alternating exacerbations and remissions.[89] Unlike rheumatoid arthritis, the rheumatism of syphilis typically does not deform affected joints or impair their function.

In the pre-antibiotic era, a high percentage of patients dying of syphilis were found at autopsy to have renal abnormalities consistent with chronic inflammation.[90] In many such cases, these were due to the ill effects of diseases other than syphilis. Nevertheless, the impression among clinicians remained that syphilis itself caused a variety of inflammatory abnormalities of the kidney, although no report exists of its having caused calcium deposits like those found at autopsy in Beethoven's kidneys, a condition now referred to as "papillary necrosis." That condition would more likely have been due to chronic analgesic abuse taken for pains induced by the underlying disorder (see above).

If Beethoven had syphilis, the questions remain, how and when might he have acquired the infection? Syphilis is an exclusively human disease. It has a worldwide distribution, although considerable evidence indicates that prior to Columbus' first voyage it was confined to the Americas.[91] It is an infection generally transmitted during sexual intercourse, and its prevalence among peoples and social classes varies according to their sexual practices. It is most often first contracted in early adult life (between ages twenty and twenty-six in men), at precisely the time Beethoven would have been infected if syphilis was the cause of his many-faceted illness.[92] According to current statistics, only 2.1 in one hundred thousand persons in the United States are infected with T. pallidum, the bacterium responsible for syphilis. In fact, the prevalence of syphilis in the United States is now so low there is hope that it soon will disappear from America, with the application of lessons learned from the successful global smallpox eradication initiative (see Chapter 2). In the early 1900s, however, syphilis was rampant throughout the world, with an estimated prevalence of six to ten percent in residents of the United States.[93] In Europe the prevalence was even higher, with the heaviest concentrations of the infection in urban areas and among prostitutes and their clients. Syphilis' prevalence among both military and urban populations typically rises during times of war.[94] Owing to the lack of a reliable diagnostic test for the infection before the turn of the 20th century,[90] the prevalence of syphilis in the (Napoleonic) war-torn Europe of Beethoven's lifetime is unknown. However, recent trending data suggest that it was at least as high as that of Europe in the early 1900s.[95]

When syphilis is transmitted from an infected mother to her child, spectacular, sometimes lethal, congenital deformities develop that are readily apparent in early childhood. These are the deformities that dominate "classic descriptions" of congenital syphilis found in modern medical textbooks. However, inapparent (latent) congenital infections also occur, in which clinical manifestations of the infection are delayed for as long as thirty-five or even fifty years.[96] In some cases, obvious disabilities never develop. If Beethoven had congenitally acquired syphilis, it would have been latent for two decades or more before revealing itself in the form of irritable bowel syndrome and evolving deafness. If he was infected in utero, his father is the one most likely to have introduced T. pallidum into the family bloodline. He was, after all, a determined alcoholic; if he ac-

quired syphilis in the course of his debauches and passed it on to the
mother of Beethoven, he would not have been the first alcoholic to
be swept into the channel of syphilis dissemination, kept open and
even enlarged by "the perverse genius of alcohol and commercial-
ized sexuality."[97]

If Beethoven was infected as a young man, the source of his infection is a mystery that will almost certainly forever remain so. Although his conversation books indicate liaisons with prostitutes
later in life, little is known for certain of his earlier sexual activities.
His principal biographer, Alexander Wheelock Thayer, provides
only innuendos of sexually activity as a young man, and thus, a risk
of acquiring syphilis early in life. In his celebrated biography of the
composer, Thayer wrote the following:[91]

> The present age must be content to find in Beethoven, with all his
> greatness, a very human nature, one which, if it showed extraordi-
> nary strength, exhibited also extraordinary weakness... in those
> years when the strict regulations of a school would have compen-
> sated in some measure for the unwise, unsteady, often harsh disci-
> pline of his father, he was thrown into close connection with actors
> and actresses, who, in those days, were not very distinguished for
> the propriety of their manners and morals...that he never suc-
> ceeded in governing his passions with absolute sway, was not be-
> cause the spirit was unwilling; the flesh was weak."

If Beethoven had syphilis and were alive today, he would be
treated with penicillin, whose capacity to destroy *T. pallidum* was
recognized almost immediately after its introduction into clinical
medicine in the 1940s. Its potency against the infection remains
undiminished to this day. In the 19th century, mercury was the
treatment of choice.[98] Mercury is one of the oldest drugs used to
treat syphilis and in Beethoven's day was prescribed for all stages of
the infection. A medley of other drugs were also tried, sarsaparilla,
guaiac, sassafrass, and gold, for example, but only mercury, in some
cases, seemed to halt progression of the infection. Because clinicians

were inclined to treat patients vigorously, symptoms of mercury toxicity were frequently added to those of the infection itself in patients of Beethoven's day. These included excessive salivation, gastroenteritis, weakness, depression, anemia, mouth ulcers, weight loss, liver and kidney disease and, occasionally, death. In view of the similarities between mercury intoxication and Beethoven's illness, some have suggested that it was the cause of at least some of his physical ills. If the recently conducted analysis of his hair is valid, and the eight strands examined were, indeed, his, the absence of mercury in the specimen suggests that of all the possible explanations offered for Beethoven's mysterious illness, mercury intoxication, at least, can be excluded from consideration.

Unlike mercury intoxication and many of the other disorders offered over the years as Beethoven's diagnosis (see Note 64), syphilis is a disease many would consider too banal, too unbecoming, to have extinguished the life of this remarkable patient. Even in his own lifetime, Beethoven was rightly regarded as one of the illuminati, and his stature has only grown with the passing of years, engendering a growing reluctance to accept the possibility that this extraordinary man might have died of an ordinary disease. It should be noted, however, that while the deafness syphilis induced certainly may have impaired Beethoven's creativity, on the other hand it may have actually *enhanced* it by forcing him to abandon his piano, thus freeing him to create the new brand of polyphonic music that was to be, perhaps, his greatest gift to mankind.

Notes

1. Solomon M. *Beethoven* (Second, Revised Edition). Schirmer Books. New York. 1998: p.158-62.
2. Forbes E. *Thayer's Life of Beethoven*. Volumes I and II. Princeton U. Press: Princeton, 1967; p.303.
3. Op cit (Forbes) p. 284,6.
4. Op cit (Forbes) p. 373-4.

5. Op cit (Forbes) p. 595.

6. Op cit (Forbes) p. 187.

7. Op cit (Forbes) p. 248.

8. A celebrated document, now known as the "Heilegenstadt Testament," dated October 6 and 10, 1802 C.E., was found among Beethoven's papers after his death. He was thirty-one when he wrote it to explain the suffering and anguish caused by his illness, which drove him to thoughts of suicide. Its full text is as follows:

> *For My Brothers Carl and Johann Beethoven*
>
> Oh you men who think or say that I am malevolent, stubborn, or misanthropic, how greatly do you wrong me. You do not know the secret cause which makes me seem that way to you. From childhood on, my heart and soul have been full of the tender feeling of goodwill, and I was ever inclined to accomplish great things. But, think that for six years now I have been hopelessly afflicted, made worse by senseless physicians, from year to year deceived with hopes of improvement, finally compelled to face the prospect of *a lasting malady* (whose cure will take years or, perhaps, be impossible). Though born with a fiery, active temperament, even susceptible to the diversions of society, I was soon compelled to withdraw myself, to live life alone. If at times I tried to forget all this, oh how harshly was I flung back by the doubly sad experience of my bad hearing. Yet it was impossible for me to say to people, "Speak louder, shout, for I am deaf." Ah, how could I possibly admit an infirmity in the *one sense* which ought to be more perfect in me than in others, a sense which I once possessed in the highest perfection, a perfection such as few in my profession enjoy or every have enjoyed. —Oh I cannot do it; therefore forgive me when you see me draw back when I would have gladly mingled with you. My misfortune is doubly painful to me because I am bound to be misunderstood; for me there can be no relaxation with my fellow

men, no refined conversations, no mutual exchange of ideas. I must live almost alone, like one who has been banished; I can mix with society only as much as true necessity demands. If I approach near to people a hot terror seizes upon me, and I fear being exposed to the danger that my condition might be noticed. Thus it has been during the last six months which I have spent in the country. By ordering me to spare my hearing as much as possible, my intelligent doctor almost fell in with my own present frame of mind, though sometimes I ran counter to it by yielding to my desire for companionship. But what a humiliation for me when someone standing next to me heard a flute in the distance and *I heard nothing*, or someone heard a *shepherd singing* and again I heard nothing. Such incidents drove me almost to despair; a little more of that and I would have ended my life — it was only *my art* that held me back. Ah, it seemed to me impossible to leave the world until I had brought forth all that I felt was within me. So I endured this wretched existence — truly wretched for so susceptible a body, which can be thrown by a sudden change from the best condition to the very worst. — *Patience*, they say, is what I must now choose for my guide, and I have done so — I hope my determination will remain firm to endure until it pleases the inexorable Parcae to break the thread. Perhaps I shall get better, perhaps not; I am ready. — Forced to become a philosopher already in my twenty-eighth year, —oh it is not easy, and for the artist much more difficult than for anyone lese. —Divine One, thou seest my inmost soul; thou knowest that therein dwells the love of mankind and the desire to do good. —Oh fellow men, when at some point you read this, consider then that you have done me an injustice; someone who has had misfortune may console himself to find a similar case to his, who despite all the limitations of Nature nevertheless did everything within his powers to become accepted among worthy artists and

men. —You, my brothers *Carl* and   as soon as I
am dead, if Dr. Schmidt is still alive, ask him in my name
to describe my malady, and attach this written document
to his account of my illness so that so far as is possible at
least the world may become reconciled to me after my
death. —At the same time, I declare you two to be the
heirs to my small fortune (if so it can be called); divide it
fairly; bear with and help each other. What injury you have
done me you know was long ago forgiven. To you, brother
Carl, I give special thanks for the attachment you have
shown me of late. It is my wish that you may have a better
and freer life than I have had. Recommend *virtue* to your
children; it alone, not money, can make them happy. I
speak from experience; this was what upheld me in time of
misery. Thanks to it and to my art, I did not end my life by
suicide — Farewell and love each other — I thank all my
friends, particularly *Price Lichnowsky* and *Professor Schmidt*
— I would like the instruments from Prince L. to be preserved by one of you, but not to be the cause of strife between you, and as soon as they can serve you a better
purpose, then sell them. How happy I shall be if I can still
be helpful to you in my grave — so be it. —With joy I
hasten to meet death. — If it comes before I have had the
chance to develop all my artistic capacities, it will still be
coming too soon despite my harsh fate, and I should probably wish it later — yet even so I should be happy, for
would it not free me from a state of endless suffering? —
Come *when* thou wilt, I shall meet thee bravely. —
Farewell and do not wholly forget me when I am dead; I
deserve this from you, for during my lifetime I was thinking of you often and of ways to make you happy — please
be so —

LUDWIG VAN BEETHOVEN

Heiglnstadt, [Heiligenstadt]
October 6th,1802

FOR MY BROTHERS CARL AND JOHANN, TO BE READ AND EXECUTED AFTER MY DEATH.

Heiglnstadt, *October* 10th, 1802, thus I bid thee farewell — and indeed sadly. — Yes, that fond hope — which I brought here with me, to be cured to a degree at least — this I must now wholly abandon. As the leaves of autumn fall and are withered — so likewise has my hope been blighted — I leave here — almost as I came — even the high courage — which often inspired me in the beautiful days of summer — has disappeared — Oh Providence — grant me at last but one day of pure *joy* — it is so long since real joy echoed in my heart — Oh when — Oh when, Oh Divine One — shall I feel it again in the temple of nature and of mankind — Never? No Oh that would be too hard. [Op cit (Solomon) p. 151-5]

9. Harrison P. The effects of deafness on musical composition. *J Royal Soc Med.* 1988;81:598-601.

10. From Franz Grillparzer's funeral oration. [Op cit (Forbes) p. 1057-8]

11. Op cit (Forbes) p. 284.

12. Op cit (Forbes) p. 1007.

13. Op cit (Forbes) p. 811.

14. Op cit (Solomon) p. 331,333.

15. Op cit (Solomon) p. 161.

16. Op cit (Solomon) p. 31.

17. Op cit (Solomon) p. 3,41.

18. Op cit (Solomon) p. 22.

19. Op cit (Solomon) p. 8.

20. Op cit (Forbes) p. 48.

21. Op cit (Solomon) p. 9,10.

22. On November 15, 1815, Beethoven's brother, Casper Carl, died of tuberculosis, leaving a widow, Johanna, and a nine-year-old son, Karl, over whom Beethoven obtained exclusive guardianship. The relationship between Beethoven and his nephew and sister-in-law was troubled from the onset, ulti-

mately driving Karl to attempt suicide in 1826. Beethoven's fateful trip to his brother's country estate in Gnelixendorf was undertaken solely to escape Viennese criticism in the aftermath of Karl's self-inflicted head wound. [Op cit (Forbes) p xii]

23. Op cit (Solomon) p. 10, 109, 297.
24. Ibid.
25. Op cit (Forbes) p. 244-5.
26. Op cit (Solomon) p. 240.
27. Op cit (Solomon) p. 196-7.
28. Op cit (Solomon) p. 339-40.
29. Op cit (Solomon) p.334.
30. Op cit (Solomon) p. 107.
31. Op cit (Forbes) p. 820.
32. Op cit (Forbes) p.283.
33. Op cit (Forbes) p. 371.
34. Op cit (Forbes) p.352.
35. Op cit (Forbes) p. 473.
36. Op cit (Forbes) p.430.
37. Op cit (Forbes) p. 506, 644-739; (Solomon) p. 281-333.
38. Op cit (Solomon) p. 333.
39. Op cit (Forbes) p.783-4.
40. Op cit (Forbes) p. 776.
41. Op cit (Forbes) p. 823,859.
42. Op cit (Forbes) p. 945.
43. Op cit (Forbes) p. 798.
44. Op cit (Forbes) p. 836.
45. Op cit (Forbes) p. 946.
46. Op cit (Forbes) p. 952.
47. Op cit (Forbes) p. 973-4.
48. Op cit (Forbes) p. 1006-8
49. Op cit (Forbes) p. 1013
50. Op cit (Forbes) p. 1016-8.
51. Op cit (Forbes) p. 1022-3.
52. Op cit (Forbes) p. 1029-32.

53. The formula for almond milk (aqua amygdalarum concentrata), the water of bitter almonds, was as follows: "Take two pounds of *bitter almonds*, bruise them well, and add — whilst triturating them — ten pounds of *spring water*, and four ounces of highly *rectified spirit of wine*. Let the mixture rest for twenty-four hours in a well closed vessel, and then distil two pounds. The product must be kept in a well stopped bottle." (From Dunglison R. *New Remedies. Pharmaceutically and Therapeutically Considered.* 4th ed. Lea and Blanchard. Philadelphia. 1843: p.55)

   "Salep" was the name given to preparations of bulbs of *Orchis mascula* and other species of the same genus. It was felt to be highly nutritious and was employed for the same purposes as tapioca. (From Wood GB, Bache F. *The Dispensory of the United States of America.* 5th ed. Grigg and Elliot. Philadelphia. 1843: p. 55 and 109)

54. Op cit (Solomon) p. 105.

55. Op cit (Forbes) p. 1041.

56. Op cit (Forbes) p. 1045.

57. A common closing line in Roman comedy. Beethoven's words to Anton Schindler on March 23, 1827 C.E., three days before he died. [Op cit (Forbes) p. 1048]

58. Op cit (Forbes) p. 1049.

59. On March 27, 1827 C.E., an autopsy was performed by Dr. Johann Wagner in the presence of Dr. Andreas Wawruch, who was Beethoven's principal physician during his final illness. In order to facilitate examination of the organs of hearing, the temporal bones (in which they are encased) were sawed out and carried away. Dr. Wagner's written report of the findings was as follows:

   March 27, 1827

   The corpse was very emaciated, especially in the limbs, and sown over with black Petechien; the abdomen, which was unusually dropsied, was distended and stretched.

   The external ear was large and irregularly formed, the scaphoid fossa but more especially the concha was very spa-

cious and half as large again as usual: the various angles
and sinuosities were strongly marked. The external auditory canal was covered with shining scales, particularly in
the vicinity of the tympanum, which was concealed by
them. The Eustachian tube was much thickened, its mucous lining swollen and somewhat contracted about the os-
seous portion of the tube. In front of its orifice and towards
the tonsils some dimpled scars were observable. The principal cells of the Mastoid process, which was large and not
marked by any notch, were lined with a vascular mucous
membrane. The whole substance of the Os petrosum
showed a similar degree of vascularity, being traversed by
vessels of considerable size, more particularly in the region
of the cochlea, the membranous part of its spiral lamina appearing slightly reddened.

The facial nerves were of unusual thickness, the auditory nerves, on the contrary, were shrivelled and destitute
of neurina; the accompanying arteries were dilated to more
than the size of a crow quill and cartilaginous. The left auditory nerve much the thinnest, arose by three very thin
greyish striae, the right by one strong clearer white stria
from the substance of the fourth ventricle, which was at
this point much more consistent and vascular than in other
parts. The convolutions of the brain were full of water, and
remarkably white; they appeared very much deeper, wider,
and more numerous than ordinary.

The Calvarium exhibited throughout great density and
a thickness amounting to about half an inch.

The cavity of the Chest, together with the organs
within it, was in the normal condition.

In the cavity of the Abdomen four quarts of a greyish-
brown turbid fluid were effused.

The liver appeared shrunk up to half its proper volume,
of a leathery consistence and greenish-blue color, and
was beset with knots, the size of a bean, on its tuberculated

surface, as well as in its substance; all its vessels were very much narrowed, and bloodless.

The Spleen was found to be more than double its proper size, dark-colored and firm.

The Pancreas was equally hard and firm, its excretory duct being as wide as a goosequill.

The Stomach, together with the Bowels, was greatly distended with air. Both Kidneys were invested by cellular membrane of an inch thick, and infiltrated with a brown turbid fluid; their tissue was pale-red and opened out. Every one of their calices was occupied by a calcereous concretion of a wart-like shape and as large as a split pea. The body was much emaciated.

(Signed) Dr. Joseph Wagner

Assistant in the Pathological Museum

[Op cit (Forbes) p. 1059-60]

60. Today, the autopsy provides comprehensive information on the cause of a patient's illness(es) and death. Usually the information is definitive. However, many of the techniques used today to establish diagnoses in post mortem examinations were not available to Dr. Wagner when he performed Beethoven's autopsy.

The autopsy (derived from the Greek "autopsia", seeing for oneself) has been used for centuries to elucidate the structure and function of the human body. "During the Middle Ages, theologians and philosophers considered the material world (including the frail human frame) to be fleeting and unimportant compared to eternity, and the body was therefore not a focus of rigorous study. Anatomical dissection, in particular, was culturally construed as desecration and thus prohibited. In the 15th century, however, a small cadre of French and Italian university professors—inspired by the humanist rediscovery of the ancients – began to use cadavers to illustrate lectures from ancient Greek and Latin texts. In science and medicine, as in sculpture and painting, the Renaissance inaugurated a period of renewed interest in the human body and human potential in this world. Prior to the mid 16th century, however, anatomical dissection was not physically performed by professors or students of medicine. The professor lectured from a chair elevated above the cadaver while lowly barber-surgeons demonstrated various structures at the professor's command. Students were completely passive—they engaged the dissected body only through their eyes and their ears, never with their hands.

Occasionally, exceptional students might inhabit the role of the barber-surgeon in demonstrating structures for the lecturer. One such student, Andreas Vesalius (1514-1564), became so enthusiastic about dissecting that he continued to dissect as a professor and insisted that his students do likewise. Vesalius' most important book, *De Humani Corporis Fabrica (On the Structure of the Human Body)*, drew on the most recent techniques in illustration and helped solidify his pedagogical innovation. Anatomy, through Vesalius and his successors, became the fulcrum of a major shift in medical education away from the study of ancient Greek and Latin texts and toward direct observation. For these Renaissance medical educators, the dissected cadaver became the definitive text and the students' own observations became a source of authoritative knowledge about the human condition."

Although the study of anatomy was not static during the 350 years following Vesalius' work, the next major advance in the field did not materialize until the latter half of the 19th century with the advent of cellular pathology under the influence of Rudolf Virchow. Not until tissues obtained post mortem were subjected to microscopic examination was the autopsy's full diagnostic potential realized. Once such examinations became routine, physicians were able "to work backwards from the cadaver to determine whether diagnoses and treatments during life" were valid and appropriate. Microscopic examination enabled the autopsy to become "the yardstick by which all diagnostic and therapeutic efforts could be measured." Unfortunately, Beethoven's tissues were not examined microscopically. (From Gregory SR, Cole TS. The changing role of dissection in medical education. JAMA 2002; 287:1180-1)

61. Op cit (Forbes) p. 1051.
62. Senior K. Did Beethoven die of lead poisoning? *Lancet.* 2000; 356:1498.
63. Op cit (Solomon) p. ix.
64. The wide range of diagnoses offered to explain Beethoven's poor health reflects the diverse array of signs and symptoms produced by his illness. Table 9-1 groups these diagnoses according to the organ system disabled by his illness.
65. "Ockham's razor" refers to the Law of Parsimony articulated by William of Ockham in the 14th century, "Non sunt multiplicanda entia praetor necessitatum," which for generations of clinicians has been loosely translated as "don't think up more diagnoses than you need [to explain your patient's signs and symptoms]." (Fitzgerald FT, Zaslaw N, Mackowiak PA: Nobel heart. *Am J Med.* 2001;110:633-40)
66. Friedman I, Frohlich A, Wright A. Epidemic typhus and hearing loss: a histologic study. *J Laryngol Otol.* 1993; 107:275-383.
67. Toxicologic Profile for Lead. Publication of the U.S. Department of Health and Human Service, Agency for Toxic Substances and Disease Registry. July 1999, p. 19-124.
68. Nriagu JO. Saturnine gout among Roman aristocrats. Did lead poisoning contribute to the fall of the empire? *N Engl J Med.* 1983;308:660-3.
69. Lucey MR. Approach to the patient with cirrhosis, portal hypertension, and end-stage liver disease. In Kelley WN, ed. *Textbook of Internal Medicine.* 3rd ed. Philadelphia: Lippincott-Raven Publishers; 1997: p. 665-73.

70. Trepo C, Pradat P. Hepatitis C virus infection in western Europe. *J Hepatol.* 1999; 31(Suppl):80-3.

71. McCabe BF. Beethoven's deafness. *Ann Otol Rinol Laryngol.* 1958;76:192-206.

72. Millodot M, Laby DM. *Dictionary of Ophthalmology.* Butterwork Heinemann. Oxford:2002, p. 143, 303.

73. Op cit (Forbes) p. 181.

74. Schwarz A: Beethoven's renal disease based on his autopsy: a case of papillary necrosis. *Am J Kidney Dis.* 1993;21:643-52.

75. Syphilis, A Synopsis. Public Health Service Publication no. 1660, Jan. 1968, p.1.

76. Stokes JH, Beerman H, Ingraham NR. *Modern Clinical Syphilology. Diagnosis Treatment Case Study.* W.B. Saunders Co., Philadelphi:1944; p. 967.

77. Ibid (Stokes) p. 1118.

78. Jeans PC, Cooke JV, Haynes RS. *Clinical Pediatrics.* Prepubescent Syphilis. D. Appleton and Co. New York: 1931, p. 166.

79. Op cit (Forbes) p. 508.

80. Moore JE. The Diagnoses of Syphilis by The General Practitioner (Supplement 23). *J Venereal Dis Information.* 1949, p. 26-36.

81. Op cit (Jeans et al) p. 144.

82. Op cit (Stokes et al) p. 850.

83. Op cit (Stokes et al) p. 852.

84. Schumacher GA. Causative factors in the production of Laennec's cirrhosis with special reference to syphilis. *Am J Med.* 1937;194:693-700.

85. Op cit (Stokes et al) p. 1183.

86. Op cit (Stokes et al) p. 816-19.

87. Op cit (Stokes et al) p. 765.

88. Op cit (Stokes et al) p. 767.

89. Op cit (Stokes et al) p. 771-2.

90. Op cit (Stokes et al) p. 1177-80.

91. The origin of syphilis is debated to this day. Its history is unique among the great diseases in that it does not appear to

have gradually emerged into the historical record but to have appeared suddenly at the end of the 15th century as a great plague which swept over the known world in just a few years. Owing to the juxtaposition of that plague with the return of Columbus from his first voyage, many believe it was one of few diseases imported into Europe from the New World. Initially, because the disease was new and had no name, early references to it tended to credit responsibility for it to others. Thus, the Italians referred to it as the "Spanish" or the "French disease"; the French called it the "Italian" or "Neapolitan disease"; the English, the "French disease"; the Russians, the "Polish disease", and so on. The Spaniards, who were the earliest victims of the infection, called it the "disease of Espanola," which at that time meant the "disease of Haiti." Spread of the disease has been traced chronologically not only throughout Europe, but also from there to other parts of the world in contact with Europe. Shortly after its introduction in Europe, the Portuguese carried it to Africa and the Orient. It reached Japan, China and India sometime there after.

Syphilis was recognized as a new disease in 15th/16th century Europe because of the explosive nature of the epidemic and because it was unlike any other genital disease encountered until that time, in that it regularly spread to the skin and vital organs. No prior references can be found in either the Occidental or Oriental medical literature of a disease of the genitals commonly accompanied by severe systemic complaints. The name of the new disease, "Syphilis," has been traced to a poem written by the Italian pathologist, Hieronymus Fracastorious entitled, "Syphilis Sive Morbus Gallicus." It describes the plight of a mythical shepherd named Syphilus afflicted with the French disease as punishment for cursing the gods. The poem recognized the venereal nature of the infection and was a compendium of current knowledge of the disease. The story of syphilis over the past five centuries has been marked by grudging progress in our understanding of the disorder and ability to treat it. In 1530 C.E., Paracelsus first suggested that the disease could be transmitted congenitally and is credited with introducing mercury as a treatment in 1508 C.E. The Arabs, however, had long used mercury to treat scabies, psoriasis, leprosy and other skin diseases. Mussa described neurological manifestations of the infection in 1532 C.E., and Ferro described joint lesions in 1537 C.E. Jean Fernel (1506-88 C.E.) recognized that the agent responsible for syphilis could not pass through normal skin, but required a break in the skin to infect its host.

In the 17th and early 18th centuries, Valsalva, Baader and others established the infection's capacity to invade the liver, spleen and kidneys. By the end of the 18th century, mercury was being administered to syphilitic patients to the point of toxicity as manifested by profuse salivation. By this time, Morgagni (1682-1772 C.E.) had demonstrated invasion of virtually all organs of the body by the germ responsible for the disorder; the multifaceted abnormalities and chronic course of congenital syphilis were established; and the classical descriptions of the disorder that continue to appear in medical textbooks today were recorded.

In 1767 C.E. John Hunter performed an experiment which resulted in a startling and unfortunate reversal in this steady growth of knowledge. His experiment he hoped would resolve the question of whether syphilis and gonorrhea were the same or two different diseases. He believed they were the same disease, with gonorrhea developing when the responsible germ was deposited on a "secreting" surface (a mucous membrane such as the urethra) and syphilis when the same germ was inoculated onto a non-secreting surface. To test his theory, Hunter inoculated a non-secreting surface, his skin, with pus from a patient with gonorrhea. Unfortunately, that patient was simultaneously infected with *T. pallidum*, which infected and ultimately killed Hunter. For the next half century, Hunter's experiment was regarded as proof that syphilis (which we now know to be caused by *T. pallidum*) and gonorrhea (caused by the bacterium *Neissera gonorrhea*) were the same disease.

The beginning of the 20th century witnessed some of the most spectacular advances in syphilology. In 1903 C.E., Metchnikoff and Roux successfully infected apes with syphilis, opening the way for future studies of the disease in animal models. In 1905 C.E., Schaudinn and Hoffman ended the long search for the agent responsible for syphilis with their discovery of *T. pallidum*. In 1906-1907 C.E., Wassermann, Neisser and Bruck developed the first practical blood test for syphilis, now known as the Wassermann reaction. In 1911 C.E., Noguchi succeeded in growing *T. pallidum* in culture. In 1909-10 C.E., Ehrlich introduced arsphenamine as a treatment for syphilis, which was succeeded by penicillin as the definitive therapy for the disorder in the 1940s C.E. (Pusey WA. *The History and Epidemiology of Syphilis*. Charles C. Thomas, Springfield, IL: 1933; p. 30-74; Syphilis. A Synopsis. U.S. Public Health Service Publication No. 1660, 1968, p. 1-16.)

92. Op cit (Forbes) p. 238-40.
93. Op cit (Pusey) p. 77.
94. Op cit (Stokes et al) p. 1189.
95. Op cit (Pusey) p. 81.
96. Dennie CL. *A History of Syphilis*. Charles C. Thomas, Publisher. Springfield, IL: 1962, p. 75.
97. Op cit (Stokes et al) p. 1185.
98. Crissey JT, Parish LC. *The Dermatology and Syphilology of the Nineteenth Century*. Praeger Publishers: New York: 1981, p. 360-1.

10   A BRIGHT BUT UNSTEADY LIGHT

This patient was as strange and as talented a figure as any in the American literary pantheon.[1] Orphaned, disowned, wedded to a child-cousin and ruled by alcohol, he overcame extreme poverty and mental torment during an all-too-brief life to become one of the most influential writers of the 19th century.

He was a Romantic poet of incomparable technical virtuosity, one who captured the actual sound of bells in a phonic experiment of hypnotic cadences and also conjured up a haunting vision of doom in a single-word refrain delivered by a raven. He was a literary critic, an editor and an art theorist; it has even been said, with some justification, that he created the science fiction genre and the detective story. He also wrote macabre stories, ones most of us read as children and have encountered again as modern-day horror films.[2]

The patient had a perverse concept of beauty, one epitomized by the death of a beautiful woman.[3] Death, in fact, was never far from his mind, and in his work took strange forms. His own death in 1849, three months before his forty-first birthday, was as strange as any he created in his many works of fiction.

Only a few details of the illness that extinguished his "bright but unsteady light"[4] are known because his physician, Dr. John Joseph Moran, used the illness to promote his own celebrity and in the process denied posterity an accurate clinical description.[5] Only Moran's letter to Mrs. Maria Clemm (see Figure 10-1), the patient's mother-in-law, can be trusted, for it was written before he began to feed the public's appetite for ever more moving and ironic details of

241

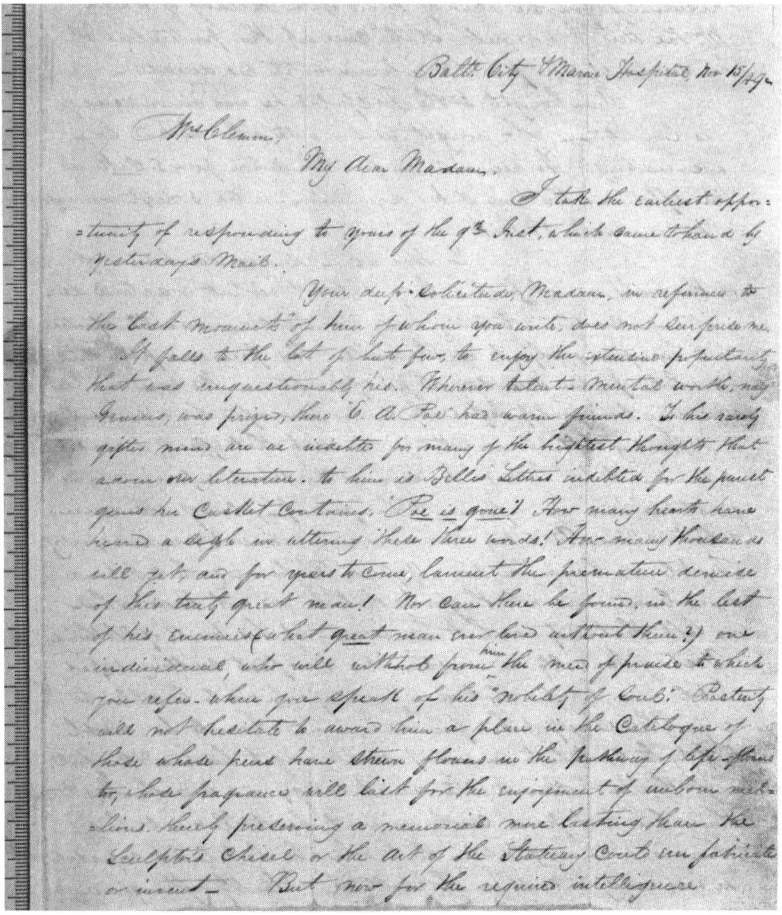

FIGURE 10-1. Dr. J.J. Moran's letter to Maria Clemm, November 15, 1849, in which he describes the patient's last hours (see Note 6).

his patient's final hours.[6] Unfortunately, the letter is brief and only modestly informative.

According to the letter, the patient arrived at the Washington College Hospital in Baltimore on Wednesday, the 3rd of October, 1849. He was delirious, with no apparent appreciation of his desperate condition, how he happened to be in the hospital or where he had been during the days prior to his admission. Earlier that day, he

242

had been found disoriented outside of Ryan's Fourth Ward polls in the heart of Baltimore and brought to the hospital by his friend, Dr. J. E. Snodgrass. In one of his later accounts, Moran wrote that the coachman who conveyed the patient to the hospital claimed that his passenger "did not smell of whiskey," fueling speculation that his fatal illness was the consequence of some disease other than the alcoholism with which he had struggled for years.

By the next morning the patient was in a tremulous state. Initially, he exhibited a busy but not violent or active delirium, marked by constant talking and vacant conversations with spectral and imaginary objects on the walls. His face was pale, his whole body drenched with perspiration. All efforts to induce tranquility were unsuccessful that first day. But by the next day, his senses seemed to clear, though his answers remained incoherent and unsatisfactory. He claimed that he had a wife in Richmond (which was untrue, although he did have a fiancée there) and that he did not know when he had left that city or what had become of his clothes and other belongings. The mystery of his whereabouts and activities from the time of his departure from Richmond until his arrival at the Washington College Hospital have never been solved.

Attempts to console the patient were met with visible agitation and an assertion that "the best thing his best friend could do would be to blow out his brains with a pistol."[6] Shortly thereafter he seemed to doze, only to awaken sometime later in a delirium so violent that two nurses had great difficulty keeping him in bed. He persisted in this state until Saturday the 6th, when, as Moran reported, he began calling for one "Reynolds." Who Reynolds was, if not simply the product of Moran's over-active imagination, has never been determined, but in an article published in the *Baltimore Sun* on the one hundredth anniversary of the patient's death,[7] James H. Bready claimed that the man was Henry Reynolds, a friend of the patient and owner of a carpenter shop near the spot where the poet was found. According to Maryland Historical Society records, this same Reynolds was also chief judge of elections at the local polling station[8] where some believe the patient fell victim to the practice of Election Day "cooping." The patient continued calling out until 3:00 a.m. Sunday, when a decided change began to affect him. Enfeebled by the strenuous exertions of the preceding three days, he seemed to rest for a short time, then, gently moving his head, he said "Lord help my poor Soul" and expired. The official diagnosis was "congestion of the brain."[9]

Whereas details of this last illness are sparse, the patient's letters and those of his family, friends and associates[10] tell us much about the man and, in all likelihood, also about the nature of the illness that cured for him "the fever called living."[11]

He was born in Boston to a twenty-two-year-old English actress who performed with some distinction in theaters throughout the northeastern United States. She died when he was two of a lingering, debilitating illness, which, although never diagnosed, was most likely tuberculosis. The patient's father was also an actor, but one decidedly less talented than his mother. He was of Irish stock, and some say that it was his Celtic flame that kindled in his son a mysticism that concerned itself with those dim regions where the relations of man and the supernatural collide. The patient's father loved alcohol more than he loved his son and abandoned the child and his wife just before she died. What became of him is unknown. Fortunately for the boy, a cousin took him in when his mother died and raised him as his foster son in a loving and privileged household. When the boy became a man, a schism developed between them and with it, the loss of both his foster father's love and financial support.

The patient had an older brother who died at age twenty-four. While the exact cause of his death is unknown, it is likely that alcoholism was involved.[12] Another relative, a paternal cousin, was also an alcoholic. The patient's sister, one year his junior, did not suffer from the disease, however, and though mentally retarded, lived until aged sixty-three in "reasonably good physical health."[13]

Although the patient spent most of his formative years in Virginia, he began his schooling at a private institution in England at age six. After five years of study there, he was able to speak French and to read Latin and was better versed in history and literature than many older, more advantaged boys. He continued to exercise his mind and his body and by the time he entered the University of Virginia at age seventeen, he showed evidence of a promising future as a man of letters. However, whereas the University of Virginia broadened his grasp of literature, it also taught him the elements of gambling, fighting and drinking. After a year, his stepfather refused to subsidize his education further because of the debts he had accumulated.

Shortly after his departure from the University, the patient enlisted in the army. He served in an artillery unit under an assumed name, Edgar Perry. Why he chose not to use his own name is not known. In his two years with the unit, he rose to the rank of sergeant major, the highest non-commissioned grade in the army. When he was twenty-one, he entered the United States Military Academy at West Point. Within a year, he was court-martialed and forced to leave the Academy. Although his roommates said that he had a "fondness for drinking," the charges against him were "gross neglect of duty" and "disobedience of orders." A biographer credited his expulsion to the fact that "he simply declined to continue under circumstances which hampered his creative work."[14]

After he left the Academy, poverty, despair and alcohol began to tighten their grip on him, even as the literary triumphs that would become his legacy were accumulating. In October, 1833, when he was twenty-four, he wrote "The Manuscript Found in a Bottle," for which he received a fifty-dollar prize for the best short story submitted to Baltimore's *The Saturday Visitor*. It was the first public acknowledgement of his literary genius. By the time he was twenty-six, he had many other published works to his credit, including "Berenice," "Morella," "Lionizing" and "Hans Phaall, a Tale." It was then that he began a courtship of his thirteen-year-old cousin, Virginia, which within a year culminated in marriage. Her companionship and that of her mother temporarily elevated his spirits. Virginia, however, was never well, and spent their eleven years of marriage succumbing to the ravages of tuberculosis. She was twenty-five when she died. He was thirty-eight, and although famous by then following publication of his poem "The Raven" in *The American Whig Review*, he was mentally and physically bereft.

Except for minor childhood illnesses and "severe ear trouble" while at the Academy, the patient's health had been good until age twenty-two. That year he wrote to his foster father of "bad health" and an arrest for a debt. The former was a recurrent theme in subsequent letters. Like his great rival, Nathaniel Hawthorne, he complained repeatedly of nervous depression.[15] He is believed to have attempted suicide at least once (see below) and was plagued by a succession of unspecified illnesses that interrupted his work for varying periods of time. He exercised regularly, at least he did until his final years, and except for an attack of cholera early in 1849, his "unspecified illnesses" seem to have been more the result of mental than physical disability.

The patient's most serious and most controversial medical problem concerned his use of alcohol. By his own admission and the statements of numerous friends and associates, he had a weakness for drink, which reflected "a perverse tendency to injure his own prospects."[16] Was the weakness indicative of some basic character flaw? It was said that he was overly sensitive, self-critical, irregular, eccentric, querulous, prideful and chronically unhappy. He also had a "wonderful fecundity of imagination,"[17] which at times culminated in fabrications concerning his personal history. He loved his wife deeply, for example, and she was devoted to him. However, after her death, pursuit of new companionship led him to claim that he had "married, for another's happiness, where I knew no possibility of my own existed."[18]

Many of the patient's later years were marked by a desperate struggle for sanity. Recurrent bouts of depression brought on by his basic constitution and his unrelenting social and financial pressures drove him ever deeper into the shadowy world of alcohol. He had both a fondness for and an intolerance of wine. If he took one glass, "the Rubicon of the cup was passed with him, and it almost always ended in excess and sickness."[19] In June of 1842, when he was thirty-three and hard at work on *Phantasy Pieces*, a new two-volume edition of his collected works, he was so "unwell" he was forced to give up and go to bed. Virginia was then dangerously ill with hemorrhage from her lungs. In September while nursing her, he was taken with a severe chill and fever himself. He was ill again in March of 1843, and also in September of that year. Although admitting to "in times past [being] given to spreeing upon an extensive scale," he claimed that he was sober then as he despaired over Virginia's deteriorating condition.[20]

Eighteen forty-six was a particularly bad year. From February to July of that year the patient was too ill to write installments of "Marginalia" for *Grahm's* and *The Democratic Review,* from which he earned his meager income. When Virginia died in January of 1847, his own long agony seemed to be drawing to conclusion. At times then he talked like a man insane, one perfectly self-possessed in all other respects, whose brain and tongue seemed beyond his control.[21] He had no memory of these spells afterwards and seems to have been under the influence of mental aberrations brought on by wine. During the first few months after Virginia's death, he experienced a complete mental collapse and had to be cared for by his mother-in-law and Mrs. Marie Louise Shew, a friend with some medical training. According to the latter, the patient was afflicted with "brain fever," which caused his pulse to race and to "beat only ten regular beats, after which it suspended or intermitted."[22]

The patient was still exceedingly ill in August of 1847. In November of that year, he made a trip to Providence of which he remembered nothing distinctly until his arrival. After a bad night, he bought two ounces of laudanum, half of which he swallowed and immediately regurgitated during his return trip to Boston.[23] At the time, he was purportedly despondent over a failed courtship, leading to suspicion that the ingestion might have been a suicide attempt. This was apparently the only time he used opiates. In spite of these "illnesses," his mind never weakened, at least not until the very end, as evidenced by "Eureka," a long prose poem of a semi-scientific and metaphysical nature that he wrote in 1846 and lectured on until shortly before his death.[24]

A little less than a year before he died, the patient was writing with renewed inspiration. However, misfortune continued to pursue him. Magazines which had accepted his work failed or suspended payment, leading to further episodes of binging and delirium for which his aging mother-in-law again had to nurse him. In the spring of 1849, somewhat recovered, he left her in New York to travel to Richmond. On the way, a stop in Philadelphia resulted in yet another binge for which he was arrested. Ultimately, faithful friends raised sufficient funds to rescue him from prison and send him on his way to Richmond.

Shaken by what had been a near fatal relapse of his struggle with alcohol in Philadelphia, and with great effort, the patient succeeded in abstaining from drink for a brief time. During this period of sobriety, he managed to obtain a promise of marriage from his childhood sweetheart, Elmira Royster, now Mrs. A.B. Shelton, a well-to-do widow. On September 27, 1849, the patient left Richmond on what was to be his final journey. The purpose of the trip is just one of many lingering mysteries surrounding his death. It has been speculated that he intended to travel to New York to retrieve his mother-in-law for the upcoming wedding,[25] and also that he was going to either New York or Philadelphia to wind up some unfinished business.[26] Whatever his reason for making the trip, he was far from well when he departed.

According to his intended, when he came to her house the night before he left, "he was very sad and complained of being quite sick."[27] When she felt his pulse, she found that he had "considerable fever" and thought it unlikely that he would be able to begin his journey the next morning.

From the time the patient left Richmond until he was found in Baltimore on October 3, nothing is known of his activities. His death, unlike his poetry, was unbeautiful. It was, however, poignant to the point of mythmaking — if, that is, the details were not fabricated *in the interest of mythmaking*, for many have sought to find fame of their own in embellishing the story of the life and death of Edgar Allan Poe, who died in Baltimore early in the morning of October 7, 1849 (see Figure 10-2).

EDGAR ALLAN POE,

FIGURE 10-2. Edgar Allan Poe. Daguerreotype. Whitman, Sarah Ellen (19th CE).
Photo Credit : Giraudon/Art Resource, NY.

***

Many diagnoses have been offered to explain Poe's death. The earliest and most persistent has been that of alcohol-induced delirium tremens. The newest and most interesting is rabies. Homicide, carbon monoxide poisoning, suicide, syphilis and mercury intoxication also have been proposed, reflecting more an unwillingness on the part of the proposers to accept an ordinary disease as the cause of Poe's death than any convincing clinical evidence of such disorders.

In 1995, during the first of the Historical Clinicopathological Conferences on which this book is based, Dr. R. Michael Benitez concluded that Poe died of rabies resulting from an unrecorded and most likely unrecognized animal exposure prior to his hospitalization in Baltimore.[28] Benitez based his diagnosis on evidence of autonomic instability (dilating and contracting pupils and an irregular pulse which alternated between rapid and slow), fluctuating delirium and hydrophobia (suggested by his adamant refusal of alcohol and difficulty swallowing water) included in Moran's later descriptions of the terminal illness.

Rabies, in fact, has much in common with Poe's final illness.[29] It is a viral encephalitis (i.e., an infection of the brain) marked by acute onset of confusion, hallucinations, combativeness, muscle spasms and seizures, all of which tend to wax and wane during the course of the illness. Autonomic instability marked by alternating tachycardia (racing pulse) and bradycardia (slow pulse), profuse sweating, lacrimation and salivation are also characteristic. The infection is virtually always fatal, with a median survival time after the onset of symptoms of four days. Poe, it will be recalled, died four days after being admitted to the hospital.

Although Poe had no known history of exposure to a rabid animal, this would by no means be unusual in cases of rabies. Of thirty-three such human cases diagnosed in the United States between 1977 and 1994, only nine had evidence of an appropriate animal exposure.[30]

Moran offered no indication of autonomic instability in the letter he wrote to Mrs. Clemm a month after her son-in-law's death. Only decades later, most likely relying on memory alone, does he mention a "very low pulse" and that his famous patient's "pulse which had been as low as fifty was rising rapidly, though still feeble and variable."[5] Likewise, in Moran's early letter, he says that although Poe regained consciousness the day after being admitted, "his answers were incoherent & unsatisfactory," implying that Poe's delirium was unremitting, not waxing and waning. Only in his later accounts does he suggest that Poe's delirium cleared for a period during his hospitalization. And with regard to suggestions that Poe might have had hydrophobia, Moran states in his later account that his patient "vehemently rejected" a glass of toddy and when given a drink of water to determine if he could swallow freely, "did this with some difficulty." No such evidence of hydrophobia appears in his earlier letter to Mrs. Clemm. Nor in any of his accounts is there mention of excessive salivation or seizures, both of which are highly characteristic of rabies.

In his account of 1885,[5] Moran theorized that prior to arriving at his hospital, Poe had been "seized by two roughs, dragged into one of the many sinks of iniquity or gambling hells which lined the [Baltimore] wharf...drugged, robbed [and] stripped of every vestige of clothing he had on" before, in effect, having been left to die. By the time he wrote this account, Moran had assumed the role of his patient's defender, declaring that he had detected no trace of alcohol on the poet's breath and later felt obligated to protect the man he initially "believed to be drunk" against the malicious accusations of his enemies. In fact, Moran's accounts of 1875 and 1885 are so replete with contradictions (e.g., regarding the time of Poe's death) and untruths (e.g., his claim of having referred to Poe's hospital record in writing his later accounts), one is inclined to doubt anything he says in them not corroborated by his earlier letter to Mrs. Clemm. His robbery/murder theory is especially suspect, because when found unconscious, Poe still grasped a valuable sword-cane he had brought with him from Richmond.

Several more recent theories are worth mentioning, if only to illustrate the determination of Poe devotees to ascribe to him a cause of death as enigmatic as his life and works. It has been suggested, for example, by an employee of a company that manufactures carbon monoxide detectors, that Poe's alcohol intolerance was a consequence of "multiple chemical sensitivity" due to chronic carbon monoxide poisoning acquired from gas lights used in Baltimore, Philadelphia and New York during the poet's lifetime.[31] Another would-be diagnostician has suggested, without supporting evidence, that Poe's alcohol intolerance was the result of a "hyperactive ear syndrome" caused by syphilis.[32] It has even been proposed that Poe killed himself by taking an overdose of calomel, a mercury-containing compound he originally obtained to treat himself for cholera.[33] If past is indeed prologue, none of these diagnoses offers a better explanation for Poe's chronic ill health and death than alcoholism.

Was Poe an alcoholic? The *Third Diagnostic and Statistical Manual* of the American Psychiatric Association divides alcoholism into alcohol abuse and alcohol dependence. According to the manual, *alcohol abuse* exists if there is evidence of alcohol-related impairment of normal life function. Alcohol abuse progresses to *alcohol dependence* when alcohol-related functional impairment is accompanied by heightened ethanol intolerance or characteristic physical abnormalities on withdrawal from alcohol. In simpler terms, alcoholism is a diagnosis given to persons whose use of alcohol causes marital strife, work-related problems, arrests, or physical disabilities, such as liver dysfunction, heart failure and withdrawal symptoms.[34]

Although there is no direct evidence that Poe's drinking created problems in his relationship with his wife, Virginia, there is evidence that his subsequent courtship of Mrs. Sarah Helen Whitman was jeopardized by alcohol. On November 13, 1848, Whitman reportedly consented to be engaged to Poe, but only if he abstained from drink, which he proved he could not.[35] That alcohol repeatedly interfered with his work is suggested by the many "unspecified illnesses" referred to above, which repeatedly interrupted his literary and editorial efforts. That at least some, if not most, of these illnesses were direct consequences of alcohol abuse is suggested by a letter written by John R.Thompson on October 17, 1848, when he was Editor of the *Southern Literary Messenger*. In it, he writes:

> Poe is not in Richmond. He remained here about 3 weeks, horribly drunk and discoursing 'Eureka' every night to the audiences of the Bar Rooms. His friends tried to get him sober and set him to work but to no effect and were compelled at last to reship him to New York. I was anxious for him to write something for me, while

he remained here, but his lucid intervals were so brief and infrequent that it was quite impossible.[36]

As noted above, Poe was arrested at least once for drunkenness. We know this because in a letter to his mother-in-law three months before he died he wrote, "I have been taken to prison once since I came here for getting drunk."[37] Although he claimed that he was not drunk "then," he nevertheless fulfilled yet another criterion of the *Third Diagnostic and Statistical Manual* for alcohol dependence.

Evidence that alcohol was exacting a heavy toll on Poe's physical condition during his later years is also compelling. As early as 1841, when he was thirty-two and working in Philadelphia as an assistant editor for *Graham's* magazine, he wrote:

> I was never in the *habit* of intoxication. I never drank drams, etc. But for a brief period while I resided in Richmond, and edited the *Messenger*, I certainly did give way, at long intervals, to the temptation held out on all sides by the spirit of Southern Conviviality...In short, it sometimes happened that I was completely intoxicated. For some days after each excess, I was invariably confined to bed.[38]

Then in November of 1847, as we have already seen, there was the trip to Providence of which Poe remembered nothing. This was not his only instance of short-term memory loss and subsequent amnesia (blackout) characteristic of both episodic and chronic intoxication. In an editorial in the *Home Journal*, Saturday, December 26, 1846, Nathaniel P. Willis describes an exhibition of patently psychotic behavior by Poe, which he had "little or no memory of... afterwards."[39]

By July of 1849, Poe's handwriting was beginning to deteriorate. In a letter to his mother-in-law on July 19, he wrote, "You will see at once, by the handwriting of this letter, that I am better...."[40] His remark implies that he was having at least intermittent difficulty with his penmanship. Although the source of this problem is open to question, based on Poe's other physical disabilities related to alcohol, it is likely that he was beginning to manifest tremors characteristic of persons who reduce their intake of alcohol after prolonged bouts of drinking.

Hallucinations and overt psychosis are common during withdrawal periods in alcohol-dependent persons. *Delirium tremens*, the most severe form of withdrawal, is dominated by confusion, agitated delusions and hallucinations and, occasionally, generalized seizures. The hallucinations of delirium tremens are most often visual hallucinations of a disturbing nature, spiders on walls, for example. Moran's description of his patient's vacant conversations with "spectral and imaginary objects on the walls"[6] suggest that Poe was having just such visual hallucinations during his final illness.

The likelihood of developing severe symptoms of withdrawal increases in the presence of concomitant medical problems (such as infection), a prior history of withdrawal seizures or delirium tremens, and in the aftermath of particularly intense drinking bouts. Most episodes begin and end abruptly. Symptoms appear within five to ten hours of ceasing alcohol intake, peak in intensity by day two or three and improve by day four to five.[21] In some series, mortality has been as high as twenty percent.[41]

Poe had episodes of both hallucinations and overt psychosis prior to his final illness. In the letter by Willis referred to above, Poe is described as:

> [talking] like a man insane. Perfectly self-possessed in all other respects, his brain and tongue were evidently beyond his control. We learned afterwards that the least stimulus — a single glass of wine — would produce this effect....[39]

Similarly, Mrs. Whitman described a visit by Poe in November, 1848 in which he came to her home in an excited state, begging her to save him from a terrible doom. A physician was called and diagnosed the case as one of "cerebral congestion,"[35] ironically, the very diagnosis that was later given as the cause of Poe's death.[9] During a stop in Philadelphia in July of 1849, Poe called on John Sartain, then editor of the *Union Magazine*. Looking pale and haggard, Poe begged Sartain for refuge from attack by two men who, he said, were on the train for New York, and were plotting to kill him. Sartain believed Poe was suffering from "mania of persecution," for he reported being in Moyamensing Prison and dreaming of a radiant young woman standing on the topmost coping of the prison's stone tower, who spoke to him across a great distance. When Sartain asked how he came to be in Moyamensing Prison, Poe said he had been suspected of trying to pass a fifty-dollar counterfeit note, when, in fact, he had been arrested for public intoxication.[42] Poe repeated his account of the dream and the radiant figure to John R. Thompson some time later. However, in the later version, the vision carried him over the housetops of Philadelphia, "turning eventually into a black evil bird, which told Poe it was cholera."[43] Later that same month, in a letter to his mother-in-law, he wrote:

> For more than ten days I was totally deranged, although I was not drinking one drop; and during this interval, I imagined the most horrible calamities. All was hallucination, arising from an attack which I had never before experienced — an attack of mania-à-potu [another name for delirium tremens].[40]

In the fall of 1849, Poe was taken to Duncan Lodge in Richmond by Dr. John MacKenzie and Dr. Gibbon Carter after two "relapses," the second of which was serious. The two physicians warned Poe at that time "that another attack of the same nature would be fatal. Poe replied that "if people would not tempt him, he would not fall."[44]

Although the liver is the organ most vulnerable to the toxic effects of prolonged alcohol excess, like the brain, the heart occasionally falls victim to such abuse. In 1973, in a letter to *The New England Journal of Medicine,* Tsung O. Cheng, MD first described a syndrome he called "delirium tremens cordis."[45] This condition, now more commonly known as "holiday heart," is characterized by cardiac rhythm disturbances (especially various forms of tachycardia) in alcoholics who have engaged in especially heavy bouts of drinking. The specific mechanism responsible for these alcohol-induced tachycardias is unknown. However, preliminary evidence points to an excitatory effect of alcohol on the sympathetic nervous system.[46]

Shortly after Virginia's death, following a period of intense drinking, Poe collapsed and was cared for by his mother-in-law and Mrs. Marie Louise Shew, a friend with some prior medical training. The latter found Poe's pulse to be rapid and extremely irregular and, in consultation with the great Dr. Valentine Mott of the School of Medicine of New York University, diagnosed "brain fever brought on by extreme suffering of the mind and body."[22] Based on her findings and Poe's long history of alcohol abuse, "delirium tremens cordis" due to alcoholic cardiomyopathy is the diagnosis today's clinicians likely would apply to his condition.

How much Poe drank and for how long can only be guessed. Clinical investigation has determined that complications of alcoholism such as those from which Poe appears to have suffered arise only after prolonged and continuous drinking at levels in excess of the equivalent of one pint, or more often one fifth, of spirits a day.[47] In view of such observations, it can be estimated that if wine was Poe's alcoholic beverage of choice, given its lower ethanol content, he had for years consumed an average of three to four fifths of the drink daily.

Why Poe drank has many potential answers. Currently, alcoholism afflicts ten percent of men and three to five percent of women at some time during their lives. Evidence from family, twin and adoption studies has shown that genetics plays an important role in vulnerability to alcoholism, with the risk increasing *pari passu* with the number of alcoholic relatives and the closeness of their genetic relationship.[48] Poe's father, brother and at least one cousin were most likely alcoholics.

Poe gave a host of reasons for why he drank. He maintained that drinking was a treatment of sorts for his "sensitive temperament [that] could not stand an excitement which was an everyday matter to [his] companions."[38] He claimed that he "was induced to resort to the occasional use of *cider*, with the hope of relieving a nervous at-tack."[38] He attributed his drinking to the death of Virginia when he "became insane, with long intervals of horrible sanity. During fits of absolute unconsciousness [he] drank, God only knows how often and how much."[49] And he blamed his drinking on his associates. He said, "I call God to witness that I have never loved dissipation.... But I was drawn to it by companions."[50]

Poe's biographer, Arthur Hobson Quinn, offers his own reasons for the drinking: Fear that one day he [Poe], like his sister Rosalie, "would pass over the line that divides the sane from the insane"[51] caused Poe to drink so that he might forget for a short time who and where he was.[51] Quinn has suggested that the sufferings caused by poverty in a sensitive, proud, educated gentleman like Poe are ago-nies indescribable that generate temptations irresistible; and that Poe's poverty was at times extreme, extending to the want of even the mere necessities of life. Pride, self-reproach, want, weariness, Quinn believed, drove Poe to seek excitement, perhaps forgetful-ness, in wine, and that the least drop of wine, which to most people is a moderate stimulus, was to Poe literally the cup of frenzy.

Of the many mysteries surrounding Poe's death, one of the most perplexing is the question of his activities between the time he left Richmond on September 23 and his appearance at the Washington College Hospital on October 3. One of the most persistent theories concerning his whereabouts and how he came to be fatally intoxi-cated is that he was a victim of "cooping."[52] This particular theory has attracted many students of his final illness because it would ex-plain how he happened to be dressed in a poor suit of thin texture not his own at the time he was discovered outside Ryan's Fourth Ward polls and yet still be in possession of the expensive sword-cane he had brought with him from Richmond. It might also explain why he might have broken so soon an oath of abstinence that he had given the Sons of Temperance shortly before leaving Richmond.

In 1849, Baltimore, like most major American cities, was plagued by election fraud. "Cooping," then a popular form of ballot rigging, was a practice whereby gangs of thugs roamed the city a few days before Election Day, rounding up drunkards and homeless persons. These captives were furnished with food and liquor while confined to a basement or back room, "like chickens in a coop." On Election Day, they were then herded to the polls to vote repeatedly for candidates of the party sponsoring the gangs. To make it harder for opponents at the polls to spot such fraud, captives were made to swap clothes after casting votes. Many believe Poe, already drunk or perhaps sick, injured or just vulnerable looking, was scooped up from the streets of Baltimore by one such gang. Critics of the cooping theory argue that Poe had too many friends, fans and family in Baltimore to have been marched through the streets without being recognized and rescued.

Given Poe's medical history prior to his departure from Richmond in late September of 1849, and the nature of the illness described by Moran in his letter of November 15, 1849 to Poe's mother-in-law, one need look no further than delirium tremens as an explanation for his death. Whether his last bout with alcohol was the result of cooping,[52] his own inability to control the craving that had for so many years driven him to drink, or a second (successful) attempt at suicide[53] will never be known. However, if one ignores Moran's later expanded description of Poe's final illness, which deviates so spectacularly from his initial description in his letter to Maria Clemm a month after his patient's death,[6] neither rabies,[28] homicide,[5] mercury intoxication,[33] nor, for that matter, any of the myriad other explanations proposed in the century and a half since Poe's death, offers a better fit than delirium tremens.

The physical consequences of chronic alcoholism were clear to physicians of the first half of the 19th century. Dr. Benjamin Rush, one of the most influential American physicians of that era, correctly identified alcohol with "sickness of the stomach," "obstructions of the liver," "jaundice and dropsy of the belly and limbs," "consumption," "diabetes," epilepsy, gout and madness.[54] He also recognized the potentially deadly consequences of these complications of the addiction. He was aware of the genetic predisposition to alcoholism. A *propos* of Poe, he believed that men who follow professions that require constant exercise of the faculties of their minds are apt to seek relief by use of ardent spirits from fatigue born of great mental exertions. He also maintained that persons under pressure of debt, disappointments in worldly pursuits and guilt, sometimes seek to drown their sorrows in strong drink. Interestingly, Rush did not believe that fermented liquors such as wine and beer contained enough alcohol to produce intoxication without exciting a disrelish to their taste or pain from distension of the stomach. Rather, he thought that when taken in a moderate quantity, such beverages were generally innocent and "often have a friendly influence upon health and life."

Rush taught physicians of Poe's era how to manage fits of acute drunkenness,[55] as well as how to destroy the desire for alcohol.[56] In the former instance, he advised first opening the man's collar and removing all tight ligatures from every other part of the body. The contents of the stomach were then to be discharged by thrusting a feather down the throat. A napkin was wrapped round the head and wetted for an hour or two with cold water. Sometimes the whole body was plunged into cold water. Other treatments included severe whippings, to excite "a revulsion of the blood from the brain to the external parts of the body" (i.e., to relieve "congestion of the brain"), profuse sweats and bleeding. Although Dr. Moran did not describe application of any of these treatments to Poe in his letter to Mrs. Clemm of November 1849, in view of Rush's considerable influence on the practice of medicine in early 19th-century America, if Moran had thought Poe intoxicated at the time of admission, it is likely that he would have resorted to at least some of Rush's recommendations.

The specific treatment recommended for delirium tremens in 1849 was articulated by Dr. Robley Dunglison, MD in his *Dictionary of Medical Science*, published in 1845.[57] Dunglison taught in Baltimore at the University of Maryland School of Medicine from 1833 until 1836. Although many of his contemporaries regarded the use of "stimulants" such as large doses of opium to induce rest as indispensable, Dunglison believed that simple supportive measures were both generally successful and more likely to result in a permanent cure than drugs.

The treatment of delirium tremens today is controversial and, in many respects, no more satisfying than Dunglison's. Like Dunglison's contemporaries, most modern clinicians treat patients with sedatives (Dunglison refers to opium as a stimulant; today it is classified as a sedative) such as benzodiazepines.[34] Because patients are confused and agitated for three to five days regardless of therapy, sedatives are used to control behavior rather than to alter the course of the delirium. Supportive measures, such as proper nutrition, vitamins, rest and hydration, are the other mainstays of therapy today.

According to Rush, the purpose of alcoholic rehabilitation programs was to destroy the desire for ardent spirits.[56] To this end, he recommended interventions based on the doctrines of the Christian religion, inducing a sense of guilt or shame, negative conditioning (using measures such as the lacing of the alcoholic's drink with tartar emetic) and "exciting a counter measure in the mind" of the alcoholic. He also advocated a diet consisting wholly of vegetables, "an oath, taken before a magistrate" and counseling regarding the potential fatal consequences of intemperance. Although some of his contemporaries recommended gradual withdrawal of spirits from the alcoholic, Rush felt that addicted persons should abstain from alcohol "suddenly and entirely."

Even today, fewer than half of alcoholics completing rehabilitation programs maintain abstinence for a year.[34] Moreover, there is as yet no accepted single best way to rehabilitate alcoholics. Most programs emphasize the importance of helping patients achieve and maintain a high degree of motivation toward abstinence and, in the process, teaching the alcoholic to adjust to life without alcohol and to reestablish a functional lifestyle through personal counseling, vocational rehabilitation, family support and sexual counseling. Sometimes disulfiram is prescribed. This is a drug that induces severe gastrointestinal distress when alcohol is consumed. Self-help groups, such as Alcoholics Anonymous, like the Sons of Temperance Poe joined just prior to his death,[58] have also been effective in helping some alcoholics manage their addiction.

Thus, had Poe recovered from his last illness, it is doubtful that he would have succeeded in his struggle against alcohol, even with the help of the Sons of Temperance. Whether his mental faculties had already suffered from alcohol to an extent incompatible with the literary triumphs of earlier years is also uncertain. However, scientific investigation has shown that whereas chronic alcoholics do not differ from non-alcoholics on most standard indices of psychometric testing, they perform significantly less well on several measures of adaptive ability, such as speech and sound perception.[47]

Although there are many secrets surrounding Poe's death, there can be no doubt that alcohol had already done great harm to him by the time he was found unconscious in Baltimore in October of 1849. Nor is there any reason to believe he ever triumphed over his addiction to alcohol. How he came to be in delirium tremens when taken to the Washington College Hospital will not likely ever be known. Based on his prior history, however, and the nature of the illness described by Dr J.J. Moran in his initial account to Mrs. Maria Clemm, there can be no doubt that delirium tremens was the disorder that carried Poe to the place: "Where the good and the bad and the worst and the best/Have gone to their eternal rest."[59]

Notes

1. Description of Poe by John Pendleton Kennedy in his journal written after Poe's death in 1849. From Tuckerman HT. *The Life of John Pendleton Kennedy.* New York: 1871, p. 376-7.

2. Weinstein A. Lecture 10: Edgar Allan Poe: Poete Maudit. In *The Brown University Guidebook. The Great Courses: Teaching that Engages the Mind.* 1997. The Teaching Company Limited Partnership. Chantilly, VA.

3. Some scholars attribute the death of Poe's young wife, Virginia, as the inspiration for "Annabel Lee." Silverman, K. *Edgar A. Poe: Mournful and Never-Ending Remembrance.* New York: Harper Perennial, 1992, p. 401-4.

4. J. P. Kennedy's description from his October 10, 1849 note in his diary: "On Tuesday last Edgar A. Poe died in town here at the hospital from the effects of a debauch. . . . He fell in with some companion here who seduced him to the bottle, which it was said he had renounced some time ago. The consequence was fever, delirium, and madness, and in a few days a termination of his sad career in the hospital. Poor Poe! . . . A bright but unsteady light has been awfully quenched." (Charles H. Bonner, *John Pendleton Kennedy; Gentleman from Baltimore*, Baltimore: The Johns Hopkins Press, 1961, p. 194.

5. Our knowledge of what happened, from the time of Poe's admission to the Washington College Hospital In Baltimore until his death depends almost entirely on the evidence of one person, Dr. J. J. Moran. His two later accounts were likely influenced by his desire to tell anyone who would listen the story of Poe's final illness and death. He even gave a number of public lectures on the subject, of which we have several newspaper reports. His most important statements, however, are contained in three documents, still extant:

(1) Moran's letter of 15 November 1849, to Maria Clemm. This letter was first published incompletely by Woodberry in his 1885 book on Poe, but with some excisions and false readings. It has been reprinted with similar infidelities. The most reliable text is the one given by Arthur Hobson Quinn and Richard Hart in 1941. The manuscript which they reproduce in facsimile, is held by the Enoch Pratt Library.

(2) His article published in the *New York Herald*, 28 October 1875, entitled "Official Memoranda of the Death of Edgar A. Poe," page 28.

(3) His book of eighty-seven pages, entitled *A Defense of Edgar Allan Poe*, published in 1885, perhaps at Moran's own expense, by the Washington firm of William F. Boogher.

The summary of Poe's 1849 hospitalization presented here is derived primarily from Moran's letter to Maria Clemm. The errors and inconsistencies contained in these three documents have been noted by some biographers, who usually ascribe them to lapse of memory, an over-developed tendency to romanticize, or to senility. Most scholars believe Moran was lying when he claimed that his several accounts of Poe's death were based on the official hospital records. If there were such records, Moran did not consult them; otherwise he would not have given different dates and hours for Poe's admission and for his death. (Bandy WT. Dr. Moran and the Poe-Reynolds Myth. In *Myths and Reality*. Baltimore: The Edgar Allan Poe Society of Baltimore, 1987.

6. Dr. J. J. Moran's letter to Maria Clemm on November 15, 1849 was as follows:

> Balt. City & Marine Hospital, Nov. 15/49
>
> Mrs. Clemm,
>
> My dear Madam,
>
> I take the earliest opportunity of responding to yours of the 9th Inst., which came to hand by yesterday's mail.
>
> Your deep solicitude, Madam, in reference to the "last moments" of him of whom you write, does not surprise me.
>
> It falls to the lot of but few, to enjoy the extensive popularity that was unquestionably his. Wherever talent — mental worth, nay Genius, was prized, there "E. A. Poe" had warm friends. To his rarely gifted mind are we indebted for many of the brightest thoughts that adorn our literature — to him is Belles Lettres indebted for the purest gems her Casket Contains, "Poe is gone"! How many hearts have heaved a sigh in uttering these three words! How many thousands will yet, and for years to come, lament the premature demise of this truly great man! Nor can there be found, in the list of his enemies (— what great man ever lived without them?) one individual, who will withhold from him the meed of praise to which you refer — when you speak of his "nobility of soul." Posterity will not hesitate to award him a place in the Cata-

logue of those whose pens have strewn flowers in the pathway of life — flowers too, whose fragrance will last for the enjoyment of unborn millions, thereby reserving a memorial more lasting than the Sculptor's Chisel or the Art of the Statuary could ever fabricate or invent — But now for the required intelligence.

Presuming you are already aware of the malady of which Mr. Poe died I need only state concisely the particulars of his circumstances from his entrance until his decease.

When brought to the Hospital he was unconscious of his condition — who brought him or with whom he had been associating. He remained in this condition from 5 o'clock in the afternoon — the hour of his admission — until 3 next morning. This was on the 3rd Oct.

To this state succeeded tremor of the limbs, and at first a busy, but not violent or active delirium — constant talking — and vacant converse with spectral and imaginary objects on the walls. His face was pale and his whole person drenched in perspiration — We were unable to induce tranquility before the second day after his admission.

Having left orders with the nurses to that effect, I was summoned to his bedside so soon as conscious supervened, and questioned him in reference to his family —place of residence — relatives &c. But his answers were incoherent & unsatisfactory. He told me, however, he had a wife in Richmond (which, I have since learned was not the fact), that he did not know when he left that city or what had become of his trunk of clothing. Wishing to rally and sustain his now fast sinking hopes I told him I hoped, that in a few days he would be able to enjoy the society of his friends here, and I would be most happy to contribute in every possible way to his ease & comfort. At this he broke out with much energy, and said the best thing his best friend could do would be to blow out his brains with a pistol — that when he beheld his degradation he was ready to sink in the earth &c." Shortly after giving expression to these words Mr. Poe seemed to dose & I left him for a short time. When I returned I found him in a violent delirium, resisting the efforts of two nurses to keep him in bed. This state continued until Saturday evening (he was admitted on Wednesday) when he commenced calling for one "Reynolds," which he did through the night up to three on Sunday morning. At this time a very decided change began to affect him. Having become enfeebled from exertion he became quiet and seemed to rest for a short time, then gently moving his head he said "Lord help my poor Soul" and expired!

This, Madam, is as faithful an account as I am able to furnish from the Record of his case.

Mrs. Chapman was not with him. But he lacked nothing which the utmost assiduity of nurses and myself could supply. Indeed we considered Mr. Poe an object of unusual regard. Medical men & Students of the House sympathized earnestly with him. Your imperative request urges me to be candid, else I should not have been this plain. Rather far would I cancel his errors than even hint a fault of his.

His remains were visited by some of the first individuals of the city, many of them anxious to have a lock of his hair. Those who had previously known him pronounced his corpse the most natural they had ever seen. Z. Collins Lee Esq. and Nelson Poe with many other respectable individuals attended his funeral — The Revd. Mr. Clemm of this city attended officially on the occasion.

I have, thus, complied with your request, Madam, and therefore subscribe myself respectfully yours

J. J. Moran, Res. Phys.

7. Baltimore Sun. 7 October 1949.
8. Bandy WT. Dr. Moran and the Poe-Reynolds myth. In *Myths and Reality*. Baltimore: The Edgar Allan Poe Society of Baltimore, 1987.

9. Baltimore *Clipper,* October 9, 1849, p. 2, col. 7. The precise meaning of "congestion of the brain" is uncertain. According to Robley's *Dictionary of Medical Science,* published in 1845 (*A Dictionary of Medical Science.* Lea and Blanchard. Philadelphia: 1845, p. 226):

> Congestion. Accumulation of blood or other fluid in an organ. It is an important symptom in febrile and other disorders. It may arise, either from an extraordinary flow of blood by the arteries, or from a difficulty in the return of blood to the heart by the veins. More often, perhaps, it is owing to the latter cause, and is termed *venous congestion, stasis* or *stagnation,* — being not unusually attended with symptoms of oppression and collapse.

Interestingly, in November of 1848, Poe was examined by a physician during an excited state, most likely the result of alcohol withdrawal. The physician diagnosed the case as one of "cerebral congestion" (Quinn AH. *Edgar Allan Poe. A Critical Biography.* The Johns Hopkins University Press. Baltimore: 1998, p. 580).

10. This version of Poe's medical history prior to his hospitalization in Baltimore is a distillate of information contained within letters and books written by Poe himself, his friends and his associates as recorded in Quinn's biography (Ibid).

11. from "For Annie."

12. Quinn, AH. Edgar Allan Poe, A Critical Biography. The John Hopkins University Press. Baltimore: 1998, p. 188.

13. Poe's sister Rosalie, "was always a pathetic figure and failed to develop mentally after she was about 12 years of age." Op Cit (Quinn), p. 93

14. Op cit (Quinn) p. 174.

15. In 1836, Nathaniel Hawthorne was discouraged in his efforts to publish *Twice Told Tales.* As a result, he was going through a nervous depression which caused his friend, Horatio Bridges, to caution him against suicide [Op cit (Quinn) p. 252].

16. Op cit (Quinn) p. 297

17. Op cit (Quinn) p. 433.

18. Letter from Poe to Mrs. Sarah Helen Whitman on October 18, 1848 [Op cit (Quinn) p. 578].

19. Written by Frederick W. Thomas in March of 1843 [Op cit (Quinn) p. 381].

20. Letter from Poe to Thomas & Dow, March 16, 1843 [Op cit (Quinn) p. 379-80].

21. Willis NP. *Home Journal*, Editorial Page, Saturday, December 26, 1846.

22. Op cit (Quinn) p. 528.

23. Op cit (Quinn) p. 579.

24. During 1847, Poe worked steadily on "Eureka," his prose poem dealing with science and the universe. To a certain extent the work was the climax of his creative achievement. According to Quinn, it demonstrated that as late as 1848 Poe was not, as had frequently been stated, entering a period of mental decline. "His mind [instead] was clear and his imaginative power was still capable of dealing with scientific problems that tax the best of modern thinkers" [Op cit Quinn p. 541, 557].

25. Allen H. Biography of Edgar Allan Poe. http://www.pambytes.com/poe/bio.html.

26. Op cit (Quinn) p. 629.

27. Letter of Mrs. Elmira Shelton to Mrs. Clemm, October 11, 1849, published by Woodberry in "The Poe-Chivers Papers," *Century Magazine*, N.S. XLlll (February, 1903) p. 551-2.

28. Benitez RM. A 39-year old man with mental status change. *Maryland Med J.* 1996;45:765-9.

29. Bleck PP, Rupprecht CE. Rhabdoviruses. In Mandell GL, Bennett JE. Dolin R (eds.). *Principles and Practice of Infectious Diseases*. 6th Ed., Elsevier, Inc. Philadelphia:2005, p. 2047-56.

30. Centers for Disease Control and Prevention. Human rabies: Alabama, Tennessee and Texas 1994. *MMWR.* 1995;44:269-272.

31. *The Sun*. January 11, 2000. p. E1-2.

32. Gordon AG. The death of Edgar Allan Poe: a case for syphilis? *Maryland Med J.* 1997;46:289.

33. Shoemaker RC. Reader suggests Poe died from mercury poisoning. *Maryland Med J.* 1997;46:288.

34. Schuckit MA. Alcohol and alcoholism. In Issebacher KJ, Braunwald E, Wilson JD, et al. Eds. *Harrison's Principles of Internal Medicine.* 13th ed. McGraw-Hill Inc. New York: 1994, p. 2422-5.

35. Op cit (Quinn) p. 580.

36. Op cit (Quinn) p. 568-71.

37. Letter from Poe to his mother-in-law, July 7, 1849. Published first by Chauncey Burr in his quarterly journal, *The Nineteenth Century,* V (February, 1852), p. 29.

38. Letter from Poe to Dr. J. E. Snodgrass, April 1, 1841. Published in the *Baltimore American* of April 4, 1881, with editorial comment.

39. *Home Journal,* Editorial Page, Saturday, December 26, 1846.

40. Letter from Poe to his mother-in-law, July 19, 1849 [Op cit (Quinn)] p. 620-1.

41. Hashimoto SA, Paty DW. The neurologic complications and consequences of ethanol use and abuse. In Kelley WN. Ed. *Textbook of Internal Medicine.* 3rd Ed. Lippincott-Raven Publishers. Philadelphia: 1997, p. 2408.

42. Op cit (Quinn) p. 616-7.

43. Op cit (Quinn) p. 618.

44. Susan A, Weiss T. The last days of Edgar A. Poe. *Scribner's Monthly,* XV (March, 1878), p. 712.

45. Cheng TO. Delirium tremens cordis. *N Engl J Med.* 1973; 289:593.

46. Greenspan AJ, Schaal SF. The "holiday heart:" electrophysiologic studies of alcohol effects in alcoholics. *Ann Intern Med.* 1983;98:135-9.

47. Turner TB, Mezey E, Kimball AW. Measurement of alcohol related effects in man: chronic effects in relation to levels of alcohol consumption. Part B. *Johns Hopkins Med J.* 1977;141:273-86.

48. Schuckit MA. Genetics and the risk for alcoholism. *JAMA.* 1985;254:2614-7.

49. Letter from Poe to George W. Eveleth, January 4, 1849 [Op cit (Quinn)], p. 536-7.

50. Valentine letters, p. 259-62 [Op cit (Quinn) p. 111].

51. Op cit (Quinn) p. 227.

52. Birch D. The last days of Edgar Allan Poe. *Baltimore Sun, Sun Magazine*. October 2, 1994, p. 5-14.

53. In the aftermath of Poe's death, Charles Baudelaire, the French poet and Poe's fervent admirer wrote:

    This death was almost a suicide, a suicide prepared for a long time" (Ibid p. 14). In fact, according to Poe's own story, his distress over Virginia's death "led him even to attempt suicide." [Op cit (Quinn) p. 572]. Moreover, in the spring of 1849, he wrote: "It is not so much ill that I have been as depressed in spirits — I can not express to you how terribly I have been suffering from gloom.... I am full of dark forebodings. Nothing cheers or comforts me. My life seems wasted — the future looks a dreary blank: but I will struggle on and "hope against hope." [Undated letter from Poe to Mrs. Charles Richmond. Op cit (Quinn) p.604].

54. Rush B: An inquiry into the effects of ardent spirits upon the human body and mind with an account of the means of preventing and of remedies for curing them. In *Medical Inquiries and Observations*. Vol I. Third Ed. Published by Carey M, Hopkins, Earle, et al. Philadelphia: 1809, p. 271-314.

55. The complete version of Rush's cure for a fit of drunkenness. Note that measures 1, 7 and 9 are specifically designed to relieve "congestion of the brain" (see note 5), the official note of Poe's death:

    (1.) The first thing to be done to cure a fit of drunkenness, is to open the collar, if in a man, and remove all ligatures from every other part of the body. The head and shoulders should at the same time be elevated, so as to favour a more feeble determination of the blood to the brain.

    (2.) The contents of the stomach should be discharged, by thrusting a feather down the throat. It often restores the patient immediately to his senses and feet. Should it fail of exciting a puking,

(3.) A napkin should be wrapped round the head, and wetted for an hour or two with cold water, or cold water should be poured in a stream upon the head. In the latter way I have sometimes seen it used, when a boy, in the city of Philadelphia. It was applied, by dragging the patient, when found drunk in the street, to a pump, and pumping water upon his head for ten or fifteen minutes. The patient generally rose, and walked off, sober and sullen, after the use of this remedy.

Other remedies, less common, but not less effectual for a fit of drunkenness, are,

(4.) Plunging the whole body into cold water. A number of gentlemen who had drunken to intoxication, on board a ship in the stream, near Fell's point, at Baltimore, in consequence of their reeling in a small boat, on their way to the shore, in the evening, overset it, and fell into the water. Several boats from the shore hurried to their relief. They were all picked up, and went home, perfectly sober, to their families.

(5.) Terror. A number of young merchants, who had drunken together, in a compting-house, on James River, above thirty years ago, until they were intoxicated, were carried away by a sudden rise of the river, from an immense fall of rain. They floated several miles with the current, in their little cabin, half filled with water. An island in the river arrested it. When they reached the shore that saved their lives, they were all sober. It is probably terror assisted in the cure of the persons who fell into the water at Baltimore.

(6.) The excitement of a fit of anger. The late Dr. Witherspoon used to tell a story of a man in Scotland, who was always cured of a fit of drunkenness by being made angry. The means chosen for that purpose was a singular one. It was talking against religion.

(7.) A severe whipping. This remedy acts by exciting a revulsion of the blood from the brain to the external parts of the body.

(8.) Profuse sweats. By means of this evacuation, nature sometimes cures a fit of drunkenness. Their good effects are obvious in labourers, whom quarts of spirits taken in a day will seldom intoxicate while they sweat freely. If the patient be unable to swallow warm drinks, in order to produce sweats, they may be excited by putting him in a warm bath, or wrapping his body in blankets, under which should be placed half a dozen hot bricks, or bottles filled with hot water.

(9.) Bleeding. This remedy should always be used, when the former ones have been prescribed to no purpose, or where there is reason to fear, from the long duration of the disease, a material injury may be done to the brain."

56. The complete version of Rush's method for preventing recurrence of drunkenness and for destroying a desire for ardent spirits was as follows:

(1.) Many hundred drunkards have been cured of their desire for ardent spirits, by a practical belief in the doctrines of the christian religion. Examples of the divine efficacy of Christianity for this purpose have lately occurred in many parts of the United States.

(2.) A sudden sense of the guilt contracted by drunkenness, and of its punishment in a future world. It once cured a gentleman in Philadelphia, who, in a fit of drunkenness, attempted to murder a wife whom he loved. Upon being told of it when he was sober, he was so struck with the enormity of the crime he had nearly committed, that he never tasted spirituous liquors afterwards.

(3.) A sudden sense of shame. Of the efficacy of this deep seated principle in the human bosom, in curing drunkenness, I shall relate three remarkable instances.

A farmer in England, who had been many years in the practice of coming home intoxicated, from a market town, one day observed appearances of rain, while he was in market. His hay was cut, and ready to be housed. To save it, he returned in haste to his farm, before he had taken his customary dose of grog.

Upon coming into his house, one of his children, a boy of six years old, ran to his mother, and cried out, "O, mother! father is come home, and he is not drunk." The father, who heard this exclamation, was so severely rebuked by it, that he suddenly became a sober man.

A noted drunkard was once followed by a favourite goat to a tavern, into which he was invited by his master, and drenched with some of his liquor. The poor animal staggered home with his master, a good deal intoxicated. The next day he followed him to his accustomed tavern. When the goat came to the door, he paused: his master made signs to him to follow him into the house. The goat stood still. An attempt was made to thrust him into the tavern. He resisted, as if struck with the recollection of what he suffered from being intoxicated the night before. His master was so much affected by a sense of shame, in observing the conduct of his goat to be so much more rational than his own, that he ceased from that time to drink spirituous liquors.

A gentleman, in one of the southern states, who had nearly destroyed himself by strong drink, was remarkable for exhibiting the grossest marks of folly in his fits of intoxication. One evening, sitting in his parlour, he heard an uncommon noise in his kitchen. He went to the door, and peeped through the key hole, from whence he saw one of his negroes diverting his fellow servants, by mimicking his master's gestures and conversation when he was drunk. The sight overwhelmed him with shame and distress, and instantly became the means of his reformation.

(4.) The of the idea of ardent spirits with a painful or disagreeable impression upon some part of the body, has sometimes cured the love of strong drink. I once tempted a negro man, who was habitually fond of ardent spirits, to drink some rum (which I placed in his way) and in which I had put a few grains of tartar emetic. The tartar sickened and puked him to such a degree, that he supposed himself to be poisoned. I was much gratified by observing he could not bear the sight, nor smell, of spirits for two years afterwards.

I have heard of a man who was cured of the love of spirits, by working off a puke by large draughts of brandy and water, and I know a gentleman, who in consequence of being affected with a rheumatism, immediately after drinking some toddy, when overcome with fatigue and exposure to the rain, has ever since loathed that liquor, only because it was accidentally associated in his memory with the recollection of the pain he suffered from his disease.

This appeal to that operation of the human mind which obliges it to associate ideas, accidentally or otherwise combined, for the cure of vice, is very ancient. It was resorted to by Moses, when he compelled the children of Israel to drink the solution of the golden calf (which they had idolized) in water. This solution, if made, as it most probably was, by means of what is called hepar sulphuris, was extremely bitter, and nauseous, and could never be recollected afterwards, without bringing into equal detestation the sin which subjected them to the necessity of drinking it. Our knowledge of this principle association upon the minds and conduct of men should lead us to destroy, by means of other impressions, the influence of all those circumstances, with which the recollection and desire of spirits are combined. Some men drink only in the *morning*, some at *noon*, and some only at *night*. Some men drink only on a *market day*, some at *one* tavern only, and some only in *one kind* of company. Now by finding a new and interesting employment or subject of conversation for drunkards, at the usual times in which they have been accustomed to drink, and by restraining them by the same means from those places and companions, which suggested to them the idea of ardent spirits, their habits of intemperance may be completely destroyed. In the same way the periodical returns of appetite, and a desire to sleep, have been destroyed in a hundred instances. The desire for strong drink differs from each of them, in being of an artificial nature, and therefore not disposed to return, after being chased for a few weeks from the system.

(5.) The love of ardent spirits has sometimes been subdued, by exciting a counter passion in the mind. A citizen of

Philadelphia had made many unsuccessful attempts to cure his wife of drunkenness. At length, despairing of her reformation, he purchased a hogshead of rum, and after tapping it, left the key in the door of the room in which it was placed, as if he had forgotten it. His design was to give his wife an opportunity of drinking herself to death. She suspected this to be his motive, in what he had done, and suddenly left off drinking. Resentment here became the antidote to intemperance.

(6.) A diet consisting wholly of vegetables cured a physician in Maryland of drunkenness, probably by lessening that thirst, which is always more or less excited by animal food.

(7.) Blisters to the ankles, which were followed by an unusual degree of inflammation, once suspended the love of ardent spirits, for one month, in a lady in this city. The degrees of her intemperance may be conceived of, when I add, that her grocer's account for brandy alone amounted, annually, to one hundred pounds, Pennsylvania currency, for several years.

(8.) A violent attack of an acute disease has sometimes destroyed a habit of drinking distilled liquors. I attended a notorious drunkard, in the yellow fever in the year 1798, who recovered, with the loss of his relish for spirits, which has, I believe, continued ever since.

(9.) A salivation has lately performed a cure of drunkenness, in a person of Virginia. The new disease excited in the mouth and throat, while it rendered the action of the smallest quantity of spirits upon them painful, was happily calculated to destroy the disease in the stomach which prompts to drinking, as well as to render the recollection of them disagreeable, by the laws of formerly mentioned.

(10.) I have known an oath, taken before a magistrate, to drink no more spirits, produce a perfect cure drunkenness. It is sometimes cured in this way in Ireland. Persons who take oaths for this purpose are called affidavit men.

(11.) An advantage would probably arise from frequent representations being made to drunkards, not only of the certainty, but of the *suddenness* of death, from habits of intemperance. I have heard of two persons being cured of the love of ardent spirits, by seeing death suddenly induced by fits of intoxication; in the one case, in a stranger, and in the other, in an intimate friend.

(12.) It has been said, that the disuse of spirits should be gradual, but my observations authorise me to say, that persons who have been addicted to them should abstain from them *suddenly*, and *entirely*. "Taste not, handle not, touch not," should be inscribed upon every vessel that contains spirits, in the house of a man who wishes to be cured of habits of intemperance. To obviate, for awhile, the debility which arises from the sudden abstraction of the stimulus of spirits, laudanum, or bitters infused in water, should be taken, and perhaps a larger quantity of beer or wine, than is consistent with the strict rules of temperate living. By the temporary use of these substitutes for spirits, I have never known the transition to sober habits to be attended with any bad effects, but often with permanent health of body, and peace of mind.

57. *R. A Dictionary of Medical Science.* Lea and Blanchard. Philadelphia: 1845, p. 226.

58. Op cit (Quinn) p. 624.

59. From "The City in the Sea."

GLIMMERING
GLOOM[1]

11

$\mathbf{M}$any believe the seed of the illness that sent this patient to bed for three decades was sown in Scutari (now Uskudar) in 1854/5, where in her mid-thirties, she began her service in a brief but bloody war that most historians view as the first truly modern military conflict.[2]

The Crimean War, that conflict, began in early 1854 after Russia destroyed the Turkish fleet at Sinope on the Black Sea and invaded Turkish provinces in the Balkans. Fearing Russia might next seize Constantinople, Britain and France landed forces in what is now Bulgaria, where they intended to engage the enemy but then decided to attack the great naval base at Sebastopol in the Crimea in hopes of destroying the Russian fleet. In early June, twenty-seven thousand British troops arrived at Varna on the western shore of the Black Sea and soon began to suffer the deadly effects of summer heat, poor sanitation and a swampy terrain. Between June and August 1854, twenty percent of the expeditionary force was hospitalized with cholera, dysentery and other disorders, with nearly one thousand lives lost before the first shot was fired. In September, a British force, poorly supplied and decimated by disease, sailed to the Crimea and with its French allies routed the Russians at a battle near the Alma River just outside of Sebastopol. Unable to capitalize on their victory, they had to settle for a protracted siege of the city. Several more engagements ensued, including the charge of the Light Brigade immortalized by Tennyson and the bloody battle of Inkerman. The patient arrived at Scutari on November 4,1854, just a day after Inkerman, and remained with the army until four months after the war finally ended on March 30, 1856 with the signing of the Treaty of Paris.[3]

During the patient's service at the front, the whole British army seemed to find its way to the wards over which she presided as nurse-in-charge. They were crammed, wounded and sick, by the thousands into four miles of beds not eighteen inches apart. With a mere thirty-eight nurses, she hovered over them day and night as an innumerable caravan of diseases claimed one man after another.[3]

The patient's power over them was awesome. In the blood-stained room where operations were performed without anesthesia, maimed soldiers, if not already resigned to their fate, begged for death rather than meet the surgeon's knife. When they saw her patiently standing near, however, with lips set and hands folded, they found the strength to submit and to endure,[4] so inspired were they by the constancy and valor she displayed in the face of so much sorrow and death.

For twenty-one months the patient served her time with the army "steeped to her neck in blood."[5] She saw thousands devoured by disease and came to understand those who have said "it is not death, but dying which is terrible."[6] The magnitude of the carnage was terrifying. During January and February of her first winter, she laid to rest three thousand brave men,[7] who perished from frostbite, gangrene, dysentery and other diseases.[8] During the height of the conflict, she oversaw the care of some twenty-five hundred such cases in the Barrack Hospital, eleven hundred twenty-two in the General Hospital and another two hundred fifty convalescents in the Sultan's Summer Palace behind the Barrack Hospital.[9] To these were added another twelve hundred sick troops from Balaclava, also dying of dysentery, fever, and frostbite, until their numbers exceeded those left manning the camps above Sebastopol.

In all likelihood, the inner strength that sustained her during her time in Scutari and the Crimea was inherited; even at an early age the patient showed remarkable independence and a tendency to challenge society's assumptions.[10] She was born in Florence, Italy, for which she was named, to British parents belonging to the "upper ten thousand"[11] of "a county where luxury had reached its height and poverty its depth."[12] As a girl, she was serious but somewhat frail. She liked to write, though her hands were so weak she was unable to form cursive script until age ten. She also had recurrent respiratory infections and unusually weak ankles, which required her to wear steel-lined boots for support. Once she reached adulthood, however, except for an episode of measles at age thirty-three, she enjoyed excellent physical health until her service in the Crimea.[13]

According to one biographer, the patient experienced a mystic's calling to the work of the Lord when she was sixteen.[14] Thereafter, she viewed service to God as her sole purpose in life. To this end, she surrendered herself to a kind of mysticism not associated with trances, renunciation of the material world or visions of an afterlife, but one dedicated to the betterment of mankind through social activism. Such dedication was not without self-doubt. On occasion, feelings of inadequacy severe enough to generate thoughts of suicide overcame her, as evidenced by the following entry she made in her diary when she was twenty-five:

> Lord thou knowest the creature which thou has made; thou knowest that I cannot live — forgive me, O God & let me die — this day let me die; it is not for myself that I say this; thou knowest that I am more afraid to die than to live — for I shall carry myself with me — but I know I shall only heap anxieties on other hearts, which will increase with time.[15]

Whereas such morbid thoughts dominated the patient from time to time,[16] there were also times when her self-doubt and longing for death gave way to exhilaration. During one such time, shortly before she went to war, she wrote:

> This is the life. Now I know what it is to love life, and I really would be sorry to leave life....I wish for no other earth, no other world but this....I am now in the heyday of my power."[17]

It was the patient's white-hot devotion to her calling, however, rather than these intermittent episodes of exhilaration, that sustained her during her twenty months with the army. She was thirty-four when she arrived at Scutari. With little training or prior experience to prepare her for the impossible challenges that confronted her, she had to work tirelessly, many times twenty hours a day, to instill her wards with a commanding authority and healing presence. Whenever a new group of sick and wounded soldiers arrived, she ignored the contagion rampant among them[18] and took the severest cases for herself. When she walked the wards, soldiers saluted her. After all of the medical officers had retired for the night, it was she as "ministering angel" who alone cared for them in the silence and the darkness, carrying a small lamp in her hand as she made her solitary rounds.[19]

When she rested, which was rare, the patient did so in quarters that offered scant protection from the harsh conditions she encountered her first winter with the army.[20] Europe was unseasonably cold then, with temperatures in the Crimea dropping to 13^0 F (-10^0 C). "Inkwells froze, toothbrushes needed to be thawed before use and icicles sometimes as long and as thick as a man's finger formed on mustaches."[21] She and her thirty-eight nurses endured these conditions in a living space originally allocated for three people. It was infested with rodents and vermin, the roof leaked and the windows were often torn off during storms. Washing facilities, privies and water supplies were inadequate, forcing the patient to take turns with others bathing from a single basin. There were no drying facilities for clothes, and when the patient was drenched in harsh weather, she had to stay in bed for hours while her soaked garments dried in front of a kitchen fire.[20] Moreover, proper food was scarce. During the worst months at Scutari, "the unvarying menu was goat's flesh and something they called mutton — black, blue, and green in color; coarse bread, rancid butter, milkeless tea."[22] During those times she fasted more often than not. It is little wonder she became disparately ill.

The patient's physical illness began with crushing fatigue on her thirty-fifth birthday (May 12, 1855). She had been with the army for five months and a week earlier had traveled three hundred miles across the Black Sea from her base at Scutari to the Crimea to inspect hospitals at the front. She arrived healthy but tired. When she became ill, she sent for the principal medical officer at Balaclava, who diagnosed "Crimean fever" and advised her to leave the ship on which she was housed, so that she might be admitted to the Castle Hospital not far away on the Genoese Heights. Her weakness was so profound by then she had to be placed on a stretcher and carried by relays of soldiers to a private hut next to those occupied by wounded soldiers. For three days she hovered near death before her doctors had reason to believe she would recover.[23]

During the next two weeks, her condition fluctuated between desperate and satisfactory, "with sudden relapses [of fever] in the morning, followed by recovery and then another relapse in the evening."[23] Her hair was cropped short for comfort, and bed rest, the only available treatment, was prescribed. Even then, the patient would not relinquish her responsibility for those dying *pro patria* and resorted to pen and paper to continue her work. Her writings rambled[24] during episodes of fever so severe, her physician, who had vast experience with such illnesses, rated her condition "as bad an attack....as I have seen."[23] For several weeks she was so weak she could neither feed herself nor speak above a whisper.

Raglan, the commander-in-chief of the British expeditionary force,[25] came to see her at the end of May. He was sufficiently reassured by what he saw to telegraph a relieved London that the patient was out of danger. A month later, he became ill himself and died in just a few days.[26]

The patient was advised to return to England to complete her convalescence, but would not. She was determined to remain with the army until the last soldier left the East for home. She did, however, accept Lord Stafford's offer to recuperate at his summer residence at Therapia, a few miles west of Constantinople. Those who saw her when she arrived described her as emaciated, weak and pale, and looking much older than her thirty-five years. Her physicians suspected that the extreme exhaustion that lingered long after the fever had subsided "was more from the previous overstrain on mind and body than from the fever [itself]."[24]

By the end of July, she was able to resume her letter writing and to take evening walks on the shore of the Sea of Marmara. Gradually her strength returned, and in August she was able to resume the full rush of her work.[24] Her doctors and friends urged continued rest, but she would not listen. So long as there remained sick and wounded in the Levant to be cared for, she was resolved to continue her work.[24]

At the beginning of October, the patient developed sciatica, followed in late November by earaches, chronic laryngitis, dysentery, rheumatism and insomnia.[23] She began to experience intermittent feelings of despair compounded by the loss of several of her nurses to the fever that had nearly taken her own life. She took their loss hard, knowing they had remained with the army primarily out of devotion to her. And yet, at no time did she harbor even a passing thought of deserting her post. She remained until the end of the war, until the last transport had sailed, working indefatigably at great cost to her own comfort and health, resolved to show that a woman, too, had the strength to suffer and to endure.[24]

To her physical disabilities and crushing workload were added the accusations of an English press growing increasingly critical of the medical and military handling of the war. The army was plagued by organizational chaos and logistical blunders obvious to even the most casual investigative reporter. The army's administrative shortcomings compounded her own problems of supervising a diverse contingent of nurses of varying social status, religion, political loyalty and level of training. Self-doubt and obsession with failure began to intrude increasingly into the patient's thoughts.[27]

When the war finally ended in 1856 and the patient returned to England, her family noted distressing changes in her appearance, personality and behavior. At thirty-six, she had become hardened and aged by illness and exhaustion.[27] She slept no more than two hours a night and complained of persistent fever and lack of appetite. She never left her room and for a month was scarcely off her sofa, feeling then much as she did when recovering from her fever at Balaclava. In spite of these symptoms, her doctors could find no physical evidence of disease and concluded that extreme exhaustion from overwork had taxed every organ to the limit. They believed that rest alone would restore her.[28] That year and the next the patient suffered from insomnia, nausea at the sight of food, irritability, nervousness and varying levels of depression. In August of 1857, when she was thirty-seven, she experienced her first attack of severe palpitations and tachycardia.[27]

In September of 1857, following an episode of fever similar to the one she experienced in the Crimea, the patient declared herself an invalid and began limiting her visitors. Within a year, shortness of breath, weakness, syncope, indigestion and flushing of the face and hands were added to her growing list of complaints. In 1861 she developed "nervous tremors" and "spinal pain" so severe she was unable to walk and had to be carried from bed to sofa. For the next six years she was confined to bed.[27]

The patient was seen in consultation by Dr. Charles Edouard Brown-Sequard, the leading specialist in spinal disease of the day, who diagnosed "congestion of the spine" caused by constant worry.[29] He advised rest and a moratorium on the patient's incessant letter writing since her return from the front. However, she was then deeply involved in efforts to reform the army (later nursing), and would not abandon her crusade even at the cost of risking the paralysis Brown-Sequard warned might develop if her spinal congestion were not arrested.[27]

In March of 1862, unrelenting pain caused the patient to long for death, even though she was only forty-two. She wrote her mother:

> Sometimes I wonder that I should be so impatient for death. Had I only to stand & wait, I think it would be nothing — tho' the pain is so great that I wonder how anybody can dread an operation. If Paget could amputate my left *fore quarter*, I am sure I would have sent for him in half an hour."[30]

Excruciating spinal pain, shortness of breath and muscle spasms plagued her from 1863 to 1866. For a time in 1866, the patient's pain was so severe she could not tolerate having her position changed for periods as long as forty-eight hours. Subcutaneous opium provided temporary relief but was accepted by the patient only occasionally. She complained that it muddled her brain and made it difficult to concentrate on her work. During the course of her prolonged illness, she also was treated with bromides (given for sedation), hydrotherapy and other forms of alternative medical therapy, such as the company of a dog and cat, reading, singing to herself, flowers, letter-writing, feeding birds and avoiding visitors.[23]

Until 1887, thirty years after she declared herself an invalid, the patient continued to suffer with intermittent spinal pain, headaches, insomnia, depression and a frequent sense of failure and worthlessness. During much of this time, she feared, as did her family, that her condition was terminal. Then, in her sixties, the saturnine veil of her illness began to lift. Gradually the pain and other symptoms resolved and the depression dissipated. The patient began to venture out of her room for visits with friends and family members. The "cold, obsessed and tyrannical" workaholic of earlier years slowly transformed into a softer, gentler matron who, at last, was able to assume "something like normal relationships with relatives and friends."[23]

The medical history of the patient's family contains no obvious clues to her own diagnosis. Her father enjoyed excellent physical and mental health throughout his life, dying suddenly at the age of eighty of head trauma sustained during a fall.[31] Her mother lived to be ninety. The patient was sixty when her mother died and too ill to attend the funeral.[32] There was one sibling, a sister, who suffered a nervous breakdown in her early thirties over the patient's increasing independence. Later she developed severe rheumatoid arthritis and died in great physical pain at the age of seventy-one.[33]

Marriage never tempted the patient. She hated the idea of being tied forever to a society life.[34] God, she believed, marked out certain women to be single and others to be wives, organizing them accordingly for their vocation. Some women, she maintained, have every reason for not marrying, and best serve humanity by educating children already in the world, rather than by bringing more into it themselves.[35] Although she had several suitors and more than one marriage proposal, she never accepted. Her meat was to do God's will and to devote herself completely to his work, so that he might dwell within her.[36] To that end she remained celibate her entire life.

The patient's life's work was as boundless as her later years were confined. The first idea she could recall from her childhood was a desire to nurse the sick. Her dreams in her early years were all of hospitals, which she visited as often as she could.[37] She more than fulfilled these early dreams. Her accomplishments as a nurse, a nurse administrator and a nurse educator earned for her recognition as the founder of modern nursing.[38,39] Her service to God and humanity also took many other forms during the feverish labors of her protracted invalidism. These included those of political activist, hospital architect and administrator, statistician, sanitarian and public health expert.[40]

When the patient reached the age of seventy-five, she began to complain of failing memory and eyesight, although visitors continued to find her lively, factual and witty. By age eighty-one, she was blind, and failing memory had progressed to dementia so profound that by age eighty-two she required round-the-clock nursing care.

Florence Nightingale (see Figure 11-1), the "Lady with the Lamp,"[1] died in her sleep at age ninety. According to the death certificate, the cause of death was, "old age and heart failure."[41]

***

Since her death in 1910, biographers, historians, nurses and physicians have argued over the cause of Florence Nightingale's strange illness. Some believe that it had an organic basis, while others assert that her symptoms were the product of a neurosis.[15] Sir Edward Cook,[23] her official, and still her best, biographer thought she suffered from "dilation of the heart and neurasthenia." In his 1982 biography, F.B. Smith[42] was less charitable. He believed she feigned illness to avoid people she didn't want to see, especially her

FIGURE 11-1. Florence Nightingale (1820-1910) circa 1865. Photograph by H. Lenthall. Photo Credit: Adoc-photos/Art Resource, NY.

sister and mother. Feminist Elaine Showalter[43] thought Nightingale created a "strategic illness" that had no physical basis. Others have suggested that she was simply mired in self-pity, which found expression as Victorian melodrama and exaggeration.[44] Nursing student lore has even maintained that syphilis contracted while serving in the Crimean was her disease, although no shred of evidence exists to support this diagnosis.[45] In a recent biography, Hugh Small[46] claims that Nightingale herself believed that the spiteful attitude of her mother and sister toward her ruined her health. Small maintains that her real problem was repressed self-loathing. He bases his conclusion on Nightingale's "habit of omitting all references to the Crimean War whenever she — rarely — praised her own achievements." He suggests that through her illness she was punishing herself "with what was virtually a sentence of life imprisonment" for her arrogance and ignorance in failing to recognize that the unsanitary condition of her wards was the reason her army perished.[46,47]

Nightingale's wards were unsanitary because by the time the British arrived at Gallipoli in May 1854, the French had already invested the choicest sites on the European side of the Bosporus near the Grand Bazaar. With no other space available there, the British set up their hospitals at Scutari, on the Asian side of the Bosporus, borrowing a Turkish hospital, which came to be known as the General Hospital. It was originally designed for one thousand patients and in only fair condition. Selimiye barracks, situated a half an hour's walk from the General Hospital, was converted to the Barrack Hospital after the Battle of Alma. During the war, it held an average of two thousand patients in space originally designed for twelve hundred. The Sultan's Summer Palace south of the General Hospital was also used as a hospital until January 1855 (Fig. 11-2).[9]

When in March of 1855 Prime Minister Palmerston sent a Sanitary Commission to the Crimea to investigate the thousands of troops dying not of their wounds, but of dysentery, diarrhea and other diseases, they discovered that the General Hospital's water supply was being contaminated by open privies and had never been cleaned out. Clogged sewers were discovered beneath the Barrack Hospital as well as a horse carcass in its fresh water supply. The hospital was, in effect, sitting atop a huge cesspool. Eventually, dead animals and hundreds of cartloads of rubbish were removed from beneath the hospitals, and a system was installed to flush out the sewers. Openings were made in roofs to improve air circulation. Rotten shelves and floors were torn out, eliminating breeding places for rats and mice. Inside walls and floors were painted with

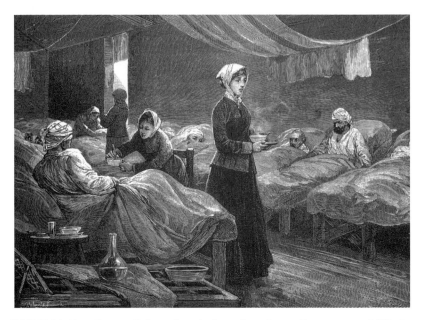

FIGURE 11-2.   Florence Nightingale in the barracks at Scutari. Engraving circa 1880. Oxford Science Archive, Oxford, UK. Credit: HIP/Art Resource, NY.

disinfectant; double rows of mattresses were reduced to one; and orderlies were assigned to empty waste containers and debris from the wards and corridors on a daily basis. Aided by improving weather and a lack of major fighting, these sanitary improvements produced striking results. By June, just three months after implementing these interventions, the mortality rate at Scutari had fallen from 42.7 deaths per 1,000 to 2 per 1,000.[47]

It has been suggested that Nightingale suffered greatly from repressed feelings of guilt over her failure to recognize these reasons for the high mortality rate among soldiers hospitalized on her wards.[46] Her guilt, in fact, might have been even worse than that of the "survivor syndrome," which induces diminished feelings of self-worth in persons surviving a major tragedy because it was guilt based on a belief that her own negligence and arrogance had contributed to the loss of the army over which she presided as nurse-in-charge. She not only survived the tragedy but, to a certain extent, compounded it by first refusing to accept its cause (blaming it on poor provisions rather than poor sanitation) and then unwisely agreeing to a cover-up in which she betrayed the men who were her patients.[46]

With such intense feelings of repressed guilt, one might ask, how was Nightingale able to continue to function as effectively as she did? Psychiatrist Katherine Wisner[15] believes an underlying bipolar personality disorder (specifically, Bipolar Disorder I, with psychotic features) was the source of the psychic energy that sustained her during and after her Crimean experience. Wisner bases her diagnosis on criteria delineated in the Diagnostic and Statistical Manual, 4th Edition (DSM-IV) of the American Psychiatric Association (see Tables 11-1 and 11-2),[48] many of which Nightingale

TABLE 11-1 DSM-IV Criteria for Major Depressive Episode

A. Five (or more) of the following symptoms have been present during the same 2-week period and represent a change from previous functioning; at least one of the symptoms is either depressed mood or loss of interest or pleasure.
  i. Depressed mood most of the day, nearly every day
  ii. Markedly diminished pleasure in all, or almost all, activities most of the day nearly every day
  iii. Significant weight loss/weight gain, or decrease or increase in appetite, nearly every day
  iv. Insomnia or hypersomnia nearly every day
  v. Psychomotor agitation or retardation nearly every day
  vi. Fatigue or loss of energy nearly every day
  vii. Feelings of worthlessness or excessive or inappropriate guilt nearly every day
  viii. Diminished ability to think or concentrate, or indecisiveness, nearly every day
  ix. Recurrent thoughts of death, recurrent suicidal ideation without specific plan, or a suicide attempt or a specific plan for committing suicide
B. The symptoms do not meet criteria for a mixed episode
C. The symptoms cause clinically significant distress or impairment in social, occupational or other important areas of functioning.
D. The symptoms are not due to the direct physiological effects of a substance
E. The symptoms are not better accounted for by bereavement

TABLE 11-2 DSM-IV Criteria for Manic Episode

A. A distinct period of abnormally and persistently elevated, expansive, or irritable mood, lasting at least a week (or any duration if hospitalization is necessary).
B. During the period of mood disturbance, three (or more) of the following symptoms have persisted (four if the mood is only irritable) and have been present to a significant degree:
  i. inflated self-esteem or grandiosity
  ii. decreased need for sleep (e.g., feels rested after only 3 hours of sleep (suspect)
  iii. more talkative than usual or pressure to keep talking
  iv. flight of ideas or subjective experience that thoughts are racing (suspect)
  v. distractibility (i.e., attention too easily drawn to unimportant or irrelevant external stimuli)
  vi. increase in goal-directed activity (either socially, at work or school, or sexually) or psychomotor agitation
  vii. excessive involvement in pleasurable activities that have a high potential for painful consequences (e.g., engaging in unrestrained buying sprees, sexual indiscretions, or foolish business investments).
C. The symptoms do not meet criteria for a mixed episode.
D. The mood disturbance is sufficiently severe to cause marked impairment in occupational functioning or in usual social activities or relationships with others, or to necessitate hospitalization to prevent harm to self or others, or there are psychotic features.

exhibited in word as well as in deed. The disorder is defined by striking oscillations between dark and bright states of mind. Nightingale revealed her dark side in numerous documents. On December 5, 1845, for example, she wrote:

> God has something for me to do for him or he would have let me die some time ago. I hope to do it by living — then my eyes would indeed have seen his salvation — but now I am dust & nothing — worse than nothing — a curse to myself & others. This morning I felt as if my soul would pass away in tears — in utter loneliness — in a better passion of tears & agony of solitude but I live — and God grant that I may live to do this."[15]

If this example of emotional passion exhibited well before the trauma of the Crimean War were not convincing enough evidence of serious clinical depression, one need only consider the one of self-doubt given in the preceding case history or the following excerpt from a private note written in 1851:

> Why, oh my God, can I not be satisfied with life that satisfies so many people? I am told that the conversation of all these clever men ought to be enough for me. Why am I starving, desperate, and diseased on it?....My God, what am I to do? In my thirty-first year I see nothing desirable but death."[17]

Nightingale's luminescent side — the manic side of her bipolar disorder responsible for her astonishing productivity — is reflected in statements such as the one reproduced in the case history in which she wrote: "I am now in the heyday of my power." Her mania, the antipode of her depression, was also evident before, during and after the war in her extraordinary creativity, her high energy level and her incredible productivity.[15]

Bipolar personality disorder might well have had a role in sending Nightingale to the Crimea and helping her cope with its aftermath, but it could not have produced the near fatal, relapsing, febrile illness she contracted there. Typhoid, typhus and remittent or "Crimean" fever were the most common fevers encountered by the British during the Crimean War.[23] "Crimean fever" was a generic diagnosis that covered a multitude of febrile disorders, of which brucellosis was one of the most important.

Although brucellosis was probably known to physicians as early as the time of Hippocrates, most authorities credit Marston, an Assistant Surgeon in the British Army Medical Department, with the first accurate description of the disorder in 1860 (four years after Nightingale's return from the Crimea).[49] The disease had many names, at least some of which reflected its geographic distribution. In addition to *"Crimean fever,"* it was called *Mediterranean fever, Rock of Gibraltar fever, Malta fever, Neapolitan fever, Cyprus fever, undulant fever, intermittent typhoid, typho-malarial fever* and *remittent fever*. David Bruce, a military physician assigned to the great naval base at

Malta, first isolated the bacterium responsible for the disorder, which now bears his name. He was assisted in his work by Dr. Caruana-Scichluna, an employee of the Government of Malta. In 1906, the Mediterranean Fever Commission identified the goat as the reservoir for brucellosis in Malta and prohibited the use of goat's milk and its products in government establishments. While the incidence of the infection remained high in the civilian population the following year, the attack rate in the Army and Navy dropped precipitously. This, of course, took place long after the Crimean conflict. Had this information been available in 1854/5, Nightingale might have been spared a near fatal illness caused by the particularly severe species of brucella found in goats, *Brucella melitensis*.

Brucellosis is not principally a human disease. Rather, it is an infection of animals that periodically spills over into human populations.[49] It is caused by a tiny bacterium able to survive and even multiply within the very cells responsible for destroying pathogenic microorganisms: phagocytic leukocytes. Infected animals (goats, sheep, cattle and swine) sometimes appear sick, but not necessarily. In fact, some of the healthiest looking are the ones that shed the largest numbers of bacteria in their milk for the longest periods of time. The milk and cheese of infected goats contain tremendous numbers of bacteria and are especially dangerous. The infection is transmitted to humans in two principal ways: ingestion of contaminated milk and milk products and direct contact with infected animals or their environment.[49] If Nightingale's "Crimean fever" was brucellosis as her symptoms suggest, her "unvarying menu [of] goats flesh....and rancid butter"[22] while in the Crimea would have been the likely vehicle by which the infection was transmitted to her.

The illness itself varies from a mild, insidious disorder to a severe affliction dominated by fever, shaking chills and extreme physical and mental exhaustion. It causes both acute and chronic symptoms. Weakness is the most prominent complaint of patients with both the acute and chronic infection. Chills, sweats and loss of appetite are the next most frequent complaints, being reported by nearly three fourths of symptomatic patients. Loss of appetite, generalized aches and pains, headache, nervousness, depression, insomnia and cough are also common. In young men, prolonged sexual impotence has been observed occasionally and adds to the psychic trauma of the disorder. Interestingly, in spite of the multitude of complaints troubling patients, physical examination typically reveals few abnormalities. The characteristic fever pattern is one with a normal or slightly elevated morning temperature that peaks in the late afternoon or evening. Soyer's report that during the acute phase of her illness, Nightingale had "sudden relapses in the morning, followed by recovery and then another relapse in the evening"[23] suggests that she had a dicrotic fever pattern (that is, one with two fever spikes each day), which, at least according to the late Wesley Spink (the United States' most noted authority on brucellosis) is not typical of brucellosis. Spondylitis, or inflammation of the spinal cord, with which Nightingale suffered greatly (recall that Brown-Sequard diagnosed these symptoms as "spinal congestion") is typical of patients with brucellosis, particularly those infected with the species of brucella Nightingale would most likely have been exposed to in the Crimea, *B. melitensis*.

The symptoms of brucellosis can linger for long periods. However, even in the absence of antibiotic therapy, only a minority of cases progress to chronic illness. In the pre-antibiotic era, the average duration of illness was fifty days.[49] In cases that became chronic, neuropsychiatric complaints (such as headache, depression and nervousness) predominated, especially among persons with prior psychiatric disorders. In such patients, brucellosis had a tendency to accentuate prior psychopathology. Occasionally, chronic neuropsychiatric symptoms were accompanied by inflammation of the lumbar spine, which manifested as severe sciatica (excruciating pain in the lower back).

Thus, both Nightingale's acute and chronic illnesses had much in common with brucellosis. Although it is possible, that her thirty years of headaches, spinal pain, depression and invalidism were the consequence of a stubborn *B. melitensis* infection, hers would have been a decidedly unusual case of chronic brucellosis. It persisted much longer than even the most refractory cases of the disorder without killing the patient. Moreover, for no apparent reason, it disappeared after creating physical and neuropsychiatric havoc for over three decades.

If Nightingale's protracted invalidism was not an atypical case of chronic brucellosis, what else might it have been? The obvious answer is a typical case of post-traumatic stress disorder (PTSD).

Scholars have long pondered the traumatic effects of war on the human psyche. Homer explored them in considerable detail in the *Iliad* over twenty-five hundred years ago, as did Plutarch and Arrian in their descriptions of Alexander's emotional collapse after returning from his conquest of Asia (see Chapter 3). However, not until the 19th century did clinicians begin to appreciate that the mind/body relationship is so tightly intertwined that in response to the stress of combat, physical signs of anxiety can mimic or even induce the symptoms of organic illness.[50]

During the American Civil War, at just the time Nightingale was experiencing recurrent palpitations,[51] shortness of breath, fatigue and pain in her "left fore quarter" so severe she pleaded with Paget to amputate it, Dr. Jacob Mendez De Costa[52] was confronted with identical symptoms in Union soldiers too ill to return to the battlefield. For reasons not then understood, the war experience seemed to have created acute cardiac abnormalities ("soldier's heart") in young men fighting for the Union, which De Costa feared would progress over time to full-blown organic heart disease.

World War I provided the deadly laboratory in which the first systematic investigations of combat-related neurosis were conducted.[53] In the seemingly endless carnage that characterized that conflict, "shell shock" was epidemic, with sixteen thousand cases recorded among the British between July and December of 1916 alone. Such cases were given diagnoses reminiscent of those applied to Nightingale during her long agony: *hysteria, exhaustion, nervous collapse, malingering, secondary gain syndrome,* and *cowardice* (more than two hundred British soldiers were executed for the latter diagnosis).

Charles S. Myers, a British military psychiatrist, coined the term "shell shock" to call attention to the importance of the physical effects of bursting shells in creating the disorder. Later, he placed less emphasis on the physical effects of exploding shells, concluding that although "abrupt changes in the atmospheric pressure, or exposure to carbon-monoxide gas or physical violence, resulting from the explosion of a shell, may each produce hemorrhages and other minute lesions within the central nervous system, and....as such may [favor "shell shock"]....it is not essential."[53]

During the conflict, an effort was made to identify risk factors for the disorder we now know as PTSD. Although many men who had no prior mental disability "broke down" under the stress of trench warfare,[54] it was widely believed that certain vulnerable personality types, those with "nervous dispositions," were especially prone to the disorder.[55] Lack of training, older age, absence of prior combat experience and rapid deployment to the front (all true of Nightingale when she arrived at Scutari) were recognized as other important risk factors. Various treatments were recommended. These varied from placing patients in a quiet environment (not so far from the firing line that they might "develop an idea of permanent freedom from military duties"),[56] to strict discipline,[56] to brutal forms of electrical therapy.[57] The ultimate aim of all forms of therapy was to return disabled soldiers to active duty as quickly as possible.[50]

During the Second World War, a new focus of combat-related neurosis research emerged: that concerned with prophylaxis.[50] These investigations examined the importance of training and sociopsychological factors (such as group cohesion, leadership, motivation and morale) on the incidence of such neuroses. The value of group psychotherapy and interventions designed to assist in resocialization began to be recognized. However, behavior psychotherapy was not systematically applied (except as an adjunct to electrotherapy) until the aftermath of the Vietnam conflict.

During the Vietnam War, the American military finally seemed to have solved the age-old problem of psychological breakdown in combat by applying preventive measures developed during World War II and the Korean War. At least initially, the incidence of combat neurosis was at an all-time low of only twelve per thousand recruits.[58] However, as the war continued, growing numbers of veterans began to exhibit symptoms of a new kind of battle fatigue, mainly intense anxiety, battle dreams, depression, explosive and aggressive behavior and problems with interpersonal relationships. Some developed these symptoms as an acute reaction to combat. However, many more with no such symptoms during their service in Vietnam began to exhibit them long after their combat experience had ended. Their *post*-traumatic stress disorder, an obscure but nevertheless previously well documented malady of World War II had returned, as it always has in the aftermath of war.

The character of PTSD exhibited by affected Vietnam veterans has much in common with Nightingale's chronic illness.[58] Veterans subjected to the most extensive carnage typically develop the most severe symptoms of PTSD. Depression has been, by far, their most serious complaint, with associated sleep disturbances, feelings of worthlessness, difficulty concentrating, a sense of helplessness and suicidal ideation. Many fantasize about living the life of a hermit, a fantasy that became reality for Nightingale during thirty years of confinement to her room. Many describe themselves as emotionally dead, an assessment shared by family members who rate them as cold and uncaring. With respect to this feature of PTSD, Young has said of Nightingale after her return from the Crimea that: "Though her aims were loving and humanitarian, as they had been in the Crimea, her personal relationships were cold at best and at worst appallingly heartless, and she maintained a cruel, tyrannical, and reproachful attitude to the relations, friends, and allies who were closest to her."[23]

Survival guilt is a common symptom of patients with PTSD, especially among nurses, ex-corpsmen and ex-medics.[58] Even though many of the casualties these caregivers treated (in many instances at great danger to themselves) were beyond medical help, they continue to suffer extremely painful memories long after their service, blaming the deaths on their own incompetence. The lifetime risk of PTSD among the seventy-two hundred women who served in Vietnam (almost exclusively as nurses) has been estimated by the National Vietnam Veterans Readjustment Study (NVVRS) as 26.9%, with the highest incidence occurring among those who worked in the presence of the dead or dying under conditions of extreme and prolonged physical deprivation.[59] Nightingale's experience, of course, was a combination of the latter two risk factors in the extreme.

Flashbacks and recurrent dreams of specific traumatic events are frequently reported by patients with PTSD.[58] In their endless struggle to suppress such thoughts and dreams, patients tend to isolate themselves and, in the process, their social skills atrophy. They also avoid situations or activities likely to arouse traumatic memories. Moreover, they become hypersensitive to social injustice, like Nightingale, who agitated relentlessly after her return from the Crimea for better treatment of soldiers, women's suffrage and sanitary reform.[40] They also have difficulty with authority figures and engage in self-deceiving and self-punishing patterns of behavior. Their only acceptable confidants - their pathway back to mainstream society - are veterans with similar histories and problems.

There is no direct evidence of Nightingale's ever having spoken or written of flashbacks or recurrent dreams of her Crimean experience. Nevertheless, in August 1856, she wrote:

> I stand at the alter of the murdered men [of Scutari]. And while I live I fight their cause.[60]

Clearly, the thousands of British soldiers who died because of the failings of the army's Medical Department, of which she was a member, haunted her long after the Crimean conflict was over. These memories must have been all the more distressing because she had no one with similar experiences or problems in whom she might have confided. As noted above, she never spoke of her wartime experiences after her return to England. Nor did she ever again personally minister to the sick or wounded. Perhaps this was her way of avoiding situations or activities likely to arouse traumatic Crimean memories. It was also a form of punishment lasting some thirty years, one consisting of a virtual self-imposed imprisonment.

The Vietnam experience has provided the following additional evidence to support a diagnosis of PTSD in Nightingale: The disorder frequently develops as a co-morbid condition in persons with underlying anxiety, depression and related disorders (such as bipolar disorder).[61] Working to excess, preoccupation with control and celibacy are frequent among trauma survivors.[62] Symptoms persist long after the traumatic experience that precipitated them has passed, with fifty percent of patients still affected thirty years later.[62]

In all likelihood, Nightingale suffered from not one but four disorders. It seems clear that she had an underlying bipolar personality disorder, which both magnified the post-traumatic effects of her Crimean experience and enabled her to carry on in spite of them. Chronic brucellosis is, by far, the best explanation for the devastating febrile illness she contracted in the Crimea, and, almost certainly, it was the PTSD that sent her to bed for thirty years. When at last she recovered from the latter disorder, she developed a form of senile dementia we would diagnose as Alzheimer's disease today. This was the one illness of the four that finally ended her relentless pursuit of the mission she believed God had chosen for her.

On her way to the Crimea in May of 1855, Nightingale wrote:

What horrors of war are, no one can imagine. They are not wounds, and blood, and fever, spotted and low, and dysentery, chronic and acute, and cold and heat and famine. They are intoxication, drunken brutality, demoralization and disorder on the part of the inferior; jealousies, meanness, indifference, selfish brutality on the part of the superior.[63]

Like all wars before and since, the Crimean War was all of these, and its trauma lingered long after fighting had ended, stored permanently in her mind, as it no doubt was in the minds of an untold number of other veterans of that conflict. Because the psychological trauma of war respects neither rank nor privilege, Nightingale's position of authority offered no protection against PTSD any more than Alexander's did in the aftermath of his conquests in Asia.

Notes

1. From Henry Wadsworth Longfellow's "Santa Filomena":
   > Thus thought I, as by night I read
   > Of the great army of the dead,
   > The trenches cold and damp,
   > The starved and frozen camp, —
   >
   > The wounded from the battle-plain,
   > In dreary hospitals of pain,
   > The cheerless corridors,
   > The cold and stony floors.
   >
   > Lo! in that house of misery
   > A lady with a lamp I see
   > Pass through the glimmering gloom
   > And flit from room to room.
   >
   > And slow, as in a dream of bliss,
   > The speechless sufferer turns to kiss
   > Her shadow, as it falls
   > Upon the darkening walls.

2. In his preface to *Crimea: the Great Crimean War, 1854-1856* (London: Palgrave MacMillan, 2004), Trevor Royle describes how this conflict, generally regarded as the first "modern war," "introduced technical changes which affected the future course of warfare."

3. Dossey BM. *Florence Nightingale. Mystic, Visionary, Healer.* Springhouse Corp. Springhouse (PA): 2000. p. 103-169.

4. Cook E. *The Life of Florence Nightingale.* MacMillan and Co., Ltd, London: 1913. p. 238.

5. Glass N. Florence Nightingale: Casting light on a disputed reputation. *Lancet.* 2002;359:1073.

6. Henry Fielding. *Amelia* (book III, chapter 4).

7. Op cit (Dossey) p. 156.

8. Briggs A. *The Age of Improvement.* Longmans, London: 1955, p. 377, 384.

9. Op cit (Dossey) p. 108.

10. Dossey has offered the following assessment of Nightingale's personality: "Strongly introverted, a perfectionist; brilliant originator and synthesizer of vast amounts of information on nursing, hospital design, sanitation (public health), army medical reform, statistics, philosophy, and religion; in later years, worked from her bed or sofa, usually meeting with only one person at a time; made only three public appearances after return from Scutari; dedicated and determined, despite poor health, accomplished great body of work after Crimea and worked almost continuously until age 75; experienced periodic mild to severe depression throughout life related to quest for meaningful work, perfection, and for the unitive life; last 15 years of her life allowed more social contact." (Dossey BM. Florence Nightingale. A 19th century mystic. *J Holistic Nursing.* 1998;16:111-164).

11. The "upper ten thousand" were the social, political and economic elite who ruled 19th-century England by virtue of their social standing and wealth and their large land holdings. [Op cit (Dossey) p. 45]

12. Vicinus M, Nergaard B. *Ever Yours, Miss Nightingale.* Harvard University Press. Cambridge (MA): 1989. p. 40.

13. Op cit (Dossey) p. 3, 10, 11, 87.

14. Op cit (Dossey) p. 325.

15. Wisner KL, Bostridge M, Mackowiak PA. A case of glimmering gloom. *The Pharos.* Autumn 2005: 4-13.

16. The following excerpt from a note Nightingale wrote to her closest cousin, Hilary, in 1845 is yet another of many examples of de-

pression: "I shall never do anything and am worse than dust and nothing. I wonder if our Savior were to walk the earth again.... whether he would send me back to this life....which crushes me into vanity and deceit. Oh for some strong thing to sweep this loathsome life into the past." [Op cit (Cook) p. 44-5]

17. Baly M (ed). *As Miss Nightingale Said. Florence Nightingale Through Her Sayings: A Victorian Perspective.* 2nd Ed., Scutari Press. London, 1991.

18. Op cit (Cook) p. 258.

19. Op cit (Cook) p. 236.

20. Op cit (Dossey) p. 122.

21. Op cit (Dossey) p. 141.

22. Bolster E. *The Sisters of Mercy in the Crimean War.* Mercer, Cork (Ireland): 1964, p. 121.

23. Young DAB. Florence Nightingale's fever. *Br Med J.* 1995; 311:1697-1700.

24. Op cit (Cook) p. 254-263.

25. Lord Raglan (1788-1855), Commander-in-Chief of the British Army during the Crimean War, lost an arm at Waterloo (for which the "raglan sleeve" was named) and served as Wellington's military secretary for forty-two years. He had never had his own command prior to his service in the Crimea. He has been blamed by historians for much of what went wrong for the British during the war.

26. Op cit (Cook) p. 259.

27. Dossey BM. Florence Nightingale. Her Crimean fever and chronic illness. *J Holistic Nursing.* 1998;16:168-96.

28. Op cit (Cook) p. 261.

29. Op cit (Vicinus and Nergaard) p. 234.

30. Ibid p. 236.

31. Op cit (Dossey) p. 263.

32. Op cit (Dossey) p. 348.

33. Op cit (Dossey) p. 354.

34. Sticker A. Florence Nightingale: Curriculum vitae. Diakoniewerk. Dusseldorf: 1965. p. 4.

35. Op cit (Cook) p. 100.
36. Op cit (Cook, Vol 2) p. 233-5.
37. Op cit (Stickler) p. 4.
38. According to Dossey, Nightingale's historic achievement in nursing was to pioneer the modern administrative role of the nurse superintendent with measurable outcomes supported by data. [Dossey (note 21)]
39. According to Small, although Nightingale's name is most closely associated with "The nurse training school that was eventually established at St. Thomas'....Most modern historians agree that Nightingale's early biographers created a myth by exaggerating the importance of this school, the independence of its nurses, and Nightingale's personal involvement in it." (Small H. *Florence Nightingale. Avenging Angel.* ISIS Publishing Ltd. Oxford (GB):2000, p. 199-200)
40. After her return from the Crimea, Nightingale spent decades in bed agitating for better medical treatment for Britain's soldiers. During the Franco-Prussian War of 1870-71, she saw to it that nurses served on both sides and advised both the Germans and the French on hospital construction and administration, provision of medical aid and nursing duties. [Op cit (Dossey) p. 324] She was active in the area of women's suffrage in that "she began her system of nursing as a service and as an education for women, believing that nursing was a constructive way of providing work for women and freeing them from oppression." [Op cit (Dossey) p. 224] She perfected the pavilion hospital design and was a leading authority on hospitals in Europe even before she went to the Crimea. [Op cit (Dossey) p. 232] Late in her career, she led the movement for sanitary reform in India, first in military stations and then in the country at large. [Op cit (Dossey) p. 267] Her contributions as a statistician included first conceiving "the idea of comparing the morbidity and mortality rates in Scutari to those of the peacetime army as well as the civilian population." [Op cit (Dossey) p. 195] For her, "statistics was not merely a method of analyzing human behavior, of giving exact results of

human experience, but also a way of understanding God's thoughts, for statistics were the measure of his purpose." [Op cit (Dossey) p. 395] During her confinement, she communicated in writing with hundreds of public health administrators on diverse matters. Her achievements in public health are difficult to quantify because her solitary method of working defies customary standards used to measure success. [Op cit (Small) p. 245]

41. Op cit (Dossey) p. 407.

42. Smith FB. *Florence Nightingale: Reputation and Power.* Croom Helm, London: 1982.

43. Showalter E. Florence Nightingale's feminist complaint: women, religion and suggestions for thought. J Women in Culture and Society 1981;6:396.

44. Op cit (Dossey) p. 337.

45. This is what the author's wife, who graduated from nursing school in 1969, and many other nurses of that era remember being told during their training was the cause of Nightingale's chronic illness.

46. Op cit (Small) p. 171-2.

47. Op cit (Dossey) p. 151.

48. See Table 11-1 for the diagnostic criteria for depressive and manic episodes (*American Psychiatric Association Diagnostic and Statistical Manual, 4th ed*).

49. Spink WW. *The Nature of Brucellosis.* University of Minnesota Press. Minneapolis: 1956, p. 3-171.

50. Weisaeth L. The European history of psychotraumatology. *J Traumatic Stress.* 2002;15:443-452.

51. According to Cook, after 1859 "Florence became a complete invalid. Weak, frail and emaciated, the least activity was liable to bring on palpitation. [Op cit (Cook) p. 174]

52. Wooley CF. *The Irritable Heart of Soldiers and the Origins of Anglo-American Cardiology: The U.S. Civil War (1861) to World War I (1918).* Ashgate, Aldershot (England): 2002.

53. Myers CS. *Shell Shock in France. 1914-1918.* Cambridge University Press. London: 1940, p. 24-75.

54. Binswanger O. Hystero-somatic symptoms in war hysteria (Hystero-somatische Krankheitserscheinungen bei der Kriegshysterie) *Monat Psych Neurol* (Berlin). 1915;38:1-60.

55. Viets H. Shell-shock; a digest of the English literature. *JAMA*. 1917;69:1779-86.

56. MacCurdy JT. War neuroses. *Psychiatric Bull*. 1917;2:243-54.

57. Bailey P. War and mental diseases. *Am J Pub Hlth*. 1918;8:1-7.

58. Williams T (ed.). Post-Traumatic Stress Disorders of the Vietnam Veteran: Observations and Recommendations for the Psychological Treatment of the Veteran and his Family. Disabled American Veterans, Cincinnati: 1980, p. 1-23; 37-47; 125-30.

59. Kulka RA, Schlenger WE, Fairbank JA, et al. Contractual Report of Findings from the National Vietnam Veterans Readjustment Study. Volume I: Executive Summary, Description of Findings, and Technical Appendices. Research Triangle Institute. Research Triangle Park (NC): 1988, p. 2.

60. Op cit (Dossey) p. 186.

61. Op cit (Kulka) p. VI-20-7.

62. Personal communication (Dr. Thomas L. Murtaugh, Project Officer, National Center for PTSD) and Op cit (Kulka) p. II-9.

63. Op cit (Cook) p. 276.

12 RACIAL CHARACTERISTICS

A t noon on Tuesday, November 16, 1915 the remains of this patient were placed into a hearse and escorted to the Tuskegee
Institute Chapel where thousands came to gaze into the casket of
their dead leader. At twenty minutes after ten the next morning, a
procession of trustees, students, faculty and alumni of the school the
patient had founded, visitors, and honorary and active pall-bearers
began inching across campus to muffled drums, finally packing
themselves to suffocation inside the chapel. Chaplain John W. Wittaker and Dean G. L. Imes of the Phelps Hall Bible School presided
over the service, which began with the choir softly singing the Negro melody, "We Shall Walk Through the Valley and Shadow of
Death in Peace." When the opening elegy had ended, Chaplain
Wittaker began the austere burial service with a few simple words,
and then Dr. H. B. Frisell, president of the Hampton Institute, offered a prayer for the soul of his school's most illustrious alumnus.
Secretary Scott next read a telegram of consolation from Seth Low of
New York, the president of the Institute's Board of Trustees. Many
others paid similar homage to the former slave for his service to his
race and his country. They included Theodore Roosevelt, William
Taft, Andrew Carnegie, John D. Rockefeller, Julius Rosenwald, the
mayor of Boston, the governor of Ohio, the governor of Alabama
and a former ambassador to the United States from Great Britain.
When the last words of the service had been spoken, the audience
moved just outside the chapel to where a vault had been specially
constructed for the sad purpose of the day. The Institute's Bandmas-
ter stood at its head and sounded "Taps." When he had finished, a

heavy-hearted crowd turned slowly away from the tomb of their fallen prophet.[1]

The patient had traveled far in his fifty-nine years to become "the most famous black man in the world,"[2] and "one of the most admired Americans of his time."[3] Born into slavery in Hales Ford, Virginia in the spring of 1856,[4] he overcame deprivation, hardship and discrimination to succeed Frederick Douglass as the leader and spokesman for black America in the aftermath of the American Civil War.

His rise to greatness began immediately with his emancipation after the war, when he began teaching himself to read. What he lacked in formal instruction he made up for in determination, and by the time he managed to secure a position for himself at a school for newly freed blacks in Malden, West Virginia, he had already mastered the rudiments of literacy. In 1872, when he was just sixteen, he walked across Virginia to The Hampton Normal and Agricultural Institute, founded just after the American Civil War as a school for former slaves. It was there that he learned the habits of rectitude, hard work and service that would guide him for the rest of his life. He performed well enough that after graduating and briefly teaching in West Virginia, he was invited back to his alma mater as instructor. His dedication and capacity for work so impressed Hampton's white principal, General Samuel C. Armstrong, he gave the patient responsibility for organizing the Institute's first night class. Under the patient's stewardship, the class thrived; all students attended regularly, even on the coldest winter nights and the hottest summer nights. Moreover, within a year, every one of them qualified for entrance into the day school, with seven of thirty-five passing the middle class examination and the others, the examination for the junior class. Thus, when in 1881 white legislators from Alabama solicited General Armstrong's advice regarding a suitable leader for a new school for blacks about to open in a farming community near Montgomery, he recommended the patient. Despite serious reservations about a black principal, the legislators took Armstrong's advice and hired the patient to oversee creation of the school that would become The Tuskegee Institute.[5]

In just two decades of unrelenting toil, the patient developed a host of political, social and business connections that enabled him to raise an endowment of nearly two million dollars, construct more than a hundred new buildings, recruit a faculty of some two hundred black men and women and attract legions of black students from around the world to his vocational institute. The school would become the power-base through which he directed numerous charitable contributions of northern philanthropists such as Andrew Carnegie, John D. Rockefeller and Sears and Roebuck magnate Julius Rosenwald to many of the nation's other black institutions and causes. The patient's influence extended to the very pinnacle of national politics; indeed, when Theodore Roosevelt and William Taft were president, they turned to him for advice on race relations and patronage appointments. No other black contemporary was as prominently involved in so many facets of national public life as this patient,[6] and some believe the "nervous strain" of these many responsibilities had a role in destroying his health.[7]

Although the patient's early years were hard to the extreme, he seemed to weather them without apparent detriment to his physical health. As a child, he frequently lacked food, shelter and clothing, and also affection, for his mother was preoccupied by overwork and ill health and had little time to devote to his upbringing. Later he was to say that he could remember not a single meal seated at a table during his nine years of slavery. He and an older brother ate whatever they could snatch from the kitchen fire or leftovers from their master's table or his livestock: cornbread one day, potatoes the next, rarely, a few scraps of meat. Shelter then was a one-room cabin, mostly taken up by the kitchen fire, over which his mother cooked for the master's family, and a potato hole. Not until the patient was eight years old did he wear shoes, even during the worst winter weather.[8]

In the slave quarters in which the patient was reared, plantation songs were a source of both comfort and entertainment. As emancipation drew near toward the end of the American Civil War, the songs increased and began to ring with bold references to freedom.

When at last the great day did arrive, a stranger dressed in the uniform of the Union Army made a little speech and then read a rather long paper, which only later the patient realized was Abraham Lincoln's Emancipation Proclamation. The soldier told them they were all free and could go when and where they pleased, at which point, the patient's mother, with tears streaming down her cheeks, leaned forward and kissed each of her children, telling them how much she had prayed for the day she feared she would never live to see.[9]

Emancipation brought with it previously unimagined opportunities, which the patient embraced by becoming one of the first freedmen to learn to read and write. However, it also brought new challenges, and all too soon the patient came to realize that in many ways surviving as a free youth was harder than it had been as a slave.[10] To do so, he worked first as a salt packer, then as a houseboy, a janitor, a domestic, a coal miner, a waiter and a teacher.[11]

Not much is known of the gene pool from which the patient sprang. His mother was a Negro woman worth $250.00 at age forty according to records kept by her master.[12] She was neat and cooked passing well[8] but was far from healthy. She had "asthma" and "palpitations of the heart"[13] and died of unknown cause when only fifty-four and the patient not yet nineteen.[14]

The patient never knew his father, nor has his father's identity ever been discerned.[15] When asked his father's name on his first day at school after emancipation, he blurted out "Washington," his step-father's first name, and it was so recorded. Though others later identified one or another man as his father, there is no evidence that the patient's mother ever told him who his father was or that he had any strong interest in the subject. "Whoever he was," according to the patient, "I never heard of his taking the least interest in me or providing in any way for my rearing....[he was just] another unfortunate victim [of the institution of slavery]."[16] There is little doubt that his father was white: although the patient had the broad nose and full lips of a Negro, his reddish hair and luminous grey eyes clearly proclaimed him as the son of a white man.[16] H. G. Wells thought the patient's adult face was "rather Irish" in character.[17] Sir

Harry H. Johnston, African explorer, British colonial administrator, soldier, scholar and writer, saw in it the "odd look of an Italian."[18] Although his unusual middle name, "Taliaferro," given to him by his mother, lent support to suspicions of Italian blood, perhaps derived from a prominent family of the same name residing some twenty miles from where he was born, its exact provenance remains a mystery.

The patient had an older brother (also of unknown paternity) and younger half sister. The latter had a stroke when she was fifty and, like the patient, died in 1915 after a year of failing health.[19] Nothing is known of the brother's medical history.

The patient was married three times: first in 1882 when he was tweny-six,[20] then again three years later after the accidental death of his first wife,[21] and finally in 1892 at the age of thirty-six after his second wife succumbed to an "anemic or tubercular weakness" the best doctors in Boston could neither diagnose nor cure.[22] His first marriage produced a daughter, his second, two sons. His older son complained of "a thumping in the head or dizziness whenever [concentrating] on a given study for any length of time."[23] He died in Los Angeles at approximately the same age as his father after a successful career in real estate.[24] When the younger son was sixteen, he developed a mysterious inflammation of his eyes, which eventually left him blind in one eye with only partial vision in the other.[24] He died in 1938 of unknown cause at the age of fifty. The health of the daughter was decidedly more robust than that of her brothers. She lived to be ninety-five.[25]

The patient never learned to play; work was an obsession that left time for little else.[26] At Tuskegee, teachers came to dread the sound of carriage wheels in the night that signaled his return; they knew that when morning came he would be out inspecting every nook and cranny of the Institute with an insatiable appetite for detail. Terse notes would come from his office in torrents, chastising those who neglected their duties and exhorting all to ever greater efforts toward ending the slovenliness that was their heritage from slavery and poverty. However deferential he might have been to those whose money or favor he sought to support his many enterprises, at home in his Institute he ruled as master of the plantation.[27]

The patient bestrode his empire like a colossus, ruling with an even temper and an unwavering will to bend every other will to his purpose, never once allowing himself to vent publicly the awful pressures of having assumed the burden of leading his race to salvation in America.[27] During his early years at Tuskegee, he rarely slept: anxiety and uncertainty over his Institute's finances kept him awake.[28] As his school flourished, so did the intensity of the stresses of managing his expanding empire. In 1884, barely three years after arriving at Tuskegee and seemingly indefatigable, the patient suddenly buckled under the strain of "making bricks without straw."[29] By October of that year, he was so exhausted and ill he had to leave his post, temporarily delegate a portion of his authority to others and crawl into bed under a doctor's care, though only twenty-eight years of age. A brief rest revived him, and he plunged quickly back into his work.[30]

The patient had a similar breakdown when he was forty-three. Influential patrons came to his aid by raising funds for an extended tour of Antwerp, Paris and London, during which he revitalized himself by sleeping fifteen hours a day.[31] It was the first time in eighteen years he "felt, even in a measure, free from care."[32]

In the fall of 1903, when he was forty-seven, the patient again traveled to Europe on one of only a few genuine vacations. Even then, the press claimed that his health "was broken down by overwork," although the patient denied such reports.[33]

If the patient used alcohol as a sedative, we have as evidence only a cryptic passage in the second volume of Louis R. Harlan's definitive biography. In it, Harlan writes:

> [His] private papers reveal occasional, even rare purchases of alcoholic beverages. These were Glenlivet and Burnt Mill scotch and expensive bourbon, the sort a host might buy to serve his guests rather than the cheaper brands a heavy drinker would buy for his own consumption. There is no direct evidence that [the patient]

himself ever drank, and much hearsay evidence from his friends
that he did not. His daughter Portia said that he drank, particularly in his later years, as ill health brought him pain. Just how
much he drank, if at all, however, is an open question."[34]

Aside from his episodes of mental exhaustion, the patient's only
other medical problem of note involved a beating he suffered when
he was fifty-five. During the mysterious incident, he received two
large gashes in his head and had an ear nearly torn off by a stick-
wielding, white assailant. Sixteen stitches were required to repair
the damage. The beating took place near the tenderloin prostitu-
tion district in New York City, leading to rumors that he was
drunk and had been stalking a white woman when attacked. Later
he would claim he had gone to the address where the beating took
place to meet a Mr. Daniel Cranford Smith, who audited the books
of the Tuskegee Institute for its trustees. Although the laxity of
morals implied by the former explanation was patently inconsistent with the patient's lifetime of rectitude and extreme discretion,
the incident nevertheless gave traction to subsequent suspicions
that a venereal disease was, at least in part, responsible for his
death. The patient recovered quickly and spoke little of the incident afterwards, perhaps recognizing (according to his principal
biographer) that if he "explained anything, he would have to explain a great deal."[35]

The patient was a short, wiry, powerful man with the medium
brown skin of a mulatto. Like his patron, Teddy Roosevelt, he was a
self-made man who loved the outdoors and the company of horses
and dogs.[36] At Tuskegee he maintained a garden in which he spent
thirty or forty minutes a day spading, planting and cultivating.[37]
Physical work of this sort provided sorely needed rest and enjoyment and for over fifty years helped give him the appearance of a
paragon of health.

Just when his health began to fail is uncertain. On reaching
middle age, he lost his boyish figure and seamless face and grew
stocky, though never fat. His reddish hair receded slightly and

began to turn gray as he drove himself relentlessly in managing the ever-increasing layers of his immense empire. His patrons and friends urged him to rest, fearing a permanent breakdown similar to those described above, but he ignored them, working without stint until his final three weeks, when he could work no longer.

In his final years, he complained of indigestion, particularly when traveling. *Bell's Papayan tablets*, a protein-splitting enzyme extracted from unripe papayas, gave temporary relief.[38] Shortly before he died, he was persuaded by Seth Bunker Capp, a philanthropist acquaintance, to drink radium water as a possible cure for his digestive distress.[39] This too seemed to help.

In August of 1915, his personal physician wrote to Julius Rosenwald, a trustee of the Tuskegee Institute, that during the preceding month the patient had "had three severe attacks of kidney trouble — [was] also suffering from high blood pressure — extremely high — and [was] taking a chance every time he exerts himself mentally as well as physically."[40] He urged Rosenwald to relieve the patient of his responsibilities completely for six months to a year.

In early November of that same year, the patient was hospitalized in New York City, a city he visited frequently to cultivate some of his most enthusiastic white patrons, for an examination by Dr. Walter A. Bastedo, a specialist in abdominal diseases. Dr. Bastedo diagnosed "serious kidney trouble" and a "blood pressure of 215 [sic]."[41] The patient, he said, had been suffering from severe headaches for more than a month and was completely worn out, aging rapidly with notable hardening of the arteries. "Racial characteristics," he suggested, were in part responsible for the patient's breakdown. Just what he meant by "racial characteristics" he did not say. However, Dr. George Cleveland Hall, the patient's long-time personal physician, claimed that the expression implied a "syphilitic history" when referring to "colored people" and that a doctor making such a diagnosis was not the right kind to treat the patient. He also said that, so far as he was aware, the patient had never had a Wasserman test (for syphilis) and did not need one, since his condition was due to other causes.[41]

Dr. Rufus Cole, an expert in gonococcal infections, also saw the patient in consultation. He reported only that the patient's condition was extremely serious and joined the other consultants in recommending that the patient cease all trips and public addresses immediately.[41]

By this time the patient's condition was deteriorating so rapidly that his physicians gave him only a few days to live; they suggested he start for Tuskegee immediately but warned that the trip might prove fatal. The patient responded: "I was born in the South, I have lived and labored in the South, and I expect to die and be buried in the South";[42] and so it was to be. Shortly after returning to his beloved Institute, Booker Taliaferro Washington, the Wizard of Tuskegee, died in his own bed at 4:45 in the morning on November 14, 1915. According to the *New York Times*,[43] "hardening of the arteries, following a nervous breakdown, caused his death" (see Figures 12-1 and 12-2).

***

Published biographies of Booker T. Washington give only fleeting glimpses of his medical history. This is partly because Washington was intensely private about his personal life and offered little information on his own health in the mountain of still extant documents he produced during his lifetime. Perhaps more important, his biographers did not have access to his medical records in writing their accounts of his life.

The clinical information contained in these biographies and presented above consists of what scholars were able to glean from a host of non-medical sources. Although constituting a far from complete medical record, the clinical information contained in biographical works such as Louis R. Harlan's two-volume exegesis tell us a great deal about the illness that cut short the life of this famous American.[2,5]

Their accounts tell us, for example, that Washington had extremely high blood pressure at the end of his life, but not when or why his hypertension developed. They tell us that he had kidney failure and hardening of the arteries but not whether these problems were the cause of his hypertension or its consequence. They tell us that he was examined in New York City by some of the country's top

313

FIGURE 12-1. Booker T. Washington. Hulton Archive/Stringer. Getty Images. Used with permission.

physicians just before he died but do not give the results of the tests performed or the specific diagnoses entertained by the attending physicians. Finally, they raise the specter of syphilis as a disorder contributing to Washington's demise by their allusion to "racial characteristics" without defining the terminology or specifying the means by which such characteristics might have brought about his death.

During the thirteenth Historical Clinicopathological Conference of the VA Maryland Health Care System and the University of Maryland School of Medicine, upon which this chapter is based, the official

FIGURE 12-2.   Booker T. Washington in Shreveport, Louisiana on his last southern tour. Gelatin silver print, 1915. National Portrait Gallery, Smithsonian Institution, Washington, DC. Photo Credit: National Portrait Gallery, Smithsonian Institution/Art Resource, NY.

record of Washington's final hospitalization on November 1-3, 1915 in New York's Hospital of the Rockefeller Institute was revealed to the public for the first time. Dr. Barry S. Coller, the David Rockefeller Professor of Medicine at the Rockefeller University helped locate it. Washington's granddaughter, Mrs. Margaret Washington Clifford, gave permission for it to be shared with the public. It answers several of the most important, lingering questions concerning Washington's fatal illness. The document reads as follows:

Nov. 1, 1915

COMPLAINT: Headache, sleeplessness, fatigue and dyspnoea on climbing stairs.

Palpitation, slight cough, occasional indigestion, loss of weight, loss of appetite, failing vision.

315

FAMILY HISTORY: Nothing known of father. Mother died forty years ago, probably of dropsy [i.e., heart failure]. Patient has one older brother who is in only fair health. One sister died this year of apoplexy [i.e., a stroke].

PAST HISTORY: About twenty years ago patient had a bad attack of malaria, lasting two or three weeks. He has always been troubled with dyspepsia. No sore throat or rheumatism. No other illnesses. Bowels are usually regular. Patient gets up two or three times at night to urinate for the past two or three years; voids large quantities of light colored urine. He drinks a great deal of water. Vision has been failing somewhat and varies from time to time. No attacks of blindness. Patient has taken no coffee or tea in the past three months. Previously, he drank one cup of coffee daily. He takes about two tablespoonfuls of Scotch whiskey daily; no beer or wine, and never to excess. He smoked one or two cigars a day up to six months ago; since then, none. Patient denies all venereal infection.

PRESENT ILLNESS: Up to one year ago patient was quite well except for occasional headaches, which he called bilious headaches. He began to feel cold feet. In February he was acutely ill with gastro-intestinal upset, and since that time he has noticed increasing ease of fatigue and dyspnoea on exertion. He has never had any oedema. Memory is good; no evidence of any mental symptoms.

PHYSICAL EXAMINATION: Patient is a middle-aged man. He lies in bed rather restless, moving constantly.

Head: Temporal arteries are dilated, tortuous and non-compressible [indicative of "hardening of the arteries"].

Eyes: Pupils are equal and regular; react promptly to light. Movements normal. Eyeballs prominent. Ophthalmoscopic examination — Right Eye, red reflex normal. Margins of disc cannot be made out. Arteries narrow, veins dilated. There are a few flame-shaped hemorrhages. The retina is pale. Left Eye, red reflex normal. Disc slightly better outlines (sic) than in other eye, but temporal margin cannot be made out. There are several flame-shaped hemorrhages. Arteries very narrow.

Ears: Negative.

Nose: Negative.

Mouth: Teeth are in fair condition; numerous fillings.

Throat: Tonsils are not visible. No inflammation.

Neck: Thyroid not palpable. No glands palpable. Superficial veins dilated and pulsate.

Thorax: Symmetrical. Expansion limited on both sides.

Lungs: No dullness or change in vocal fremitus or voice sounds. There are a few fine râles over both bases at the end of deep inspiration.

Heart: No impulse is visible over the precordium. Area of cardiac dulness is [14.0 cm from the midline in the fifth interspace]. Apex is barely palpable in the fifth interspace 10.5 cm. from the mid-line. At the apex is a blunt first sound, followed by an accentuated and reduplicated second sound. At the left of the lower end of the sternum a low-pitched systolic murmur follows the first sound. At the base the sounds are the same as at the apex, but not so loud. The rate is rapid. The rhythm is perfectly regular.

Pulses: The two pulses are equal in volume and in time. Blood pressure is 225 systolic, 145 diastolic, right arm, patient lying down.

Abdomen: Not distended or tender. Liver palpable 5 cm from the costal margin in the mid-clavicular line. Upper limit of dullness is in the fourth interspace. Spleen is not palpable.

External Genitalia: Negative.

Extremities: No epitrochlears [i.e., lymph nodes near the elbows not palpable]. No oedema. No scars. Knee jerks present, not exaggerated. Radial arteries not easily compressible; palpable when compressed above, not beaded [indicative of "hardening of the arteries"].

Nov. 2, 1915 (Dr. Cohn)

Two weeks ago patient had palpitation. He gets tired more quickly now, especially if he is excited. He does not do a day's work now, formerly worked from 9 to 5 and in the evening. He has never had any pain in the chest or cough. If he lays out a regular program he gets on fairly well. He has headache in the frontal region for one or two days out of every eight or nine. He thinks that last night's headache came on because he ate too much, when he is not used to eating supper. When he lives [sic] regularly, his stomach gives him no or little trouble. When it gets upset, it is as a sense of unrest and feeling of nausea. He rarely vomits, but often induces vomiting and says that that relieves his headache. He is not so fit for work as he formerly was. Mentally, he thinks he is slower than he was and requires more concentration. If he is to make speeches, he finds it is necessary to master all the details first; he is now unwilling to trust himself to impromptu speeches. Blood pressure — 220 systolic, 150 diastolic. Area of cardiac dullness is [14.0 cm to the left of the sternum]. Action is rapid, no irregularities. Sounds are slightly distant and poor, there being almost no muscular quality. The second sound is reduplicated at the apex. At the base of the sternum a systolic murmur is not always present; it is in quality, like the shuffle [sic] of the pericardium, but is of course, only single [a pericardial rub (see below) usually has three components]. It is post-systolic and ends in the second sound. At the base the second sound is accentuated in the second left interspace. The right radial pulse is larger than the left; it is thick. No plaques are felt. The upstroke of the pulse is slow, only fairly sustained.

Lungs: There are a few rales at the left base. Liver is not felt. There is no oedema.

Examination of eyes (Dr. Schirmer).

Right Eye: Beginning cataract in periphery. Vitreous clear. Fundus — outlines of disc very hazy and indistinct. Color of disc grayish red. Temporal half paler than nasal. Veins are dilated and slightly tortuous. Arteries narrowed. There is slight haziness of retina and disc. Great many yellowish spots (fatty degeneration) around posterior pole of the eye... The ordinary regular arrangement around the fovea is missing. The number and size of retinal hemorrhages is scarce in comparison with the yellow spots.

Left Eye: Disc and surrounding retina and retinal vessels show about the same changes as in the right eye.

Diagnosis: Papillo-retinitis albuminuris, with relatively few and small hemorrhages.

Laboratory Studies:

Wassermann reported negative (Dr. Jagle).

Hypertension is typically defined as a blood pressure of 140/90 mm Hg or higher. Thus, according to Washington's Rockefeller Hospital record, he did indeed have hypertension, with a blood pressure so high (225/145 mm Hg) today's clinicians would treat it immediately as a hypertensive emergency with high doses of anti-hypertensive medication. Prior to the advent of such medication, a sustained blood pressure like his was virtually always fatal;[44,45] when untreated, a blood pressure of the magnitude of Washington's destroys blood vessels throughout the body, especially those supplying the brain and kidneys, and places a strain on the heart that first causes it to hypertrophy and then fail. Washington's hospital record contains evidence of extensive damage of this kind, suggesting that he had had severe hypertension for a long time prior to his admission to the Hospital of the Rockefeller Institute.

Systemic hypertension is primarily a *vasospastic* disorder, that is, one in which blood pressure rises because of spastic contraction of small and medium-sized arteries throughout the body in response to hormones released most often from the kidneys, less commonly from the adrenal or thyroid glands. Over time, unrelenting spasm, and perhaps the elevated blood pressure itself, destroys the normal architecture of the arteries responsible for maintaining blood pressure at a rate only roughly proportional to the height of the blood pressure. First, the muscular middle layer of the vessels' wall begins to hypertrophy and then degenerate. Eventually, the inner-most lining of the artery thickens and fibroses, causing a progressive narrowing of the lumen and reducing the flow of blood through it to vital organs.

Although arterial damage of this sort occurs throughout the body, it is especially prominent in the heart, brain and kidneys. It also affects the eyes, where it is a cause of "failing vision," "flame-shaped hemorrhages" and a "great many yellowish spots" (exudates) of exactly the sort described by Washington's physicians in his hospital record.

The principle effect of sustained hypertension on the heart is to cause the muscular wall of the left ventricle to hypertrophy, much like that of a body-builder's biceps in response to the daily "pressure" of "pumping iron." Initially, the hypertrophy has a beneficial effect on cardiac performance by strengthening the left ventricle, but then cardiac efficiency falls as the enlarging musculature distorts the normal ventricular architecture and outstrips the capacity of the blood vessels supplying it to deliver sufficient nutrients for its heavy workload. Washington's hospital record is replete with evidence of left ventricular failure, almost certainly due to chronic, severe hypertension. His "fatigue," "dyspnoea on climbing stairs," "palpitations," "slight cough," "[getting] up two or three times a night to urinate for the past two or three years," "superficial [neck] veins dilated and pulsate," and "fine rales over both [lung] bases at the end of deep inspiration" are all signs and symptoms of advanced left heart failure (see Chapter 4).

The renal complications of systemic hypertension are related primarily to the arterial abnormalities described above. Destruction of the kidneys' vasculature by hypertension, a process known as *nephrosclerosis*, produces progressive loss of renal tissues, culminating in total destruction of the kidneys. Results of the few laboratory tests performed on Washington at the Rockefeller Hospital show evidence of just such kidney destruction. According to the hospital record reproduced above, Washington's blood level of urea nitrogen (one of many "waste products" normally cleared from the blood by the kidneys) was dangerously high, so high (fifteen times normal) that today's clinicians would label him "uremic" (see Chapter 8) at the time of his final hospitalization. When kidney failure causes the blood urea nitrogen (and other unmeasured waste products) to rise to Washington's level, *uremic pericarditis* (waste product-induced inflammation of the pericardial sack surrounding the heart) can develop. When it does, it produces a scratchy pericardial sound (called a "pericardial rub") over the anterior chest each time the inflamed pericardium rubs against the outer surface of the heart during a cardiac contraction. Although the sound generated by a pericardial rub generally has three distinct components, it is possible, given the height of Washington's blood urea nitrogen level, that the "single" component sound "like a shuffle of the pericardium" heard by one of the Rockefeller Hospital examiners was a pericardial rub of uremic pericarditis.

Systemic hypertension also damages the brain in a variety of ways, at least some of which seem to have affected Washington. By promoting the vascular abnormalities described above, chronic hypertension compromises blood flow to the brain, causing cerebral atrophy and microscopic areas of infarction. Strokes are perhaps the most feared complication of chronic hypertension and can take the form of hemorrhage from cerebral vessels rupturing in response to the elevated intra-luminal pressure or infarctions due to atherosclerosis, vasospasm or thrombi, all of which are accentuated in the presence of systemic hypertension. The frontal headaches, mental slowing and sleepiness of which Washington complained for a considerable period before he died, are some of the only hints hypertensive patients have of the existence of the high blood pressure that is silently killing them. All too frequently, the first sign of the disorder is a massive stroke that alters their lives irrevocably in an instant.

The other critical piece of information provided by the Rockefeller Hospital record concerns the notation "Wasserman reported negative (Dr. Jagle)." The Wasserman test is a highly sensitive test for syphilis. The fact that Washington had the test, and it was negative, proves beyond all reasonable doubt that he was not infected with syphilis.

Thus, based on the information contained in the record of Booker T. Washington's evaluation at the Hospital of the Rockefeller Institute just before he died, it is clear that he did not have syphilis but did have hypertension so severe and so protracted (so "malignant") that by the time of his final hospitalization, it had destroyed his kidneys, damaged his heart and brain and would shortly take his life. What is less clear is why he developed such malignant hypertension or what more might have been done to prevent its fatal consequences (see Figure 12-3).

Even today, physicians rarely identify a specific "cause" for the elevated blood pressure of hypertensive patients. Most of the time, because no underlying disease known to elevate blood pressure can be found, the hypertension is labeled "essential," as if to imply that it is the disease itself, rather than simply a sign of some underlying defect that has caused the blood pressure to rise inappropriately.

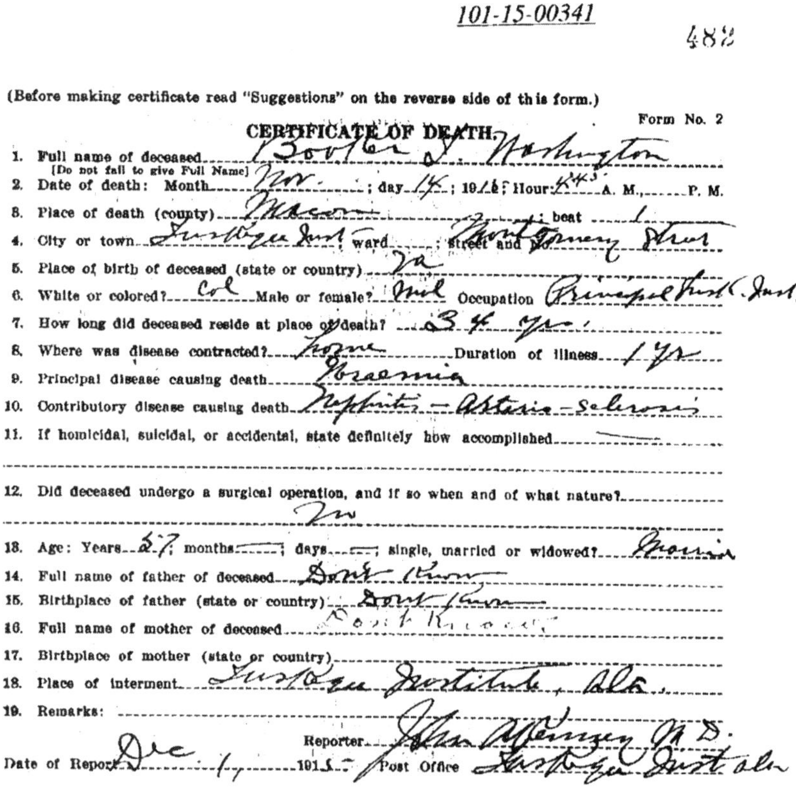
101-15-00341

482

(Before making certificate read "Suggestions" on the reverse side of this form.)

Form No. 2

CERTIFICATE OF DEATH.

1. Full name of deceased Booker T. Washington
[Do not fail to give Full Name]
2. Date of death: Month Nov. ; day 14 ; 1915 ; Hour 4:45 A. M., P. M.
3. Place of death (county) Macon ; beat 1
4. City or town Tuskegee Inst ; ward ; street and No. Montgomery Street
5. Place of birth of deceased (state or country) Va
6. White or colored? Col Male or female? Mal Occupation Principal Tusk. Inst.
7. How long did deceased reside at place of death? 34 yrs.
8. Where was disease contracted? Home Duration of illness 1 yr
9. Principal disease causing death Uraemia
10. Contributory disease causing death Nephritis – Arterio-Sclerosis
11. If homicidal, suicidal, or accidental, state definitely how accomplished
12. Did deceased undergo a surgical operation, and if so when and of what nature? No
13. Age: Years 57 ; months ; days ; single, married or widowed? Married
14. Full name of father of deceased Don't Know
15. Birthplace of father (state or country) Don't Know
16. Full name of mother of deceased Don't Know
17. Birthplace of mother (state or country)
18. Place of interment Tuskegee Institute, Ala.
19. Remarks:

Reporter John A. Kenney M.D.

Date of Report Dec 1, 1915 Post Office Tuskegee Inst. Ala.

FIGURE 12-3. Booker T. Washington's death certificate (Alabama Center for Health Statistics). Reproduced with permission from Mrs. Margaret Clifford Washington, granddaughter of Booker T. Washington.

Prior to the advent of microbiology, physicians regarded fever in much the same way — as the disease itself, rather than simply a physiological response to an infection or some other febrile disorder.

Occasionally, an underlying disorder known to raise blood pressure is found in hypertensive patients. Such "secondary" hypertension tends to involve higher blood pressure, more damage to vital organs and poorer response to therapy than "essential" hypertension, in which no cause for the elevated blood pressure can be found. Diseases causing secondary hypertension include hyperthyroidism, hyperactive adrenal or pituitary glands, strictures of the aorta or renal arteries, diabetes mellitus and a host of chronic kidney disorders. Washington's hypertension could have been secondary to one of these disorders. However, the lack of appropriate diagnostic testing, the absence of associated symptoms of such disorders (such as thyroid enlargement, heat intolerance, emotional lability, bulging eyes) and the fact that rarely are such disorders identified in hypertensive patients, it is more likely that Washington's hypertension was "essential."[6]

Why patients like Washington develop malignant essential hypertension is far from clear, even today. Environmental and behavioral factors seem to play a role in predisposing at least some patients to such hypertension, and these predisposing factors might have been important in precipitating or accentuating Washington's high blood pressure. Excessive dietary sodium, obesity, physical inactivity, excessive alcohol intake and unrelenting psychological stress are currently recognized as the most important modifiable risk factors for hypertension.[46] Of these, psychological stress is the one most likely to have contributed to Washington's hypertension. Harlan's statement above regarding Washington's use of alcohol also raises the possibility, though certainly does not prove, that excessive alcohol intake had a role in his hypertension. Excessive dietary sodium also might have been a contributor. However, again, we have no reliable information on this aspect of Washington's dietary history. The remaining two risk factors, obesity and physical inactivity, do not apply.

Of all of the factors predisposing to hypertension, especially the malignant form that took Washington's life, none seems to be more important than race. In virtually every relevant survey of the disorder, persons self-identifying themselves as African American have a higher prevalence of hypertension, develop hypertension earlier in life, respond poorer to certain antihypertensive drugs and have higher blood pressures and more strokes, heart disease and kidney failure than other American racial groups.[47] The prevalence of hypertension, for example, is three to seven times higher in African Americans than among persons self-identifying themselves as white. The rate of end-stage kidney disease due to hypertension is twenty times higher, the rate of stroke several times higher and the incidence of left ventricular hypertrophy three times higher in African Americans than in whites.[48]

Why persons who identify themselves as African American are predisposed to hypertension is a source of continuing debate. Is it because, as intimated by Dr. Bastedo, they possess certain "racial characteristics" that render them more susceptible to high blood pressure? If so, what are the characteristics and in what way do they bring about chronic hypertension?

To begin to answer questions of this sort, one must first deal with the fundamental one concerning race itself. What, for example, was there about Washington that made him "African American" as opposed to, say, "Italian American," when only half of his genetic complement came from an African parent?

Racial categories were first systematized by Carl Linnaeus in the 1700s in his *Systema Naturae*, in which he divided the human species into what he perceived as its four subspecies: *Afer niger* (African black), *Americanus rubescus* (American red), *Asiaticus luridus* (Asian yellow) and *Europaeus albus* (European white). As recently as 2002, the United States *National Vital Statistics* continued to sort Americans into these same four groups formulated by Linnaeus in the 1700s. The U. S. Census Bureau has also preserved these categories intact, except for the recent addition of "Native Hawaiian or other Pacific Islander" to its catalogue.[49]

Generally, persons are allocated to one racial category or another based on how they "self-identify" themselves. Because there is no scientifically validated litmus test for race, such categorizations are imperfect, if not patently arbitrary. In some surveys, for example, while ninety-three percent of self-reported whites are found on admixture analysis to have predominantly European ancestry, only four percent of those identifying themselves as "African American" have predominantly African ancestry on similar analysis.[50] Because such assignments ignore mixed ancestry, some experts insist that today's racial categorizations are purely social and devoid of genetic content.[51] Francis Collins, director of the (U.S.) National Human Genome research Institute, for example, maintains that *race* and *ethnicity* are "poorly defined terms that serve as flawed surrogates for multiple environmental and genetic factors in disease causation."[52]

When considering the relationship between race and health, many now believe that poverty, not race, is the critical factor in health disparities between racial groups such as African Americans and whites.[53] Nevertheless, mounting scientific evidence suggests that there are differences in the frequencies of certain genes among the various (self-identified) racial groups in America, which might influence the incidence of the diseases affecting them and their response to therapy.[51] Are such differences responsible for the higher prevalence and greater severity of hypertension among African Americans?

African Americans, it would seem, are predisposed to virtually all of the diseases of western society. Aside from hypertension, they have more coronary artery disease,[54] more breast cancer,[55] more heart failure,[56] more obesity,[57] more AIDS,[58] more hepatitis C,[59] more strokes,[60] more lung cancer,[61] more accidents[62] and more sleep apnea[49] than their white counterparts. Is their predisposition to such a wide array of disorders determined by uncommonly bad genes, or as some have suggested, is it more likely that the relatively poor health of African Americans is the consequence of environmental factors, perhaps related to their relatively low socioeconomic status?

Those who favor the latter explanation point out that migrating populations tend to acquire the diseases of their "adopted" homelands.

325

Hypertension is a case in point. When low blood pressure populations such as Eskimos, Australian aborigines, Kenyan nomads, Congolese pigmies, Melanesians, Polynesians or South American Indians move from non-industrialized to industrialized habitats, they frequently become hypertensive.[63] In Ethiopians migrating to Israel, for example, the incidence of hypertension increased three-fold after they settled in their new homeland. Similarly, just as American blacks have higher blood pressures than American whites, American blacks (and blacks elsewhere in the Western Hemisphere) also have higher blood pressures than blacks in Africa.[64] Blacks in Mississippi, for example, have the highest known prevalence of hypertension (thirty-five percent) in the world, whereas blacks in Kenya have one of the lowest (five percent). Could genes responsible for the low prevalence of hypertension among Africans in their ancestral home also be responsible for the high prevalence of hypertension among those displaced to new lands in the West? Some experts would say "yes," but only if certain "hypertensive genes" were selected for during the displacement process.

These experts believe that natural selection might have favored such genes during the era of slavery, when Africans forcibly removed from very low salt areas in tropical West Africa (where the capacity to retain salt was a physiological asset) were subjected to a lethal combination of salt deprivation (due to malnutrition) and salt loss (due to vomiting, diarrhea and sweating) during their trans-Atlantic shipment to the Americas and early years of work there. According to the theory, current-day African Americans and other western blacks are the products of a process of accelerated Darwinian evolution that took place between 1500 and the mid-1800s, when forced human migration unlike any other in recorded history saw over twelve million black Africans transported to the West and made to labor under conditions lethal to a great many. An estimated ten percent of African slaves died shortly after their capture, fifteen percent on board ship, five percent while awaiting sale in the Americas and another ten percent during the hottest seasons of their first two years in bondage.[64] Interestingly, those born in captivity in the

Western Hemisphere had a lower mortality rate than those arriving as slaves, suggesting that descendants of survivors had become better suited (perhaps genetically) to the new environment in the West than their African forbearers.

A genetic transformation of this sort might have taken place if death was not random during the early period of high mortality but tended to eliminate (from the gene pool) those recently enslaved Africans lacking some special genetic trait that favored survival. Grim[64] has suggested that the genetic trait in question was one of enhanced salt (sodium) retention, which protected slaves from the lethal effects of sodium deficiency due to poor sodium intake and excessive sodium losses from sweating and diarrhea. According to his theory, this same enhanced ability to retain sodium, which favored survival during the era of slavery, became a physiological liability with the advent of the modern high-sodium Western diet because it favored the development of salt-sensitive hypertension. We, of course, have no way of knowing for certain if Washington was a salt-retainer with salt-sensitive hypertension. If he was, restricting his intake of sodium, whether or not his dietary intake had been excessive, might have had a salutary effect on his blood pressure if instituted early during the course of his hypertension.

Experts have also argued that it is not bad genes (selected during the process of accelerated natural selection described above) but something in the social environment of the New World that drove and continues to drive African Americans toward hypertension and other aspects of poor health. Low socioeconomic status, an unremitting burden of African Americans since the slavery era, is thought by many such experts to be that something. Low socioeconomic status is closely associated with all manner of disease and death.[53] Moreover, low socioeconomic status seems to have a greater negative impact on the health of blacks than on that of other American ethnic groups.[65] Although the biological and behavioral basis for the association is uncertain, many suspect that fewer options for safe outdoor exercise, limited access to healthy foods and medical care, aversion to traditional medical treatments, greater exposure to environmental toxins such as lead and tobacco products and the heightened physical and psychological stresses of an under-privileged living environment are the features of low socioeconomic status most important in predisposing to ill health. In the case of hypertension, limited access to healthy foods, in particular access to foods low in sodium and high in potassium and calcium, is especially problematic. Repeated surveys have shown that today's African Americans have diets substantially lower in potassium and calcium and higher in sodium than white counterparts.[64] Because diets high in sodium tend to raise blood pressure, whereas those high in potassium and calcium do the reverse, at least some of the excess hypertension of African Americans seems to be due to dietary factors.

Could Washington's hypertension have been due, at least in part, to such socioeconomic influences? As noted above, not much is known about his diet at the time his hypertension reached full flower. He had a fondness for corn[66] reaching back to the earliest days of his childhood, and there is a suspicion, based on his daughter's comment (referenced above) that he might have consumed more alcohol than was healthy late in life. However, we know nothing about his intake of sodium, potassium or calcium. Moreover, by his mid- to late-thirties he was well-to-do by any standard: his Tuskegee machine was running full-throttle, and he was being courted by some of the richest and most influential men in the country. Nevertheless, his formative years were as deprived as any of today's poor, and the adverse effects of such early deprivation can be long-lasting. Numerous studies have shown that low socioeconomic status during childhood adversely affects health during adulthood, regardless of how prosperous, educated or wealthy the child becomes as an adult.[67] Epidemiological studies, for example, have established a link between birth weight and the development of adult hypertension,[68] as well as obesity,[69] coronary artery disease,[70] osteoporosis[71] and diabetes.[72] In view of such observations, it has been suggested that a deprived fetal environment can alter patterns of cellular proliferation and differentiation in the fetus that adversely affect adult organ physiology, morphology and/or metabolism.[73] If so, then the health of Washington's mother while carrying him might have been as important to the development of his hypertension as his own health habits.

Thus, Washington's unhealthy childhood environment might have had lingering adverse physical effects, regardless of how healthy his adult habits and environment came to be. Were his adult habits and environment healthy with regard to his blood pressure? As already mentioned, he seems to have exercised adequately and eaten well when in Tuskegee, although we know little about his food preferences. He had access to excellent medical care, at least late in life, and he had a safe and comfortable home environment, again, late in life. Additionally, he is not known to have been exposed to environmental toxins late in life, except for daily cigars and, perhaps, too-frequent whiskey. But was his environment healthy? With regard to his blood pressure, some would say definitely not, even when his socioeconomic status had risen to a level enjoyed by very few Americans of his day, for the price of his personal prosperity might have been hypertension, a disorder long felt to be the special burden of the "keen and ambitious man....whose engine is always at full speed ahead."[74]

In African Americans like Washington, it has been speculated that incongruity between the socioeconomic status of the individual and his/her personal goals and expectations creates an environment conducive to hypertension, one typified by young blacks who, despite a lack of requisite resources, strive by hard work and determination to overcome the disadvantages of limited educational opportunities in a racist society. At least some scientific evidence suggests that such struggles result in a chronically aroused autonomic nervous system that tends to raise blood pressure.[64] Although Washington's (successful) struggle against myriad insurmountable obstacles was not likely the *cause* of his malignant hypertension, several studies have shown that patients prone to hypertension, as well as those with chronically elevated blood pressures, have an exaggerated blood pressure response to behavioral stressors such as the ones to which Washington was subjected daily.[75] In view of these observations, it is possible that the stress of Washington's rise to greatness accelerated the course of his hypertension and hastened his demise, even though it was not actually the cause of his high blood pressure. Similarly, "racial characteristics" inherited from his slave mother, which might have favored sodium retention, were not likely solely responsible for his elevated blood pressure. Rather, his hypertension was more likely the result of a combination of factors, which included a relentlessly stressful lifestyle and a diet rich in salt, saturated fat and alcohol superimposed upon a genetic constitution maladapted to a way of life drastically different from that of the African ancestors from whom he derived genes responsible for a tendency to retain sodium.

When Washington died in 1915, he was attended by some of America's most distinguished physicians. According to the Rockefeller Hospital record, they did nothing to treat his hypertension, nor did those physicians who cared for him in earlier years recommend anything more than rest and relaxation as treatment for the elevated blood pressure that was silently killing him. What was their understanding of the mechanisms, consequences and appropriate treatment of hypertension? Based on what was known at the time, could they have done anything more to control Washington's hypertension?

Hypertension did not emerge as a clinical concept until the invention of the inflatable cuff by Scipione Riva-Rocci in 1896.[76] Before this, physicians suspected the existence of hypertension but had no simple, reliable method for measuring blood pressure clinically. Moreover, since hypertension kills slowly and silently and is defined by numbers rather than symptoms, its importance as a cause of disease and death was slow to be recognized. Even Dr. Theodore Janeway, a pioneer in the field of hypertension, who practiced in New York City shortly before Washington's hospitalization there, maintained as late as 1913 that: "The relation of the height of the blood pressure to prognosis is doubtful....The exact height of the blood pressure does not seem to have much bearing on the expectancy of life."[77] It was investigators working for life insurance companies who first recognized the adverse effect of hypertension on survival and in 1905 began including blood pressure measurements in examinations of life insurance applicants. They also began screening applicants for albumin in the urine, which they came to recognize as a feature of Bright's disease, a kidney disorder associated with both heart failure and hypertension.[77] As indicated above, Washington had a high concentration of albumin in his urine (listed as "+++" in his Rockefeller Hospital record) just before he died, most likely because his kidneys had been severely damaged by long-standing hypertension.

Concepts of the pathophysiology of hypertension were also slow to evolve. At the beginning of the 20th century, when Washington's high blood pressure was already well on its way to destroying his heart, kidneys and blood vessels, disorders of the adrenal glands were widely believed to be the principle cause of hypertension. Over time, kidney diseases, disorders of other endocrine glands (e.g., the thyroid) and salt imbalance came to be recognized as causes of hypertension. Ultimately, through the pioneering work of the great French physiologist, Claude Bernard, investigators determined that *internal secretions* derived from the kidneys were the principle mediators of the elevated blood pressure in most hypertensive patients. In a series of elegant experiments, Tigerstedt, a Finnish physiologist, and Bergmann, a Swedish physician,[78] demonstrated that the kidneys produce an active substance, which under normal conditions passes into the bloodstream and causes arterioles to constrict and elevate blood pressure. They named the substance "renin." Interestingly, many recent surveys,[48] although not all,[79] show that renin levels are lower in hypertensive African Americans than in whites, and that hypertension in African Americans is more responsive to sodium restriction than hypertension in whites.

Harry Goldblatt, another physiologist, extended work on the renal origin of hypertension by developing a reliable animal model for the disorder after noting consistent abnormalities of the arterial network of the kidneys of autopsied hypertensive patients. In a series of experiments, he showed that when blood flow to the kidney is inhibited by constricting its principle artery, hypertension develops even in the absence of destruction of renal tissue or loss of excretory function.[80] Several groups subsequently demonstrated that renin is not the actual kidney hormone responsible for raising blood pressure under such conditions. Rather, renin exerts its vasopressive effect by releasing a second peptide called "angiotensin" from a plasma precursor.

Over the years, clinicians have used a surprisingly diverse array of remedies to lower blood pressure. Until the 1920s, treatment of hypertension was based on pathophysiological theories having little rational basis. Nevertheless, by 1904, the principles behind dietary salt restriction were known (though not yet incorporated into clinical practice) thanks to the work of Ambard and Beaujard[81] showing that sodium restriction (then called "chloride unloading") lowers blood pressure in patients with Bright's disease. It has been estimated that seventy percent of high blood pressure in blacks can be reversed by drastically reducing their intake of sodium.[64] If this is true, Washington's physicians had the tools, though not yet the knowledge, to have effectively managed his hypertension, at least early in the course of his illness.

In cases of apoplexy (strokes such as the one which took the life of Washington's sister), specific treatments were limited to bloodletting, diet and drugs such as opium, digitalis and amyl nitrate. *Iodid of soda* (potassium iodide) was sometimes used to calm patients with "a tendancy to high-tension and progressive deterioration of the heart muscle."[82] Medical advice included prohibitions against alcohol, fencing, bicycling, horse riding, cold baths and trips to the seaside or mountains and recommendations for hydrotherapy (warm baths) at spas. Electricity ("Darsonvalisation"), fever therapy ("pyrotherapy"), milk diets, and x-rays were also used to treat hypertension.[83] Washington, it will be recalled, drank radium water at the urging of his associate, Seth Bunker Capp, not as a treatment for his hypertension, however, but in an attempt to relieve his chronic dyspepsia.

In 1946, pentaquine, an anti-malarial agent, was the first drug shown to have anti-hypertensive activity. In 1958, thiazide diuretics became available and then "beta-blockers" (drugs blocking the sympathetic nervous system), "calcium channel blockers," "converting enzyme inhibitors" and a whole host of medications custom-made to inhibit specific steps in the physiological pathway responsible for hypertension. As of 2003, sixty-six such drugs, including twenty-seven combinations (twenty-four with a diuretic) were available to treat hypertension.[84] If Washington had lived today, he would likely have been treated with a combination of three or more such agents along with a program of lifestyle modification that would include sodium and caloric restriction, regular exercise and moderation in alcohol consumption.

Booker T. Washington, however, lived over a century ago in a world very different from ours, one in which little could be done to stay the course of the silent killer that took him when he was only fifty-nine. Many years would have to pass before there was reason to hope that medicine might find the means to cure his malignant hypertension, or that America might find the way to end slavery's legacy of social injustice against which he fought until he could fight no more.

NOTES

1. Paraphrase of the description of Booker T. Washington's memorial service in *The Tuskegee Student.* 1915;27:2.
2. Harlan LR. *Booker T. Washington. The Wizard of Tuskegee, 1901-1915.* Oxford University Press. New York; 1983, p. 266.
3. Ibid p. 127.
4. Louis Harlan's research led him to conclude that Washington was born in the spring of 1856 (see note 5). Washington himself did not know the actual date of his birth but suspected he had been born in either 1858 or 1859 (Washington BT. *Up from Slavery.* Corner House Publishers. Williamstown, MA: 1978. p. 1).

5. Harlan LH. Booker T. Washington. *The Making of a Black Leader, 1856-1901.* Oxford University Press. New York: 1972.

6. Wright JT Jr., Brundage WF, Mackowiak PA. A 59 year-old man with "racial characteristics." *J Clin Hypertension.*

7. During his early years at Tuskegee, Washington slept little because of constant anxiety and uncertainty over his Institute's finances and his fear that if the enterprise failed, the whole Negro race might be injured. Later he would write of intense "nervous strain" of never knowing from one month to the next if he would find the money to meet these heavy financial obligations; and when he spoke before large crowds, sometimes at four separate functions in a single day, the "nervous strain" was so great, he resolved each time never again to speak in public. [Op cit (Washington) p. 145, 187, 242, 247]

8. Op cit (Harlan, vol. I) p. 14.

9. Op cit (Washington) p. 21

10. Ibid p. 28.

11. Ibid p. 32, 39, 56, 71, 79, 80.

12. Ibid p. 8.

13. Ibid p. 29.

14. Ibid p. 71.

15. Washington was deeply troubled by his ignorance of his family's history, believing that a proud family history and family connections were powerful stimuli, which helped children "overcome obstacles when striving for success." [Op cit (Washington) p. 36-7]

16. Op cit (Harlan, vol. I) p. 3.

17. Op cit (Harlan, vol. II) p. 284.

18. Ibid p. 286.

19. Ibid p. 126.

20. Op cit (Harlan, vol. I) p. 137.

21. Ibid p. 147.

22. Ibid p. 155.

23. Op cit (Harlan, vol. II) p. 115.

24. Ibid p. 122.

25. Ibid p. 120.

26. Ibid p. 438.

27. Op cit (Harlan, vol. I) p. 272.

28. Ibid p. 139.

29. From the title of Chapter X in Up From Slavery (Note 4).

30. Op cit (Harlan, vol. I) p. 151.

31. Ibid p. 238.

32. Op cit (Washington) p. 276.

33. Op cit (Harlan, vol. II) p. 282.

34. Ibid p. 400.

35. Ibid p. 382-395.

36. Op cit (Harlan, vol. I) p. 306.

37. Op cit (Washington) p. 265.

38. Op cit Harlan, vol. II) p. 439.

39. Ibid p. 445.

40. Ibid p. 447.

41. Ibid p. 450.

42. Ibid p. 454.

43. "Dr. B.T.Washington, Negro Leader, Dead", *The New York Times.* November 15, 1915.

44. Keith NM, Wagener HP, Barker NW. Some different types of essential hypertension: their course and prognosis. *Am J Med Sci*. 1974; 268: 336-345.

45 Kincaid-Smith P, McMichael J, Murphy EA. The clinical course and pathology of hypertension with papilloedema (malignant hypertension). *Q J Med.* 1958; 27: 117-53.

46. Kaplan NM, Opie LH. Controversies in hypertension. *Lancet.* 2006; 367: 168-76.

47. The Sixth Report of the Joint National Committee on Prevention, Detection, Evaluation and Treatment of High Blood Pressure. *Arch Intern Med.* 1997; 157: 2413-45.

48. Yancy CW. Heart failure in African Americans. *Am J Cardiol.* 2005; 96 [suppl]: 3i-12i.

49. Barr DA. The practitioner's dilemma: can we use a patient's race to predict genetics, ancestry, and the expected outcomes of treatment? *Ann Intern Med.* 2005; 143: 809-15.

50. Sinha M, Larkin EK, Elston RC, Redline S. Self-reported race and genetic admixtures. *N Eng J Med.* 2006; 354: 421.

51. Risch N. Dissecting racial and ethnic differences. *N Eng J Med.* 2006; 354: 408-10.

52. Collins FS. What we do and don't know about 'race,' 'ethnicity,' genetics and health in the dawn of the genome era. *Nat Genet.* 2004; 36: S13-5.

53. McCain J. Does race have a place in biotechnological research? *Biotechnology Healthcare.* 2005; December: 54-60.

54. LaRosa JC, Brown CD. Cardiovascular risk factors in minorities. *Am J Med.* 2005; 118: 1314-22.

55. Tammemagi CM, Nerenz D, Neslund-Dudas C, et al. Comorbidity and survival disparities among black and white patients with breast cancer *JAMA.* 2005; 294: 1765-72.

56. Ferlinz J. Heart disease and the color of the skin. *Am J Cardiol.* 2005; 96: 1031-3.

57. Pereira MA, Kartashov AI, Ebbeling CB, et al. Fast food habits, weight gain, and insulin resistance (the CARDIA study): 15-year prospective analysis. *Lancet.* 2005; 365: 36-42.

58. Racial/ethnic disparities in diagnosis of HIV/AIDS – 33 states, 2001-2004. *MMWR.* 1006; 55: 121-5.

59. Pearlman BL. Hepatitis C virus infection in African Americans. *Clin Infect Dis.* 2006; 42: 82-91.

60. Regional and racial differences in the prevalence of stroke – 23 states and District of Columbia, 2003. *MMWR.* 2005; 54: 481-4.

61. Haiman CA, Stram DO, Wilkens LR, et al: Ethnic and racial differences in the smoking-related risk of lung cancer. *N Eng J Med.* 2006; 354: 333-42.

62. American Heart Association. African Americans and cardiovascular diseases: statistics.http://www.americanheart.org/downloadable/heart/1103831662755FSO1AF05.pdf.

63. *A Century of Arterial Hypertension.* 1896-1996. edited by Postel-Vinay N (Translated by Edelstein R and Coffin C). John Wiley & Sons. Chichester: 1996, p. 147.

64. Grim CE, Henry JP, Myers H. High blood pressure in blacks: salt, slavery, survival, stress, and racism. In *Hypertension. Pathophysiology, Diagnosis, and Management.* Laragh JH, Brenner BM (Eds.). Raven Press, New York: 1995, p. 171-207.

65. Kessler RC, Neighbors HW. A new perspective on the relationship among race, social class and psychological distress. *J Health Soc Behav.* 1986; 27: 107-115.

66. Op cit (Harlan, vol. I) p.7.

67. Braverman PA, Cubbin C, Egester S, et al. Socioeconomic status in health research. One size does not fit all. *JAMA.* 2005; 294: 2879-88.

68. Alexander BT. Fetal programming of hypertension. *Am J Physiol Regnl Integr Comp Physiol.* 2006; 290: R1-10.

69. Power C Jefferis BJMH. Fetal environment and subsequent obesity: a study of maternal smoking. *Int J Epidemiol.* 2002; 31:413-9.

70. Barker DJP, Osmond C, Forsen TJ, et al. Trajectories of growth among children who have coronary events as adults. *N Eng J Med.* 2005; 353: 1802-9

71. Javaid MK, Crozier SR, Harvey NC, et al. Maternal vitamin D status during pregnancy and childhood bone mass at age 9 years: a longitudinal study. *Lancet.* 2006; 367:36-43.

72. Sperling MA. Prematurity – A window of opportunity? *N Eng J Med.* 2004; 351: 2229-31.

73. Robillard JE, Segar JL. Influence of early life events on health and diseases. *Trans Am Clin Climatol Soc.* 2006.

74. Osler W. *Lectures on Angina Pectoris and Allied States.* Appleton. New York; 1897.

75. al Absi M, Devereux RB, Rao DC, et al. Blood pressure, stress reactivity and left ventricular mass in a random community sample of African-American and Caucasian men and women. *Am J Cardiol.* 2006; 97: 239-44.

76. Op cit (Postel-Vinay) Forward.

77. Ibid p. 35.

78. Ibid p. 73

79. Wright JT Jr., Rahman M, Scarpa A, et al. Determinants of salt sensitivity in black and white normotensive and hypertensive women. *Hypertension*. 2003; 42: 1087-92.

80. Op cit (Postel-Vinay) p. 75.

81. Ibid p. 177.

82. Bishop LF. *Heart Disease and Blood Pressure. A Practical Consideration of Theory and Treatment.* 2nd Ed. E.B. Trent & Co. New York: 1907, p. 3-119

83. Op cit (Postel-Vinay) p. 105.

84. Joint National Committee. The seventh report of the Joint National Committee on Prevention, Detection, Evaluation and Treatment of High blood Pressure (JNC-7 Express) *JAMA*. 2003; 289: 2560-71.

EPILOGUE

Just as the child is father to the man, so health is parent to disease. To fully understand the complexities and contradictions of the nature of a man or woman and those forces that, in rare instances, carry a person from a pre-glorious state to one of greatness, one must study the experiences that shape the adult being. So too must one follow a patient's condition from the pre-morbid state to that of disease (and death) to understand fully how health is lost and the means by which disease ends a life.

These twelve famous patients exemplify these principles. Their tortuous paths to greatness are shrouded in ambiguity and contradictions. The disorders that plagued them are no less confusing — in part, because they were mysterious in character, but also because the descriptions we have of them are incomplete. In some cases, the disorders had obvious and profound effects on these patients' legacies (e.g., that of Joan's voices on the course of her mission), in others, effects of a less certain and more subtle nature (e.g., that of Beethoven's evolving deafness on the structure of his later compositions). Rarely were the disorders as extraordinary as these patients whose lives they troubled and then took. Whereas some might argue, for example, that small pox was a worthy destroyer of Pericles and his Golden Age, many more would dismiss syphilis, kidney failure and alcoholism as disorders too ordinary to have extinguished lives and talents as extraordinary as those of Beethoven, Mozart and Poe.

However, disease is an egalitarian *non plus ultra* — the ultimate equalizer — a destroyer of great and small alike. In choosing its

339

victim it has no respect for power or position or devotion to God or unbreakable will or creative genius or oratorical skill. In the end, all must "pay the debt to the divine jealousy" (1), regardless of worldly accomplishments, by succumbing to a disorder not of their choosing.

(1) Plutarch, *The Life of Alexander*

INDEX

341

INDEX

INDEX

ABOUT THE AUTHOR

Philip A. Mackowiak, MD, MBA, MACP, is Professor and Vice Chairman of the Department of Medicine at the University of Maryland School of Medicine and Chief of the Medical Care Clinical Center of the VA Maryland Health Care System. A graduate of Bucknell University (BS, Biology), the University of Maryland (MD), and the Johns Hopkins University (MBA), he began his career in academic medicine as an Epidemic Intelligence Officer with the Centers for Disease Control in the early 1970s. In 1975, he joined the faculty of the University of Texas Southwestern Medical School in Dallas, where he taught until joining the University of Maryland School of Medicine in 1988. He has published more than 150 articles, editorials, and chapters on a variety of medical topics. Perhaps Dr. Mackowiak is best known for his work on fever. His *Fever: Basic Mechanisms and Management* (second edition, 1997) was the first comprehensive monograph on the subject since 1868.

For almost a decade, Dr. Mackowiak has served as host to an internationally acclaimed series of Historical Clinicopathological Conferences in Baltimore. His work in this area has been the basis for many articles and the forthcoming *Imperial Furies: Impact of the Julio-Claudians and Their Illnesses on Roman History.* With the publication of *Post Mortem,* Dr. Mackowiak has established himself as one of today's most accomplished medical historians.